AUTOMOBILE ACCID
IN LAS VEGAS

By Steven M. Burris, Esq.

CHAPTERS

CHAPTER ONE

PREFACE AND STATED PURPOSE OF BOOK

The purpose of this book is to provide the intended audience with an overall view of what is *actually* important to know about automobile collision cases in Las Vegas, Nevada, from the perspective of a lawyer who has been doing them, strictly on the plaintiff's side, for over 40 years. By 'actually important,' I mean to say that which makes a *real* difference in winning, losing, evaluating and clearing money from an auto accident case involving personal injury. Most books written by lawyers with titles like this book are bland, scratch-the-surface tomes laying out the obvious stuff, to be used as adjuncts to marketing schemes. True, I am hopeful0 that this book will give me some added marketing punch, but I decided, that when I wrote it, I was going to have some fun writing it, and the only way to do that was to lay out stuff that actually mattered, and that, an intelligent client or newbie lawyer, or paralegal, might find worthwhile knowing. I admit, when I edited the book, I had to remove a lot of stuff because it was perhaps too over-the-line in terms of bluntness, but, as you will in the coming chapters, I am not too fearful of 'telling it like it is.' There is a lot in this book that smacks of an old curmudgeon railing against the 'world falling apart,' I admit; but, besides being a lot of fun to write, I, like every old timer before me, think that it's not just a crank complaining, but, the valuable voice of experience. Probably, it's a mixture of both.

A lot of what's in this book isn't just about automobile cases, but, personal injury cases in general. So, if you were expecting a book that focused only on things that have to do only with car accident cases, this isn't that book. However, to be fair, I have not discussed 'general' type topics that do not have specific application to automobile cases. And, I do not get into topics that would primarily concern "big damage" trials, because, frankly, the vast majority of automobile cases are not 7 figure type cases.

I graduated from Stanford University and became a lawyer in Nevada in 1978. I went to work for the then well-known law firm owned by James Rogers and Bruce Woodbury, both of whom gentlemen accomplished quite a bit in their professional lifetimes. The firm had a general civil practice, but it was not long before I was handed many of the automobile accident cases that came in. I liked this part of the practice, and when I began my own law firm in 1983, personal injury work, in particular, automobile accident cases, was a large focus of what I did. (Ultimately, I limited my practice to personal injury, only; and for many years, most of that was automobile accidents. Now, I personally handle mostly health care negligence cases, but, my office continues to do a lot of automobile work, and I continue to go to trial on a lot of motor vehicle collision cases.)

The intended audience for this book are people who have their own personal injury claim stemming from automobile collisions, and paralegals, legal assistants and attorneys in their first, say, first few years of practice, who may not be familiar with some of the basic practicalities that can only be learned through experience. I also suspect that many older practitioners will find this book helpful, as there are many who skated by with only surface knowledge for many years.

Lawyers who have specialized in auto cases for at least 5 years should know the stuff in this book; but, if you are lawyer who has been mostly out getting clients ('rainmaking'), and were not actually in the trenches doing the stuff, you, too, probably can benefit quite a bit by taking 4 hours of your time and reading this book.

This book is particularly intended to deal with aspects of automobile accident cases in Las Vegas, Nevada, as opposed to other jurisdictions. We have our own laws, our own local court rules, and our own jury pools here, as opposed to other places, and so much of this book will not be useful in other cities or states. I am writing this book in the year 2018, and probably it will be largely outdated within 10 years, as the law, and the perceptions of the public, tend to change and turn over in major ways in every 10 years or so.

I am hopeful that my own clients, who are entitled to get a free copy of this book if they wish, will be able to use this book to educate themselves about the process, and that they will be able to avoid some of the common misconceptions that often cause misunderstandings otherwise; and they will have more realistic ideas and perceptions of what is going on behind the scenes. I am hopeful that interested members of the public, who might get this book, will learn that the insurance companies have successfully executed a public relations campaign on America that has created an undeserved folksy image of what they are; that they are not the "trust the good hands people," or like "Flo" from Progressive. And, I am of course hoping to give some people the idea that not all the plaintiff's lawyers are like the "all hat no cattle" posers who give all the rest of us a bad name.

By the way, this book is copyrighted by me, and I will go after any other lawyers, in particular the "posers," who try to copy and paste parts of it into their ghost-written internet blog sites. (Yes, I know how you operate.)

Steve Burris, Las Vegas, Nevada 2018

CHAPTER TWO

BASIC CONCEPTS BEHIND THE PERSONAL INJURY TORT SYSTEM

It might surprise many people to know that England, America, Canada, and Australia are among the very few countries in the world that have a system that compensates victims of wrongdoing through a legal system that enforces monetary damages. And similarly, these countries are fairly unique in having a system where civil matters are decided by a "jury of peers." There are numerous flaws in the system which have been well documented, and to a large extent, exaggerated, in the public media; but as they say, the proof is in the pudding: The United States has the most stable legal system in the world, and largely as a result, the world "banks" its money in the U.S.

The word "torts" just refers to that branch of the law that deals with the liability (fault) of persons and companies to other persons and companies for damage caused to person (body) and/or property, typically through negligence (carelessness.) Every first year law student gets two semesters of "torts,' which includes study of not only 'accidents,' but, defamation, pollution (toxic torts), drug and medical device injuries, malpractice, fires, and product defects (e.g. automobiles that are unsafe.)

Although the possibility of civil unrest, military coup, revolution, etc., are possible in the United States as they would be in any other country, it is much less likely to happen here than anywhere else. Why? I think it is largely because we have a legal system that takes care of civil disputes in the courtroom in a manner that is largely trusted by the public. Very rarely, there have been instances in the history of our judicial system wherein jurors have been "bribed" or otherwise compromised, but for the vast majority of cases, jurors in civil cases are not being "paid off" by anyone. People know this because ordinary citizens (i.e., ordinary folks) have all been called to serve upon juries and know from their own experience, and that of their friends and relatives, that this system is not rigged in the jury box. Think about it: in how many other countries, ever, has that been the case?

On a basic human, moral level, we all understand that if you hurt somebody, it is appropriate to compensate them in some way, in order to balance the scales. While in ancient times, and even today in many cultures, the way of balancing the scales is to quite literally take "an eye for an eye," the English system of justice formed hundreds of years ago decided that rather than balancing the scales by "taking an eye for an eye" it was appropriate to use monetary damages. The English also realized that in order to assure that things were decided fairly, and not by persons who could be "paid off", it was

10

best to have a jury decide things. (Although juries at first were only males who owned land, the system evolved. Today, in the US, no one can be denied jury duty on the basis of wealth, race, sex, or religion.)

I am not the first to point out that there is yet another aspect to this civil system, where the jury not only sits on civil cases to decide compensation, but, also, sits as a "conscience of the community." It is their job to make Las Vegas a safer place. If those driving on the highway know that the penalty for, say, speeding and causing an accident, or, driving drunk and causing an accident, might be more than just the traffic ticket (which in Las Vegas, for a moving violation will cost you between $150 and $350 currently), but could also subject you to having to pay money out of pocket, via having very high insurance rates for several years (a total cost much more than the ticket), they will be more careful, and the streets will be safer for all of us. Knowing that it is going to "cost you in the wallet" if you drive in an unsafe manner makes people drive more safely. Even if they don't care about the wellbeing of kids on the streets, they will care about their pocketbooks!

If we had no system to enforce the safety rules, by assessing civil damages, then the rules would have no meaning; they would lack the 'teeth' it takes to make people pay attention. Without a civil justice system that actually enforces the safety rules, it would be like some types of substitute school teachers who would like students to obey; but the students suspect that the substitute wants to avoid any conflict and does not want to create paperwork , and so when the substitute teacher is there, it is "play day" for the classroom. Were we not to have a system where rules of safe driving are enforced by the "conscience of community," i.e., the jury, then it would be, in effect, as if the substitute teacher was in charge of the classroom every day.

I did not come up with this 'conscience of the community' stuff, by the way. These concepts have been refined and wonderfully developed for use in the courtroom by what is generally known as the "reptile" group of lawyers, founded by the famed lawyer Don Keenan of Atlanta, and Prof. David Ball, of Duke University. I give them credit for a lot of the concepts expressed in this book, particularly those involved with juror/trial psychology. In turn, a lot of what the "reptile" has to say about things is derivative from a very great trial lawyer of decades before, Moe Levine. Videos of him and copies of his closing arguments, and print versions of his lectures, are still best sellers among lawyers in the know. Levine, in turn, probably got the ideas from someone else; a good lawyer stands on the shoulders of the great lawyers.

If you are a beginning plaintiff's lawyer who wants to get a head start on figuring everything out, civil jury wise, I would much recommend you look into the very excellent books available at a publisher called Trial Guides (which puts out the basic Reptile text, and the Rules of the Road books by

12

Pat Malone and Rick Friedman); and the Jury Bias Project books at AAJ. These books will not give you the 'secret sauce,' but they will get you pointed in the right direction of things. Note: just reading the beginning texts, or, worse, just scanning them, will NOT give you the whole picture, nor, even, the essential parts of it. These are just the movie trailers, not the films. You're going to need to go to many out of town seminars and workshops, and, more importantly, step into the arena yourself a few dozen times to actually "get" it.

I would encourage everyone to think of what our world might be if we did not have our civil tort system with jury trials enforcing monetary damages against those who threaten our safety by breaking the safety rules. What if the rules were not enforced in a meaningful way, in other words? Well, you have to look no further than a few hundred miles to the south of Las Vegas.

Have any of you ever had the pleasure of driving in Mexico City, or other urban areas of Mexico? How careful are the drivers there? Have any of you had the "pleasure" of being in an accident in the country of Mexico? I single out Mexico here only because of its proximity to Las Vegas. The same could be said of the large majority of other countries today.

The basic take away of this chapter is that the civil justice system for torts, in particular, automobile cases, should not be looked at in the law school sense of "law plus facts = money," with only the lawyers and judges truly understanding what's inside the mysterious black box called the 'law.' It's more than that; frankly, it's mostly NOT that. And, it should be understood that jurors, biased against us by all the Chamber of Commerce "frivolous lawsuit," still have a deeper sense of community safety, and balancing the scales for harms and losses, that can transcend the "Macdonald's coffee" and "doctors leaving the state" fake news mindset cultivated by the multi trillion-dollar insurance industry.

CHAPTER THREE

WHY DO WE HAVE INSURANCE COMPANIES AND WHAT DO THEY DO?

Originally, the concept of "insurance companies" came about when consortiums of merchant shipping companies (many of them based in Holland at the time) wanted to spread the risk among themselves of losing cargo on ships that succumbed to storms, and I suppose, pirates. The ship owners would each put money into a pool of funds, and if one of the ships went down, the ship owner could collect from the pool. This was the forerunner of the famous "Lloyds of London" exchange.

In theory, the idea makes a lot of sense: everyone chips in, and the risk is spread. As time goes by, we go from the model of a non-profit collection of merchants pooling the risk, to the model of professional managers who calculate risks precisely, and make a profit by making sure that the amount of claims paid out are less than the amount of money that is taken in.

There was a time when we had many insurance type associations that were essentially non-profit. These would-be organizations that would insure, say, a particular class of members such as government workers. Of course, the temptation was always there for the people at the top of such organizations to take extravagant salaries and live luxurious lifestyles. But, the non-profit nature made these associations attractive to join because the rates were generally cheaper than a fully for-profit corporation owned by stockholders and subject to the manipulations of Wall Street.

When I first practiced law, there were many such insurance associations, i.e., non-profit risk pools, involved in auto insurance type situations. Today, such groups are virtually non-existent. Companies that, in the past, insured certain classes of individuals (i.e., Geico insuring government workers; Horace Mann insuring teachers; USAA insuring military members) have gone out of existence, or, changed so much that they are only nonprofit or exclusionary in the broadest, i.e. phoniest, sense of the word. (USAA, for example, extends the definition of 'military members and their families' so broadly now that few people cannot find a way to qualify.)

Insurance companies have become extremely profitable, due in large part to the ability of computer algorithms to calculate, precisely, risk groups, levels of risk, and so forth. Many of the auto insurance companies now (in my opinion, most of them) in the United States are owned primarily by people and investors in other countries. It should not surprise the reader to know that many of the flag waving (on television commercials) American auto insurance companies are actually owned by consortiums in Saudi Arabia, Switzerland, etc. The famous billionaire George Soros, from Eastern Europe, essentially owns Progressive insurance company; Farmers is owned by a group based in Zurich, etc. Geico is owned by, essentially, Warren Buffet's Berkshire Hathaway hedge fund. Buffet's hedge fund has made billions investing the "float" money generated by the Geico policy holders.

In principal, the idea of insurance companies being run for profit is not in of in itself detestable. The theory is that they will compete with each other and the open marketplace will keep rates lower. Unfortunately, with the amounts of monies involved (trillions of dollars), and the huge amount of profits that are being made, such amounts of money can corrupt the 'free market' system, and the people who service it. For example, individual doctors are paid hundreds of thousands, sometimes millions, of dollars to write "reports" calling honest citizens fakes and cheats. Insurance company lobbyists fill the hallways of every state legislator building, including Carson City, Nevada, and are heavy contributors to organizations such as the "Republican Attorneys General Association." In my 40 years of practice, I have seen the insurance company lobbyists, and their attorneys, become more and more arrogant, as though they are "bulletproof, " and treat the interests of consumers and their lawyers in an increasingly condescending fashion. The insurance industry is second only to maybe the NRA in terms of their financial contributions to state and federal legislators.

But, I have also experienced the other side of the coin, i.e., having the government own and control an insurance type organization. When I was first an attorney, Nevada's workman's compensation system was run by something called the Nevada Insurance Commission, or NIC. They had a monopoly on workman's compensation. Service to the workers was slow; very slow, actually. Nobody cared, essentially, as long as the forms were filled out on time. However, this was probably preferable to the current workman's compensation system in which the amounts of profit and money are so huge that there are specialized clinics and doctors, etc., who limit themselves to treating injured workers on behalf of the insurance conglomerates, and who tend to make the injured workers into "targets" to be shot down with ever increasingly nasty reports and insinuations. There is real "gold in them thar hills," insofar as being a doctor or a clinic that will do the bidding of the insurance company on a workman's compensation claim. Same is true for the doctors who sell a piece of their soul to auto insurance companies to do "IME" exams and reports saying what the insurance company pays them to say about people whose only crime was to get hit by a negligent driver. So, there is no perfect world. A government-controlled system is slow, tedious and uncaring; a for profit system leads to corruption, with the financial motivation for making innocent victims into "targets" for unscrupulous "IME" physicians and "biomechanical engineers" to defame.

The main point here is that the original function of insurance, to spread the risk, is a good idea. Allowing insurance companies to make profits is, *in theory*, a legitimate idea (to encourage persons and companies to get into what, otherwise, might not be attractive), *if* there were proper and effective watchdogs who were not, themselves, looking to get jobs in the insurance industry after they left their governmental posts.

People who are hurt in automobile accidents should understand that the insurance companies are not their friends. They are there to make money. The people who work for insurance companies do not care about claimants, they are there to get promoted in their jobs, and, of course, they get promoted by making money for the insurance company. For someone to expect something differently is, well, very naive.

The insurance companies have television commercials trying to convince members of the public that they are caring, family-oriented businesses where the agents and adjusters really care about people and "USAA has been a part of my family for three generations," "Allstate is the good hands people," "My State Farm agent is there to save me money," " "Farmers agents are there to protect you from the loopholes because they have seen a thing or two," "Flo is your friend," "Geico is the friendly, good natured Gecko," etc.

If you buy into that nonsense, then shame on you. Insurance companies are not evil *per se*, but they are there to make money, they will try to get away with what they can when the watchers aren't watching, and they are there to help themselves, not you.

There is a reason that the richest men in the world. e.g. Warren Buffet, and George Soros, have been putting billions, if not the bulk of their fortunes, into auto insurance companies in the last decade. It is because auto insurance has become the most profitable business this side of the legal marijuana industry.

CHAPTER FOUR

WHY DO WE NEED CONTINGENT FEE LAWYERS?

Insurance companies are solely purposed to make money. That is how it is and we need to understand that.

But what about the contingent fee personal injury lawyers on the other side of automobile insurance claim? Are they really the caring "good guys" that are promoted on their television ads? Why do we need lawyers anyway, why can't people just deal directly with insurance companies?

We know that insurance companies are vastly powerful and that they know how to game the system in their favor (e.g. by paying "experts" huge amounts to say what they want said.) Adjusters are there to make money for their company, which means paying as little as possible. This is not evil. It is just their job and we need to understand that. Their lawyers are there to bill hours of time by, among other things, grilling innocent victims for hours to intimidate them, while, at the same time, enriching the law firm's hourly billing income (ever wonder why the insurance law firms are the ones in the fanciest office buildings in LV? I know one such firm in LV that pays $150,000 a month just in rent! In

21

other, bigger, cities, they pay multiples of this amount.)

So, having a professional on your side of the fence, such as a legit p.i. attorney, makes a lot of sense in theory. Otherwise, you would be run over by big money forces (and the people who work for them) who think of you as a 'target.' Because common folk individuals rarely have money to pay for attorneys on an hourly basis, we allow attorneys to work on a "contingent fee" basis in the United States, to level the playing field. A 'contingent fee' means that the lawyer advances his own time and money to prosecute the case, and, does not get paid until the case is resolved, at which times he takes a percentage of the recovery. (As I know from hard experience, the same 'contingent fee attorney' also gets paid nothing if the case is lost.)

Of course, the contingent fee system has its pro's and con's. On the 'pro' side, people can get high quality lawyers without spending money out of their pocket. On the 'con' side, there are lazy or inexperienced lawyers who do poor jobs for contingent fee clients and settle for the last offer that comes their way every time.

Attorneys are, governed by the State Bar Associations who will, in Nevada at least, go after lawyers who are dishonest or who give exceptionally poor service. A lawyer will lose everything if he loses his license to practice law, so these bar associations do give a public a measure of some assurance.

Unlike the political appointees in various states that regulate insurance companies, the state bars are not subject to the influence of lobbyists and politicians. I can say for sure that in the state of Nevada the state bar office is as effective as its budget allows, and honest in its dealings.

There are many exceptional attorneys out there who do take personal pride and want to furnish very good service to customers. They are professionals, and they want their craft to be practiced at the highest level, and they wish to earn their money. They are, of course, motivated to get as much money as they can for their clients, but again, what is wrong with that?

So, the idea of having contingent fee attorneys is necessary to have a robust, and fair, civil justice system. There are plenty of good, and, plenty of bad, personal injury attorneys working on a contingent fee basis. The bad ones are bad for our society, overall, just as the doctors who lie for insurance companies are bad for society. But, the good contingent fee lawyers do a real service for our society, and help to keep it safer (see above discussion) for everyone, including the children of our community.

For the individual, whether the particular contingent fee attorney is good or bad depends on who is picked. See the next chapter.

CHAPTER FIVE

HOW TO SELECT A PERSONAL INJURY ATTORNEY

I would say the best way to find a good attorney is to ask other attorneys in the area, who practice other forms of law (i.e., who are not themselves personal injury lawyers) who would they recommend? If their relative was hurt in a car accident, who would they recommend their relative to go see? Other lawyers know who the better lawyers are because they are members of the legal community. Unfortunately, most people don't know, off hand, a lawyer to call to ask for such recommendations.

In choosing a personal injury attorney for a car accident case there are certain rating services that furnish some guidance, although these services are increasingly not as useful as they once were. It used to be for an attorney to receive a rating of "AV" from Martindale-Hubbell meant a great deal. It used to be that Martindale-Hubbell would send out "blind" ratings sheets to attorneys in the community to rate each other. An attorney could not manipulate the system in those days. Now, it is my impression that Martindale is not as discriminating in who receives an "A" rating, as it was, say, 25 years ago, as I have noticed some characters, who, to my knowledge, never go to trial, advertising that they had received "A" ratings. I can say for sure that these characters would not have received an "A" 25 years ago in LV. But, these grumblings aside, an "A" rating from Martindale is probably a very good first step for a consumer to separate the wheat from the chaff.

Other rating systems than Martindale have yet to become firmly established, in my opinion, and so are of unproven value at this time. Hopefully, with time, one of them might emerge as being as discriminating as Martindale was once upon a time.

There is an organization called ABOTA, American Board of Trial Attorneys, which only allows attorneys who have had proven numbers of jury trials under their belt, and who are peer-reviewed, to become members. They admit both insurance and plaintiff attorneys. Having a plaintiff's attorney who is a member of ABOTA, and, has an "A" rating from Martindale, is a good way to choose a plaintiff's personal injury attorney. ABOTA does have member lists publicly available on the internet.

I would also say that if an attorney has been president of the local State Trial Lawyers Association, which in Nevada is now called the NJA, and was formerly called the NTLA, this is also some indication that the person is well thought of by his peers. (I say with pride I was the NTLA president in 1997-1998, and I was on their Board of Governors for many years until I retired from it; and, I was the editor of their publication for many years as well.)

If you are lucky enough to know a judge or bailiff, or court clerk or judicial executive assistant, in the local district court system, they can give you a good idea who actually goes to trial, and who is good in court.

Last, just use your common sense. An attorney who goes on television and makes a joke of himself is not someone you want in court. Also, attorneys who go on television and try to look menacing, and brag about how aggressive they are, usually in reality, the least feared members of the legal community. Did you really think it was different than that? There are some good lawyers who advertise on television, but their commercials do not portray them as 'jokes,' nor, do they try to get business by making angry faces for the camera etc. They do not self-proclaim themselves to be 'pit bulls' of whom the insurance is supposedly afraid. (Older readers will know of the "Andy Griffith Show" on television, on which the main comic relief was a character called "Barney Fife," portrayed by the great Don Knotts, whose schtick was to be, in actuality, a coward, but, who would put on a front of being a 'tough guy.' The audience would laugh when Barney would slap his gun, talk tough, and chew on a tooth pick like John Wayne or James Dean, because they knew he would fold like a cheap deck of cards if a real situation confronted him.)

Ask yourself: if my case went in front of a jury, would I want the jury to see this lawyer's commercial before they heard my case? If the answer is no, then you do not want to hire that lawyer.

CHAPTER SIX

CAN I JUST DO THE CASE WITHOUT A LAWYER?

If you are not a lawyer, of course you are expecting me to say that you should always hire an attorney on a personal injury automobile accident case. After all, that is the company line to take, right?

My answer is probably close to what you expect, but not exactly.

Up until, maybe 10 years ago, I think that there were many automobile accident personal injury cases where a person could do as well or better by not hiring an attorney, as compared to hiring one. The difference between now and then is the change in subrogation laws.

Going way back, 25 or more years ago, it was unlawful for most health insurance companies to get reimbursed for what they paid on medical bills related to an automobile accident case. And, most people had 'regular' health insurance through their employer. So, for example, if a drunk driver hit you, caused some pretty serious injuries, and you went to UMC Hospital where they ran up a huge bill taking numerous CT scans, then putting a cast on your arm, the drunk's insurance company was going to give you the drunk's minimum policy limits of $15,000 whether or not you had an attorney. If your health insurance paid all the medical bills, and they did not have a right to get reimbursed, then you could go to the drunk's insurance company, collect your $15,000 check, and put it all in your pocket, more or less. Even though such sorts of accidents and cases would be rare, "back in the day" you would not need an attorney on that type of case.

But -- and it is a big *but* -- things have changed!

Now, as subrogation laws have changed to favor the interests of health insurance companies, union health plans, and big employer group plans; and governmental plans that are pseudo -health insurers (Medicare, Tricare, GEHA, etc.), in the above example of the drunk with minimum limits, there would be numerous hands trying to reach in and take all or most of the drunk's $15,000, leaving you with nothing. To make matters worse, hospitals and doctor's offices have now learned how to "game the system" wherein they will selectively bill or not bill health insurance, so that they can directly reach into the "pie" to take the money. There are so many hands trying to reach into the pot to get the money, that, unless you have an attorney, you are not going to get very much money if anything. And this is not because the attorney is taking some of it, it is because health insurance companies and healthcare providers are trying to reach in and take all the money for themselves (even though you, through your payroll deductions, and taxes, have already paid for the benefits. The laws in the last 25 years have changed to favor the interests of these corporate interests over the rights of ordinary citizens. No, I am not a "liberal" griping about republicans over democrats or whatever; I blame both parties for selling out to money men, and now, when a regular Joe gets hurt, he has to give more and more of his settlement to United Health, Cigna, Medicare, Humana Healthcare, Health Plan of Nevada, Healthsouth Corporation, and scores of other big money entities who believe that they need more and you need less, even when you are out of work for 6 months because a drunk took out on the I 15 freeway.)

An competent attorney who knows what he is doing with subrogation liens (and unfortunately there are not that many of them out there; not the "ethical" part, but the "competent" part) can actually help you to clear more money (even after paying the attorney fees) on the above described case (drunk driver with minimum limits causing serious injuries), as compared to how well you could do for yourself without an attorney.

Most attorneys, in the case where the bills are huge, and the policy limits are small, will not take a fee greater than what the client clears. This means the attorney will try very hard to get all the liens knocked down to where the client gets a fair share of the money. Sometimes this requires the attorney to file an action known as a "complaint for declaratory relief" with the court to force lienholders to take only their fair share.

The law regarding subrogation liens has become extremely complex over the last 10 to 15 years. Myself and another former Nevada Trial Lawyers President, Tim Williams, (recently, Chief Judge of our local court of general jurisdiction in Las Vegas) wrote a small book on the subject and taught a state approved seminar, teaching attorneys how to deal with these liens years ago. The seminar was always a sell out and was a big fundraiser for the Nevada Trial Lawyers Association. It sold out because the law is so complex that one has to make a concerted effort to study it, and keep up with the changes.

Even today, I noticed the Trial Lawyers fundraising seminars still involve a "latest development in subrogation lien laws" all day event.

I would think every lawyer who handles auto cases these days would want to attend these seminars. But typically, there are only 40 to 50 people that go, according to my observation. That means there are probably a thousand attorneys in Las Vegas who are handling car accident cases, but have only vague law knowledge about the latest changes in the various subrogation laws.

As I noted in the foregoing chapters, insurance adjusters are not going to give you special credit because you did not hire an attorney. To trick you, they may infer this, or even actually say it out loud, as though the fact you did not hire an attorney makes you especially honest in their eyes and therefore a trustworthy person who they will treat like gold. This is, of course, hogwash. Every claimant is viewed as a "target" to be manipulated and taken down like an elk in the crosshairs of a hunter's scope by the adjuster.

Let's say you have a relatively minor accident, and you think: I won't hire a lawyer, and I will just let my family doctor/Primary Care Physician treat me and then settle the case on my own. The problem with this scenario is that most PCPs who treat patients under health insurance want nothing to do with accident cases. There is a lot of extra paperwork involved and they may be subjected to antagonizing depositions taken by insurance lawyers. So, if you were to call up the PCP family doctor's office and say I want an appointment, I just got in a car accident, you will probably hear from the front office person "doctor doesn't take car accident cases. He says you should go to a chiropractor." Sometimes the front desk person has been "gifted" by various chiropractic offices to refer you to one of them in particular.

The chiropractic office will then say, "We are not going to take your case unless you have an attorney. The attorney guarantees us we will get paid. He will make sure that you win the case and he will make sure we get paid." The chiropractors know that if people are not represented by attorneys, they will oftentimes "accidentally on purpose" forget the chiropractor bill once the case is settled.

So, the basic sum of things is this. If you are in an accident and you are injured, 99 percent of the time you are better off with an attorney than not having an attorney. The other one percent of the time, you might do better without an attorney, but chances are, unless you are particularly skilled at matters involving paperwork and sneaky people trying to take advantage of you, you will not do very well.

CHAPTER SEVEN

IS IT CHRISTIAN AND MORAL TO SUE?

It is somewhat of a joke among personal injury attorneys that, perhaps as many as 50 percent of the persons who come into the office righteously proclaim, "I'm not the kind of person who sues." The implication of this is that people who do sue are morally unfit, and I suppose, by inference, those who assist them, i.e., plaintiff's attorneys, are disgraced in some manner as well.

Much of this perception has been created, intentionally, by insurance companies, who spend billions of dollars in public relation campaigns and on psychological experts, focus groups, etc., to carefully, and insidiously, go about influencing the public's perception of the tort system. I have heard from reliable sources that the insurance companies that are owned by foreign entities (e.g . German and East European conglomerates), and, foreign manufacturers of automobiles who get hit with products liability suits, have been particularly involved in this sort of thing.

I can give you a personally observed example of the effects of this. I am what I guess would be labeled "an evangelical Christian." I have been attending a Southern Baptist church for over 30 years.

I remember, years ago, the pastor was giving a sermon, and it involved telling a story about a man who had begun a scholarship fund to help underprivileged youth. By way of making a joke, he said something to the effect that the philanthropist was a real Christian because he prohibited the fund from assisting any student who wanted to become a lawyer. As though that were not bad enough, about half of the congregation laughed heartily at this remark, some of them glancing over in my direction to see if I minded. (I did.)

I later complained to the pastor and he said he was truly sorry for having made the remark. He said it was a cheap joke and it was only afterwards he realized that there were a couple lawyers who were members of the congregation, and he had insulted them. But, as was said by Shakespeare, "many a truth is told in jest," and the remark reflected the view of many people.

When I first became a Christian, back in 1982, the first church I attended, where I was baptized, was headed by a new pastor, who had given up the legal profession to become a full-time pastor. I believe that it was a matter of divine providence that I was directed to this church initially, because otherwise I might have gone to a church where the pastor made "lawyer jokes" as noted above, and, at that point in my life, that would have been a big stumbling block for me.

This original pastor was a very intelligent man, who had recently graduated from the Fuller Seminary, which is a very respected Protestant seminary. So, he was freshly familiar with the academic study of the Bible. I also guessed, correctly, that given his past, he had paid particular heed to those sections of the Bible study that dealt with the question of whether being a Christian, and being part of the civil tort system, were inherently opposed philosophies.

The basic answer is: "No," the Bible does not say that the American civil justice system is evil, or that lawyers are evil; in the New Testament, it simply recommends that Christians going to the same church try to settle matters among themselves, perhaps using church elders as mediators, before they go to a secular court, because, among other things, it would look very un-seemingly to outsiders to see members of the same congregation suing each other in the Roman court system.

In the latter part of the Old Testament, particularly those chapters written by the "minor prophets," there is much criticism of the Jewish 'court system' in those days being "rigged" to favor the rich against the poor. The sections involved do not call for the abolition of a 'court' system, but point out that then, as now, there is a danger of the wealthy using the court system as a sword to oppress those without money. How ironic that insurance companies have been able to convince the public that the poor, i.e., consumers, are oppressing the insurance companies unfairly through the court system now. Talk about propaganda!

In the first part of the Old Testament, there are scores of chapters devoted, in rather minute detail, to an ancient system of compensation for what amounts to acts of negligence. A neighbor who allows his mongrel goat to impregnate a 'show goat' must pay damages. The person who builds a weak fence around his roof, and someone falls off the roof as a result, must pay. Someone who negligently causes someone else to lose an eye must pay money; if the act was intentional, such as in a fight, he must lose one of his own eyes. In addition to the Old Testament itself (e.g. Deuteronomy), there are thousands of pages of other rabbinical texts that give even more detailed laws for compensation for this or that act of negligence of one person injuring the property or person of another.

The New Testament warns that if you do not settle the case and go to court, you do not know what will happen. It might go poorly for you. So, the New Testament does not say that the tort system is evil, or that lawyers are evil; it simply advises that for matters involving one Christian who has a beef with another Christian, particularly in the same church, a peaceful settlement is superior to having a secular court trial (because in court, you never for sure know what might happen in the end.)

I advise clients to settle whenever the offer is fair. This is Biblical. But, not every offer is fair.

Another aspect of the New Testament is the advice of Christ to "turn the other cheek." This has been the subject of countless books and sermons trying to discern the exact meaning. For example, if someone at a ball game cursed at you, I think it fair to say that this scripture would be advising you not to respond in kind. On the other hand, when the US responded to the Japanese attack on Pearl Harbor, I do not think anyone would say this was "against the Bible." We had to defend ourselves. For what it's worth, I take this scripture to mean, in terms of the American justice system, that it is not to be used for purposes of revenge, as opposed to compensation, or, enforcing rules.

Of course, the Bible is strong in demanding that Christians be honest. In court, an oath is given "so help me God." It is, quite literally, an oath to God Himself that the witness will be truthful. I am often surprised at how blithely certain individuals, in particular, witnesses paid tens or even hundreds of thousands of dollars by insurance companies, can be in terms of taking an oath to God, and then, saying things that they know, in their hearts, are not true, and that hurt innocent persons who simply had the bad fortune to be hurt by the negligence of another person. I do not know how these 'witnesses' sleep at night.

But, in a broader societal view, what good does it do to ever do to go to court? After all, are not there too many lawsuits? Are not the court systems flooded with personal injury cases and greedy lawyers seeking to win the "lawsuit lottery", as the insurance company propaganda machine would have us believe?

The fact is, the civil court system, in Las Vegas at least, is not currently flooded. The voters have wisely decided to fund enough courtrooms and judges that, compared to 30 years ago, we are nowhere near "over capacity." And the large majority of cases that are filed are not personal injury cases. In Federal Court, on the civil side, most of the "action" is taken up by companies suing other companies, in particular, involving intellectual property/patent disputes that can go on for years.

The vast majority of personal injury cases are either settled, or dropped along the way when it is found out they lack sufficient merit. The ones that do find their way to trial are not, as many potential juror panel members think, there because the plaintiff is being greedy, but because there are legitimate differences between the insurance company and the plaintiff that could not be settled because one side or the other was particularly stubborn (sometimes with reason); or because it is the insurance company, not the plaintiff, who is being a "bully."

Having cases go to court is a way of enforcing our community's conscience about what should be the rules of behavior that govern all of us. The jury cannot be "bought" like, say, some politicians. They are selected randomly from members of the public. Although there certainly can be "wacky juries," at least we know they are not being paid off to render their decisions.

And, when they do find against someone, in a very meaningful way, it sends a message to the community that certain kinds of behavior will not be tolerated. So for example, if there are a lot of deaths and injuries being caused by drunk drivers and the drunk drivers are getting off with $500 fines and seven day partial driver's license suspensions (which was the case until recently), then the jury enforcing rules against such people in trials helps to make up the ground that might be lacking in the criminal system. Or, companies can be forced to pay more attention to safety. For example, trucking companies can be forced to make sure that their drivers are not taking amphetamines, driving crazy hours, and the trucks, particularly the brakes, are maintained safely. Without a civil justice system, there would be little reason for trucking companies to do this, as the fines that they pay from the interstate trucking commission are mere slaps on the wrist.

Auto collision trials also make sure that John Q Public knows we will not tolerate speeding, reckless driving, running stop signs, texting while driving, etc. If we do not occasionally have such people go to trial and lose, then there would be little reason for people to pay much attention to these laws, since oftentimes a policeman is not there to see the violation, and so issues no ticket, and even if caught, they can reduce their traffic tickets to parking violations and pay a couple hundred bucks and skate. The civil justice system makes sure that people know that driving recklessly involves more risk than just paying an expensive parking ticket.

As noted above, having a civil justice system for motor vehicle cases helps us to ensure that in the United States we have, overall, the safest roads and the safest drivers in the world. If you do not believe me, just try going to Mexico City sometime, and drive an automobile there. Or Rome, or Athens, or Bogata, etc. Without an effective tort system, what happens is that everyone drives in a totally selfish manner, because there are not consequences.

Last, I have to remark on the oft quoted phrase from Shakespeare that "the first thing to do is to kill all the lawyers." Many have said this to me as proof that "even Shakespeare hated lawyers." The fact is that this is a quote from Polonius, who is a buffoon, and is made as humorous example of the buffoonery of Polonius.

Lawyers can be good, or can be evil, as is true with most things. But, there is nothing in the Bible that says that the civil justice system, and those that participate in it, are evil or immoral. The public

41

perception that somehow the tort system is evil or Satanic was promoted by those who profit from such beliefs being propagated, and who want to do away with our jury system, and instead, have everything decided by appointed administrative judges and agencies.

In the end, the tort system is run by us, the citizens of the United States who sit on the juries. It is truly where the 'rubber meets the road' in a free democracy.

CHAPTER EIGHT

IS IT BETTER TO SETTLE OR GO TO TRIAL?

I would say that 95 percent of the time, the automobile accident cases I handle are, client-wise, better to be settled than go to trial. Settlements are certain; and you are not waiting around for several years for appeals to take place before you get your money. In order to get a fair settlement, oftentimes we have to file a lawsuit, and litigate right up until the day before trial; lawyers who always settle without *ever* going to trial are known to the insurance companies as softies, and they get bad settlement offers.

But there is a five percent or so of cases that need to go to trial. Normally, the reason a case goes to trial is because the insurance company is not even "in the ballpark" with their offer. The reasons for this are numerous, but the most common reason is that the first adjuster who evaluated the case for settlement put into the computer system for the insurance company erroneous data about the case, and once something like that is entered into an insurance company's computer system, it takes an almost an act of God to change course. The computer evaluation system used by most auto insurance companies these days will say the case is only worth a "top" value of such and such; and even though the computer analysis might be based on faulty data input, the bureaucracy at the insurance company is such that no one dare question the decision (lest they be called weak), and, unless the client wants to take an absurdly low amount of money, the case goes to trial (unless someone on the insurance side has the fortitude to say, "wait, the computer was wrong." Such people exist, but, are rare given that they risk being called 'soft.')

The insurance companies know which lawyers will go to trial and which ones will not; which ones go often to trial, and which ones very rarely go. I am happy to say that our office is one of those that are in the "will go to trial" category. I get a publication called the "Trial Reporter" put out by a publisher in Arizona. It lists each and every jury verdict that comes in every month in Clark County, so I read this and I know, for sure, which lawyers actually go to trial and which ones do not.

I am particularly disgusted by "poser" lawyers who go on television advertising that insurance companies fear them because they go to trial, and act critical of those who do not. Many of the lawyers I have seen doing these sorts of commercials on TV are among those who very rarely go to trial, and some of them have never even been in a trial, to the best of my knowledge. I guess they figure that the best way to counter this embarrassing fact is by telling the "big lie" on television.

There are actually not that many plaintiff law firms in Las Vegas that regularly go to trial for anything other than the 'one day' jury trials for cases under $50,000. . There are probably only about a dozen civil cases that go to trial in Clark County each month. Most of these are auto cases that are tried as one-day jury trials, with a maximum value of $50,000. About four to five civil cases a month that are tried in Clark County are in the regular court system for cases worth over $50,000. Our office does about 10 to 15 percent of all the cases that go to jury trial in Clark County, Nevada, and, we are only four lawyers. (There are more than 10,000 lawyers in Clark County, total). So, that gives you a pretty good idea of how many lawyers actually go to trial on a regular basis in Las Vegas. Pitifully, the answer is not many.

There are some cases that just have to be tried. By that I mean there is a legitimate dispute over who is at fault, and there is no way the case can be settled f. For example, there could be a case involving serious injuries where one driver says he had the green light, and the other driver says no, I had the green light. This is a case that will go one way or the other, with no in-between. You might say: Well, why don't the plaintiff and the defendant just settle the case for 50 percent of its value, figuring it is a coin flip as to who wins? True, a lot of cases might get settled on this basis, but a lot of the times a plaintiff cannot accept the 50 percent type settlement, because their needs are so high that they would be just as well served by taking zero as taking half a loaf, as a 50% settlement would all go to subrogation lien holders, leaving the plaintiff with zero. Such cases are rare but they do happen.

By far the majority of the cases involving auto collisions that go to trial in Las Vegas involve rear-end collisions, and are in the one-day jury trial system for under $50,000 cases. Typically, these cases involve minimal outside damage to the car, and the claim by the insurance company that no one could have been hurt by that 'minor" collision. Jurors in such cases need to be educated that most of the damage in a rear-end collision is underneath the bumper, and since the bumper is made out of rubber plastic material, it will not show much of the force, among other things. Unfortunately, the majority of these "minor impact" cases are decided in favor of the insurance companies. The insurance companies have come up with something called a "biomechanical engineer" which is actually just an engineer who writes reports for the insurance companies saying that he can tell just by looking at the bumper whether someone was hurt or not. This sort of evidence is along the lines of predicting something on the basis of astrology, or palm reading, in my opinion, but jurors sometimes are impressed by these "experts." The truth is, no one can tell just by looking at a photograph of a bumper whether someone was actually hurt or not. This is the same as someone telling whether eggs are cracked just by looking at the outside of the carton.

The two biggest drawbacks to a trail, vs. a settlement, for the plaintiff are as follows. If you

46

go to trial, it could take over a year to get the trial date, and then, years on top of that if there is an appeal. Second, there is a penalty for the losing side: they will be ordered to pay some or all of the other side's legal expenses, which can be high. This later disincentive is not as daunting as it may appear at first glance, since most persons are 'judgment proof' in the sense that they can declare bankruptcy in a worst-case scenario; and, most of the time, the insurance companies will waive the fees and costs if the plaintiff does not file an appeal. Still, some insurance companies will not waive, and, no one likes to have their credit rating ruined for 5+ years with bankruptcy on their record. So, plaintiffs usually find it preferable to settle if there is an offer on the table that their (presumably competent) lawyer advises them to take.

The biggest upside of a trial is that you can ask the jury to award adequate amounts, and juries can and do make awards that exceed greatly the amount offered by the insurance company, sometimes a lot more (of course, juries sometimes give zero to someone who was offered a lot before the trial.) Both sides are taking a chance when they put their fate in the hands of 8 strangers.

CHAPTER NINE

LIABILITY - WHO IS AT FAULT IN A CAR ACCIDENT - AN OVERVIEW

Just as I have explained to my clients at scores of mediations, the question of "how much is my case worth" is, ultimately, "how much would a jury give you?"

In a similar vein, whether or not someone is at fault depends on whether or not the jury says someone is at fault. It is not something simply determined by interpreting statutes regarding culpability, or one's own personal belief of 'the truth' of what happened. To put it another way, in order to predict ultimate 'fault,' we must ask this question: if a typical juror was listening to this case, and heard both sides, who would he or she think is at fault?

In order to answer this question, it is probably best to start with the pattern jury instructions that are read to the jury in every automobile accident trial in Clark County, Nevada.

The pattern jury instruction for negligence states:

When I use the word "negligence" in these instructions, I mean the failure to do something which a reasonably careful person would do, or the doing of something which a reasonably careful person would not do, to avoid injury to themselves or others, under circumstances similar to those shown by the evidence. It is the failure to use ordinary or reasonable care. Ordinary or reasonable care is that care which persons of ordinary prudence would use in order to avoid injury to themselves or others under circumstances similar to those shown by the evidence.

The law does not say how a reasonably careful person would act under those circumstances. That is for you to decide.

[You will note that the person whose conduct we set up as a standard is not the extraordinarily cautious individual, nor the exceptionally skillful one, but a person of reasonable and ordinary prudence.]

There is also an instruction for "negligence per se." This means that negligence can also be established by proof that someone violated a traffic statute. That instruction states:

There was in force at the time of the occurrence in question [a traffic code] which read as follows:

[Read applicable traffic code]
A violation of the law[s] just read to you constitutes negligence as a matter of law. If you find that a party violated a law just read to you, it is your duty to find such violation to be negligence, and you should then consider the issue of whether that negligence was a [proximate] cause of injury or damage to the plaintiff.

As regards to negligence per se instruction, many people, quite rationally, think that, "The other driver got the ticket. Doesn't that automatically mean he is at fault?"

The answer, is no, it does not. The reason is that, one, most people know how to go down to court and "fix" their tickets so that they have them reduced to non-moving violations. Once the ticket is reduced to a non-moving violation, there is nothing to bring up in court as "proof" of violation of the statute based simply upon the issuance and payment of the ticket. More recent cases from the Nevada Supreme Court are to the effect that even if someone pleads "no contest" or similar to a ticket and pays the fine, this cannot be used as 'automatic proof' of fault.

We cannot, in an automobile insurance case in Clark County, bring up the fact of whether or not someone got a ticket, or the policeman thought that someone was at fault. Jurors are often left wondering, I think, "Who got the ticket?" This most reasonable of inquiries is not allowed to be answered in an automobile jury trial due to case law we have in Nevada. This can give a real leg up to otherwise entirely "guilty" defendants, who can, through their attorneys, give juries the misimpression that the reason we are here in court today is because the defendant did not get a ticket, and even the policeman was not able to determine fault.

The uncertainty of fault determinations is further compounded by the fact that, in reality, jurors rarely closely listen to or follow the instructions at the end of the case. I recently heard a friend of mine, retired Chief Judge Gene Porter (he was at one time in charge of all the judges at the court system that hears the automobile accident cases) tell me, half in jest," there are two things I can tell you for sure. Jurors do not listen to expert witnesses, and they do not listen to the instructions." He related how, over the course of hundreds of jury trials he had presided over, he never heard, even once, comments from jurors after the verdict was reached to the effect that "we really were looking at instruction number such and such, trying to figure out how to apply it to the facts." He said that they go back and start just talking about their own opinions about things, what they think is right and wrong, etc., and typically pay no attention to what was read to them as a jury instruction, which are, after all, written in 1920's legalese typically. I will let you in a trade secret: even lawyers have a hard time understanding jury instructions.

All the above being said, the reality is that most cases involving auto collision are pretty clear cut on most fault issues, and the defendant risks getting the jury angry by denying fault. But, oft times, the insurance companies and their attorneys just can't help themselves.

Insurance lawyers have perfected the art of crafting stories for their clients to tell that cast doubt on things that are even clear, in terms of fault. Why do I say the insurance lawyers have made up the stories? It is because over the course of 40 years doing automobile accident cases, I have heard defendants, in typical situations (rear-end collisions, left-hand turn violations) come up with exactly the same excuse/story, using almost the same words, time after time. It is beyond statistical probability that all these people could come up with the same words with the same excuse time after time. (Frankly, I am a little bit disappointed, but not surprised, that many guilty people apparently are willing to not take seriously the oath to tell the "whole" truth, but will apparently let the insurance lawyer suggest/script for them of what to say in answer to the essential questions.)

With modern technology, and modern cars, if you take your foot off the brake of a car that is stopped, it does not suddenly lurch forward with acceleration. However, I have heard, hundreds of times, the story that, "I was stopped. I took my foot of the brake. And suddenly my car started to accelerate forward until it tapped the other car." The word "tapped" is always used. I would guess that, since the 1970's, this has never actually happened to anyone, because cars do not have carburetor systems, as opposed to fuel injection; the gas pedals and brakes are not rarely , mechanically linked directly to the brakes and throttle;   but still, the story persists in virtually every rear end case I have. Or, how many times have I heard, in left-hand turn cases that, "I didn't see them but now that I look back on it, his headlights must have been off." (This only works if it is a nighttime accident.) In today's world, automobiles almost all have the feature that makes their lights come on automatically when it gets dark. However, the headlights being turned off seems to be something that happens to virtually every driver making a left-hand turn at night. When I point out that my client's car had the automatic light feature, it is stated, "Well, you can turn that feature off if you want." For every client I have that is on a motorcycle, the defendant says, "he was going really fast, maybe a hundred miles an hour, darting in and out of traffic. That's why he was hard to see." (This begs the question: if he was 'hard to see,' then how do you know he was going a hundred miles an hour?)

My clients will oftentimes say, "That is not fair. They are lying." It is unfair, but like comedian Flip Wilson used to say, while in character of a scoundrel, the attitude of many insurance companies is "a lie is as good as the truth if you can get someone to believe it."

Sometimes, insurance companies realize it is better to admit fault at time of trial, because then the jury might think they are the good guys trying to be fair, and your client is unfairly trying to take advantage of their honesty. In such cases, the jury may not know that the insurance company denied fault all the way up until the day the jury trial starts. Unfortunately, in these sorts of cases, when the plaintiff tries to point out that the defendant and his attorneys are just now admitting fault after having

53

fought it for 18 months, the defense insurance lawyer will say, "Well, that is a collateral issue your honor. The fact is we are admitting fault now so let's not get sidetracked onto that." Judges may, out of a sense of judicial economy, i.e., not wanting the trial to take any longer than it should, will grant such request, thus helping the insurance company to perpetrate a false impression.

So, the typical insurance company posture in most auto cases that actually go into litigation (as opposed to pre-litigation settlement) is to deny fault and fight it, in hopes that the plaintiff will "cave" and agree to a cheaper settlement, but then, when trial begins, act humble and folksy and say "we have admitted it is our fault all along, and now they want to get way too much money in the lawsuit lottery. Shucks, we almost wish we had not been so honest now."

CHAPTER TEN

THE "RULES OF THE ROAD" AND "REPTILE" APPROACH TO AUTO LIABILITY

Around 10 years ago, attorneys Rick Friedman and Pat Malone came out with a brilliant book called "Rules of the Road." It was a book setting forth a simplified approach to trying the liability side of personal injury cases, and it has application to automobile accident cases as well as virtually any kind of personal injury case.

Rick Friedman and Pat Malone are both brilliant trial lawyers, and the concept of the book is startlingly simple. If you are a plaintiff's lawyer and you do not have this book, you need to order it. It, and a number of very good books of modern plaintiff trial practice, are available from a company called Trial Guides.

The book advocates boiling down the wrongful conduct of the defendants into a few simple rules that virtually can understand. For example, "A driver must always be aware of other drivers on the road, and avoid collisions with them whenever possible." (I just made that up, and it is not a particularly good "rule" to be used at trial, but it gives you the flavor.)

Writing a good "rule" is actually much more complicated than it seems at first. On the big damages cases, devotees of this approach may spend quite a bit of time developing the rules they intend to use at trial, and then test them with focus groups to find exactly which rule resonates the best. Much time has to be spent in cleaning up the language and simplifying the language as much as possible.

But then, at trial, imagine trying to prove a simple "rule" that anyone can understand, as opposed to proving violation of a motor vehicle statute, which is usually written in language that not even most lawyers can understand. It is a way to make the trial process much cleaner.

Trial consultant David Ball and "Inner Circle" lawyer Don Keenan took The Rules of the Road, and combined this concept along with some other concepts related to damages (which concepts David Ball was instrumental in developing), and together with the groundbreaking psycho-social analysis offered by authors such as Rapaille (who helped engineer the campaigns for several Fortune 500 companies on their products, as well as the stunning Republican party victories during the Bush years) , and themes being used by top plaintiff's lawyers for many years, put these ideas together into what is generally termed the "reptile." ("Here, the "Reptile" is mostly just a catchy title, but, it has been adopted as a shorthand way of referring to Keenan and Ball's methodologies.)

The reptile way of litigating depends, among other things, upon using the "rules of the road" methodology for the liability (fault) portion of the case, and the Ball methods on the damages.

(As all of these authors would admit, none of what they have to say is entirely original. They, like us all, stand on the shoulders of giants. Friedman gives a lot of credit to Gerry Spence. Keenan gives a lot of credit to Moe Levine. Ball gives a lot of credit to the psychology department at Duke. All three admit that Dale Carnegie's "How to Make Friends and Influence People" is a seminal work in the field of trial psychology, believe it or not. Rapaille's work on 'culture codes,' and the psychology agencies who use it for commercial purposes, used most famously by the Republican Party/Karl Rove, and Fox News 'gurus,' is given much credit for 'opening eyes' to what was being used by the 'enemies' of trial lawyers for 'tort reform,' and gave insight into what Fortune 500 companies were spending billions of dollars upon to influence the American public on a variety of topics.)

I wish to express my gratitude here to the law firm of Claggett and Sykes for greatly helping me and others to participate in reptile discussion groups and seminars.

I have taken quite a few, maybe most, of the reptile courses, and attended most of their "colleges" on various subjects. In general, it is all very worthwhile. My only criticism might be that the "reptile" theory of litigation works very well on cases that are called, generically, "reptile cases," i.e., cases that meet certain criteria for jury appeal. As a matter of fact, they tell you right up front in the reptile classes that the most important part of the theory is selecting cases whose various aspects match up well with the reptile theory of what matters most to jurors. Unfortunately, most practitioners do not have the luxury, or, discipline, of turning down every case that does not fit the "reptile" criteria. So, we do our best with what cases we have in our file cabinets. Cases that do not meet reptile criteria are not "bad" cases in the sense of there not being actual fault, or actual damages; they just do not have the "sex appeal" of cases that get people angry at defendants. I over simplify, but the basic premise is solid: A pure "reptile" approach to things works best on cases that are "reptile cases" in the first place.

Even though the "reptile" system may work best on cases that meet the "reptile criteria" of success factors, I would say that the "rules of the road" approach works on virtually any case, whether it is a "reptile" or not. Especially if one takes the time to hone a couple very good "rules of the road" to use in the trial, it makes the process of trying the case much simpler.

I have only scratched the surface here of the "rules of the road" and the "reptile." To have even a working understanding of these, an attorney will need to spend hundreds of hours absorbing the materials and taking the seminars and course. The beginning books on the subjects really only scratch the surface as well, and thinking you understand the subjects by just reading the main, initial texts, is not going to do the job. But, you have to begin some place.

Thankfully, in Nevada, we had a recent ruling from our Nevada Supreme Court that more or less decided the debate, among various trial court judges, of whether the "reptile" style argument was permissible, or not. In the case of Pizzaro v. Cervantes, it was decided that the 'reptile' is just another variation of long established permissible arguments, by plaintiff's lawyers, and is not objectionable. Thus, Nevada has joined the large majority of other jurisdictions whose appellate courts have given their stamp of approval on the 'reptile' style of case theming.

CHAPTER ELEVEN

HOW LIABILITY DRIVES DAMAGES

You might think at first: What difference does it make whether a jury kind of hates something the defendant did or *really* hates something the defendant did insofar as liability is concerned? Once you have liability decided, then the jury goes to make a separate decision on damages, right? One sort of liability is just as good as another, right?

The fact is, study after study, and experience and observation, have shown that "liability drives damages." In other words, the more egregious or dislikeable the defendant's behavior is in a car accident situation, then the better the verdict. Even the simplest "colossus" type algorithm program used by insurance carriers recognize this fact. Close behind the galvanizing effect on the jury of egregious behavior, is behavior that is really dangerous (i.e. someone could have been killed, but, luckily, no one was, etc.). Oft times, egregious and dangerous are the same thing, but not always.

Perception of what is dangerous driving, and what is not, is driven, in no small part, by media coverage.

If you have a case where there is driving under the influence, or, an accident while the defendant is using a cell phone device, then you will have a much easier time getting an adequate damages award. Other things falling under this category might be an illegal immigrant behind the wheel of a car without a driver's license; a racing or road rage situation; an overly tired trucker who made false log entries about rest ; poorly maintained trucks or buses; hit and run;   and, in general, taxi cab drivers. I think that, in the next 5 years, we will see a lot more examples, as testing for different intoxicants improves with law enforcement, of persons causing accidents under the influence of marijuana, and opiates, and these will become hot button media topics.

Jurors actually appreciate it when a driver apologizes after an accident, and conversely hold it against drivers who act like 'jerks' after accidents. Although, technically, an apology might be used against the defendant as an indicium of guilt, jurors tend to appreciate the defendant driver who has the class to see if everyone is alright and apologize. Defendants who act like real "jerks" after the accident, trying to blame everyone else but themselves, etc., unwittingly drive up the value of the case in the courtroom.

As noted above, insurance lawyers are well aware of this phenomena, and will oftentimes fight the case on liability, but, on the day of the trial will "magnanimously" admit fault, and then try to make it appear to the jury as if their client has admitted fault all along. They can be assisted in this ruse by judges who buy into their argument "since we admitted fault, your honor, all this evidence about what happened beforehand just takes up time in the courtroom and is unnecessary."

There are ways for the plaintiff's lawyer to make sure that the defendant's "jerk" behavior at the scene gets into evidence, even if he later admits fault through his attorney. Such behavior causes emotional distress to the plaintiff, so an allegation of emotional stress caused by such behavior, will (or should) assure the admission into evidence of the behavior of the defendant post-accident. Allegations of punitive damages (if proper) can also get the behavior into evidence, even if fault is admitted (note: you need to have some kind of reckless, or "whoa dude" type behavior to allege punitives; alleging punitives in, say a typical rear ender without drugs, alcohol, or cell phone distraction is not likely to get far.)

Another way to get the liability facts into evidence, after they are admitted the day before trial, is to argue that your client was put through emotional distress by having to undergo litigation that falsely accused him of being at fault, and therefore, potentially liable to pay the other side's attorney's fees, etc., and thus, part of your damages claim. (This is not just a story; it is usually true to some extent.)

Plaintiff's counsel needs to give some thought as to how to make sure, if there is egregious conduct by a defendant, or factors in his or her driving that amount to "aggravated liability," that this gets into evidence before the jury, even if there is last minute, phoney, statement of contrition by defense counsel to try to keep everything out of evidence.

CHAPTER TWELVE

LIKEABILITY OF PLAINTIFF AS AFFECTING LIABILITY VERDICT

Above I have discussed that liability is based upon the law of negligence, encapsulated by the jury instruction on negligence. I have also explained that we can sometimes simplify the rules of fault by putting them into what are called "rules of the road."

But, to be candid with the reader, there are factors that go beyond the facts and the law that influence whether or not you are going to win the case on fault, or not. Chief among them is this: does the jury like the plaintiff or dislike the plaintiff?

Since the jury only gets to see the plaintiff in an artificial environment, and only gets to hear the plaintiff speak while on the witness stands, judgments about 'like' and 'dislike' are necessarily based on extremely limited, and in many ways, artificial, data; nevertheless, the perceptions of the plaintiff's personality and character still figure to be a huge factor in the odds of trial success.

Jurors like plaintiffs who have good employment histories; speak plainly and directly, and do not try to be 'tricky' with their answers; who are not self-pitying or whiney; and who answer the 'tough' questions directly without trying to dodge. Being able to communicate well is a plus; people who have a hard time just talking in everyday life might have a difficult time (on the other end of the spectrum, people who talk a lot and try to 'sell' everything are mistrusted.) Plaintiffs who are involved with their churches, community activities, charities, etc. have better credibility than those who do not.

Jurors tend to distrust plaintiffs who have criminal backgrounds; who live on public assistance, even if they are legitimately trying to find a job; who try to exaggerate, 'forget' or pretend not to remember negative facts; or try to blame everything that has happened negatively in their lives on the accident, and seem to be self-pitying too much. Instead of "laying it on thick," it is much better for a plaintiff to be understated about the injuries as opposed to over emphasizing the pain. Jurors also, at least at the time of writing this in 2018, are suspicious of persons who are taking a lot of opioid pain medications, no matter how legitimate their need for doing so might be.

Plaintiffs going to jury trial need to be mindful that unusual 'hip' or rebellious clothing, jewelry, hairstyles, tattoos, and the like will make many, if not most, of the jurors dislike them. I tell my clients that when they go to court, they need to dress like they would if they going to church (at least, church in the 'old days.')

There is a saying that there 'are no sinners in the jury box.' This means that even though the people sitting in the jury box are just like you and me and everyone else, not perfect, once they get in the jury box, they tend to judge others by a standard of perfection they themselves do not possess.

Many people make dumb mistakes in their 20's. If I know about it ahead of time, I can oft times file a motion and keep it out of evidence as being irrelevant. But, if I don't know about it ahead of time, it can and will be brought up by insurance lawyers during a trial, and jurors are, as I said above, quite judgmental (no pun intended.)

Even if the evidence is otherwise clear that the other driver is at fault for the accident, if the jury dislikes the plaintiff enough, it may find that the plaintiff is at fault. Defense lawyers know this, and so try to 'dig for dirt' in the course of discovery.

There is a famous case studied in law school about this phenomenon. There was a famous silent film star who had had an extramarital affair with a young woman, who later sued the actor for child support when she had a baby. The actor denied paternity. In those days, they did not have DNA testing, but they could sometimes rule out paternity by means of non-matching blood types. In this case, the blood types were such that it was scientifically impossible for the silent film star to have been the father. Yet, the jury ruled against him anyway, because they were so angered by his lack of character in having an affair with a minor (in those days, under 21 years was a 'minor.')

But, before the reader becomes too disheartened, keep in mind that if a plaintiff is of good character and 'likeable,' this can work in the opposite direction, and cause the jury to favor the plaintiff on the close issues.

Also, *as long as the plaintiff's lawyer knows about it ahead of time* (i.e. his client is truthful with him), he can usually keep out of the evidence the 'dirt' that has nothing to do with the case. So, if you in personal injury lawsuit, make sure that your attorney knows about anything that might come up to 'bite' you in trial, well before the trial takes place. This would include prior criminal arrests and convictions; prior lawsuits or injury claims; prior work comp claims; prior health issues involving the same body parts that are at issue in the case; history of alcoholism or drug addiction; immigration issues, particularly involving any false i.d's; allegations of child abuse (e.g. made in a divorce case by an angry ex-spouse; being in arrears on child support payments; etc.   As attorneys, we are not at all shocked or even impressed by these sorts of things, as we are dealing with situations all the time that are not "G" rated, due to the nature of being a lawyer, so, don't worry about what I may think of you because you have a skeleton in the closet. I just need to know so that I can file a motion with the judge to keep out the 'dirt' that has nothing at all to do with your car accident.

CHAPTER THIRTEEN

WHY CAN'T WE JUST GET THE VIDEO FROM THE TRAFFIC CAMS?

When questions about fault come up, my clients frequently say: "I know they have little cameras in all the stoplights. Why can't we just get the video of the accident from the stoplight cam?"

The short answer is, no, we cannot get such video.

If you call the Nevada Department of Transportation or the various agencies who have access to these cameras, they have a story, which I personally do not fully accept. The story is that these cameras are only used for traffic control purposes, i.e., regulating the flow of traffic by programming stoplights. For example, if the camera shows a bunch of cars backed up on a certain road, then supposedly that would affect the computer system that controls the stoplights that are causing the backup. I am sure that there is some function like that served by the cameras, and no doubt that that is the primary function.

But when the people on the other end of the phone tell you that no video recordings are made, that is when I find it hard to believe. The truth might be:

there are no video recordings made that people like you or I can get.

I have noticed that, when there is a high profile, say, murder investigation taking place, the police will somehow or other be able to get the traffic camera recording that show the suspect's car going down the road, or similar. Bravo. I am glad that the police can get the recordings so that the bad guys can get caught.

I am guessing -- and I have no evidence for this, it is just my guess -- that the function of these cameras recording all the various cars and license plates and so forth could be very useful to agencies charged with keeping the security of our city, e.g. preventing terrorists. That's a good thing!

But, to answer the question originally posed. Can I/we get the "video" from these stoplight cameras, in order to prove who is at fault in civil car accident case? For whatever reason, the answer is no. The story given to the public is such video do not exist and that is not going to change any day soon.

Occasionally there will be videos available from cameras at gas stations and convenience stores on the corners, which will partially show traffic on the streets outside. But the operators of these business are loathing to give access to these tapes to people like personal injury lawyers. They will claim that they have to erase the tapes every 30 days because it is just much too   to save recordings longer than that. In this day and age of five-dollar flash drives that can save gigabytes of information, this is an absurd claim, but for probably other reasons (good ones from their perspective -- they are not in business to help personal injury lawyers), it makes sense to erase everything so that they can be "left out of" legal proceedings to help "other people." Again, the old adage "I got mine, Jack," comes to mind.

Recently, there has been a surge in people putting dashboard cameras on their cars in order to, themselves, record what happens in an accident scenario. (Cabs in LV have had such cameras for many years.) I think this is basically a good idea, but not because we need such cameras to prove this or that in court, although that is a good thing. I like the idea of them because we have so many hit and run accidents here; persons who are not legally here, or, who have warrants out for them, or, who have been smoking weed or drinking, will simply flee the scene, and then claim that their car was stolen (if someone was fortunate enough to get the license plate.) These "scofflaws" cause a lot of harm to innocent people, and oft– too often– get away with it. I also think that if enough people have these cameras, it will greatly reduce the incidents of road rage, which is a real menace in LV. The idiots who purposely cut you off or wave a gun at you on the freeway to get even for some perceived slight will think twice. Last, the trucks that have rocks flying off the back end, which have demolished the windshields on two of my cars over the years, will not be able to get away with it if there is a dash cam. The truck will be identifiable and 'caught in the act.' I once heard that rocks flying off trucks in LV cause over a million a year in damages to vehicles here.

I also hope that these dash cams will help to catch more drunk drivers. I have, on at least two occasions, called into NHP to report a drunk weaving about on the freeway. By the time the actual cop gets there, it's too late, and later, if they catch the suspect, without the camera showing him weaving about, he can lie and say he had drinks after he got home.

CHAPTER FOURTEEN

CAN WE FIND WITNESSES AND GET STATEMENTS? I KNOW SOMEONE MUST HAVE SEEN IT.

Many times, I have clients say to me, "There were several witnesses but none of them stuck around. They just drove by. Can't we find them somehow?"

The basic answer is "no."

Back when I was first an attorney, it was not uncommon for people to run ads in the newspaper saying "anyone who saw the accident yesterday at Main and Charleston, please call attorney listed below to tell us what you saw." No one runs those ads anymore.

One might ask: Why? One reason is that the RJ charges a huge amount of money to run even a little ad like that these days. I am guessing to run such an ad (1/8 page in the Nevada section) for even one day would cost $1,000. And, frankly, how many people under the age of 40 even read a paper newspaper anymore?

Probably the greater reason is that if you ran such an ad in the paper, or, more cheaply, say, on a social media site of some kind, you are going to attract nut jobs; and people who actually did not witness the accident, but are willing to lie and they said they did as long as you pay them. The chance of a real witness calling in response to the advertisement is close to zero. As is oft said, people just do not want to get involved anymore. Even if they are helping another citizen prevent someone else from lying about what really happened, people know that if they get involved they might get called to a deposition, called to court, lose a day of work, and be subjected to lawyers picking at their every word. It is easy to understand why people do not want to get involved. Maybe, in the future, we will figure out ways for people to give their testimony without having to miss work and being unduly subjected to "aggressive" paid-by-the-hour insurance lawyers hassling them for two hours over 10 minutes' worth of testimony.

Sometimes, clients will give me the names and phone numbers of good citizens/witnesses who stick around the scene and provide this information. I will sometimes have my investigator call them to give tape recorded statements over the phone. Such statements, although not admissible in a jury trial, are admissible in arbitration proceedings; they are useful in persuading adjusters that attempts to deny fault will ultimately fail; and they prevent witnesses from suffering memory lapses (unintentional and otherwise) in the future. Unfortunately, it is getting harder and harder to get people to cooperate in giving even recorded statements; this is due largely to the shift of everyone to smart phones. Especially among millennials, generation x and generation y, the concept of answering a phone and talking to someone is foreign. When my investigator calls, and they don't recognize the number, they don't take the call, and flip it over to voicemail. Mostly, they don't even listen to voicemail (real 'friends' text them); and even if they do, they are put off by talking to someone they don't know, since there are so many scams and telemarketers these days using false stories to get through. Investigators will often, now, have to track people down in person to get a statement, rather than just on the phone. This is more expensive, and it will cost me $300 to get a statement that, 10 or 15 years ago, I could probably get for $50 in investigator fees. Also, in LV, about half the population moves every year (or, so it seems), so just tracking someone down is a hassle; and, given the 24-7 nature of the work here, knowing or predicting when someone might be home and not asleep is difficult. These are problems that lawyers in cities other than LV do not face.

The point is that my clients think that, like on TV, we can just go out and get statements from witnesses very easily. Well, in LV, real life is not even close to TV lawyer/detective shows.

CHAPTER FIFTEEN

WHAT ABOUT THE "BLACK BOXES" INSIDE CARS? WOULDN'T THEY SHOW WHAT REALLY HAPPENED?

We have all heard about the "black boxes" inside airplanes. Every time there is an airplane crash there is a mad scramble to find the "black box" in the cockpit that will hopefully tell investigators just how and why the airplane crash happened.

You will note that even when these "black boxes" are found, rarely do they yield enough information to tell us the how and why of what really happened to the plane.

The black boxes inside airplanes are very sophisticated and track multiple streams of data. Keep in mind that with the "black box" inside a plane, highly paid investigators still are usually not able to tell us the *why* part of things– why did this or that engine fail. For this, they need to find and examine the actual engine part.

The "black boxes" that are inside modern cars are much less sophisticated than the ones in airplanes. They record only some basic data. They might be able to show that at a given point in time a car came to a sudden stop, but not why it stopped.

There is a new "cottage industry" among insurance companies. This industry has vendors, who call themselves "bio mechanical accident reconstruction experts," who claim that by examining the black box information in a car, they can not only tell who was at fault, but can tell if someone was really hurt or not. (Inevitably, the black box tells them that the plaintiff is lying and was not really hurt.)

(These same 'biomechanical engineers' also claim to have a similar, ouija board like ability, to divine the same information from looking at a photograph of the car damage.)

Pseudoscience has the veneer of truth, because, after all, we are talking about *computerized* data from a *black box*. Shouldn't that be able to tell us everything about who is *really* hurt? The scientists on CSI are able to find the murderer with much less! MRI machines can tell what's really wrong with you! Shouldn't the BLACK BOX that plugs into a COMPUTER tell all?

The truth is, the data that comes from an automobile's black box is very limited and does not tell anyone if someone was really hurt or not.

Unfortunately, judges sometimes will allow the 'black box' voo doo testimony in court. There are scoundrel engineers who are more than eager to stand in a courtroom, and, for $10,000 to $25,000, tell a jury that the black box has told them that no one was hurt, and that the plaintiff is lying.

The black boxes can furnish some information, but it is limited. Very limited. It cannot tell us, with any precision, what exactly were the forces, angle of forces, etc. on the plaintiff's body; how the plaintiff's body was positioned, exactly; and whether the plaintiff already had a weak spine from aging process etc.

There are "black box" type instruments on large semi-tractor trailer rigs. These devices, which oftentimes incorporate GPS satellite tracking data, furnish much more information than the current car 'black boxes.'

And I also am aware that technology is rapidly changing and improving, and it is quite possible that the "black boxes" in cars in the future may be able to give a lot more information, of greater relevance, than what we have now. And maybe my experience with black box testimony has been confined to some experts who are not the best; e.g. I have not heard black box testimony from an expert with both an MD and Phd in bio-engineering, who is not being paid $15,000 by an insurance company to "testa-lie." But what I am seeing right now is the misuse of "black box" information by insurance companies to fool juries into thinking that they can "scientifically prove" that a plaintiff was not hurt.

Insurance companies take advantage of jurors' overreliance on technology experts, a la CSI, to come up with phony "biomechanical" experts using black box printouts and "computer analysis of photographs" to give "proof" that the plaintiff is lying.   This is science on the same level as the "bio- electricity   machines" of the early 20th century that were "scientifically proven" to cure most diseases.

CHAPTER SIXTEEN

CAN SOMEONE BE HURT IN A "MINOR IMPACT"?

Cars are built now with bumpers that are made out of rubber plastic material. If they get hit, they show little if any damage. Oftentimes there is damage underneath the plastic material, but you cannot see it unless you remove the bumper covering (which requires an auto body shop.)

Therefore, in most rear end collisions, it looks as though the car that was hit has little or no damage, even when the hit was significant.

Insurance companies have found ways to use this phenomena as a tool to deny plaintiffs any compensation for what they call "minor impacts." (They also use the term "MIST," which stands for "minor impact soft tissue." The phrase 'soft tissue' refers to muscles, ligaments and fascia, which are the anatomical components injured in a 'whiplash' type scenario.)

The insurance lawyers bring out the photograph of the plastic-rubber bumper covering and say to the jury "see, there is no damage here. Just a scratch. How could anyone be hurt?"

Then they bring in the "biomechanical expert" who says he can tell by looking at the bumper that no one was hurt, and that your client is lying. He then waves the photo around of the rubber bumper covering and says see, no damage.

All of this is a phony show, something that Penn and Teller could have dreamed up to fool people were they paid to do so.

But, juries eat it up like kids eating candy. The minor impact verdicts have been dismal for many years now. (I do know of one local attorney who has done well on these cases, though: Ben Cloward. It is no mistake he has done well. He actually went to the famous Croft school of bio mechanic forensics in California, and received his certification from them. He knows the science far better than the phony 'bio mechanical engineers' the insurance company brings out against his clients.)

The basic theory behind all this is commonsensical: the harder you get hit in a car, the more likely you are to get hurt. The harder the hit, the greater the injury. Within certain very broad boundaries, this is true.

But, the laws of physics still apply, even in car accidents involving insurance company 'experts.'

If you think about it, from high school physics class, you know that the total force of an impact is equal to the velocity times the amount of mass.

For example, you could have something going very fast, but if it had no mass (for example, say it was a tiny, tiny speck of atomic material), then, when it hit you, it would not cause injury. We know this because every day we go out into the world and we are bombarded by tiny atomic particles traveling at the speed of light or close to it, yet we are not hurt.

By the same token, something of very great mass, traveling extremely slowly, would cause harm.

Keep in mind that a person walking quickly probably goes between two and three miles an hour. You know this if you are on a treadmill: if you put the speed at 2.5 miles an hour, that is a pretty good walking pace.

If someone who was the size of a football linebacker, say, weighing 260 pounds, was walking at a good pace, and you were stopped, and they suddenly walked into you, do you think that might be enough to hurt you? Of course. It would certainly be enough.

Well, what about a rear end car accident where the car is typically traveling at around five miles an hour? The car weighs typically 6,000 pounds. A 6,000 pound car hitting you going even, say three miles an hour, is like *20 linebackers* hitting you all at once at a fast walking speed. That is enough force to cause you to be injured. It is not a fantasy, it is physics.

Seatbelts protect you from going through the windshield. They do not protect you from getting jolted by a rear end collision. A car going even three miles an hour is going to cause a lot of physical force.

Whether you actually get hurt or not by a "minor impact" depends on a lot of factors which cannot be taken into account by a "black box" or photographs of a bumper. Are you young and flexible, or old and inflexible? Is your spine in good shape, e.g., that of a young person, does it have a lot of arthritic spurs and inflexibility, i.e., anybody over the age of 40?

Was your neck turned (where flexion is not possible), or was it straight? What was the exact position of your body when you were hurt, i.e., were you looking left or right for traffic, looking with your neck turned in the mirror, etc. All of these things go into whether or not you are "really" hurt or not.

Insurance experts oftentimes compare the force of a car collision minor impact to a "bumper car" at the fair. There is a big difference here: Does the bumper car weight 6,000 pounds? Remember, the force of an impact is velocity *times mass*.

The best argument to a jury in a MIST case is that, when you buy a carton of eggs, you look inside to see if any are cracked, because just by looking at the carton on the outside, you cannot tell.

None of us likes to think about how dangerous it is to go out on the roadway. Just for our own peace of mind we imagine that it is pretty safe out there most of the time. We do not like to think that minor impacts could cause significant injury. We might be afraid to go out on the roadway if we knew that. So, we choose not to believe it. But like a lot of things that we choose to believe, just to make our lives less anxious, turn out not to be true.

Just as we are now discovering that letting kids play tackle football is a risky thing to do, in terms of exposing them to head injuries with existing helmets (injuries that can cause them to have problems later in life), we are now slowly starting to acknowledge how dangerous car accidents can be, even the "minor" ones. Cars will eventually have safety systems designed to prevent these types of accidents; within my lifetime I do not think there will be anymore rear end collisions, due to automatic stopping radar type systems that are being put on most new cars. So that is a good thing. But saying that "minor" rear end collisions do not or cannot cause injuries is just not true.

But in terms of the "reality of the courtroom," jurors will typically believe that people with minor impacts are faking their injuries to get money. It takes a very good lawyer to get around this belief system. I consider myself a very good lawyer, but my track record on winning minor impact cases is only 50-50; yet, that is better than most out there.

CHAPTER SEVENTEEN

DAMAGES IN A TORT CASE – AN OVERVIEW

I think a good overview as to the purpose of damages can be taken from a shortened version of a brilliant closing argument set forth in Rick Friedman's book "Polarizing the Case," which section was taken largely from his sometimes co-counsel, Don Bauermiester, from Anchorage, Alaska. I have, myself, used this as part of my closing arguments in many cases. My own experience is that older jurors really like this closing argument. Younger jurors, in particular Millennials, are, for whatever reasons, not as impressed and act somewhat bored by it; but, frankly, I have not yet figured out how to connect with Millennials on damages arguments (that is a work in progress for me!)

The concept of awarding monetary compensation for injury is nothing new.

We find mentions of the basics of such a system in the code of Hammurabi, a Mesopotamian system that predates the Bible.

In the old testament, there are hundreds of examples wherein, if, for example, your fence is insecure, and your mongrel goat breaks through and impregnates the prize female goat of another adjacent farmer, thus causing the female goat to skip having an otherwise prize batch of little goats, you have to pay the other farmer several goats to make up the difference.

We have all heard the expression "an eye for an eye." I read just recently wherein a middle eastern country, this penalty was actually enforced. A member of one family had, in a moment of anger, struck another family member's son and caused him to lose an eye; that family was allowed to take out the eye of the guilty party

Of course, in our civilized world, we do not want to countenance ancient systems of justice wherein actual body parts are taken to even the scales, or, sometimes death is used as a means to even the scales.

We cannot turn back the clock to make it as if the incident did not happen. The best we can do is to use money to compensate the victim.

There is another purpose to awarding money for injury. Perhaps, if you are old enough, you will know what I am talking about. There used to be a Woolworth's dime store in my town. They had on display several attractive glass or ceramic figurines. When I was a boy, I would shop there to buy my mom a gift for Mother's Day. There is a little sign attached to the cabinet upon where they had the ceramic figures on display. It says,

"Delightful to look at, even better to hold, but if you break it, consider it sold."

One time, a friend of mine was horsing around in the shop and the friend broke one of the figurines. He ran out the door home. The shop owner knew who he was (we lived in a small town), and he went to the parents of the boy and said he needs to pay six dollars, the cost of the figurine. The father offered to pay the shop owner for the damage caused by his son, but the shop owner said that is not going to teach him a lesson. I want other boys to learn that it is not okay to horse around in the store. So the young man was required to go to the store and sweep the floors for a couple hours in order to pay off the debt. All the other boys in the neighborhood then knew not to horse around or we would face a similar penalty. They knew it wasn't just a sign, it was something that would happen for real. So by enforcing a system of making the wrongdoer pay, it created a safety enforcement system.

There is a saying. Conduct ignored is conduct rewarded. If we do not seek to compensate persons who are hurt by the wrongdoing of another, then it creates an unsafe society.

This being said, how much money is appropriate compensation?

Let me tell you about an example that will make clear what your job is, when you back there figuring out what the harms and losses are in this case.

Let us say some boys are playing in a vacant lot that is next to a house owned by an older woman. They are drinking beers and throwing the football recklessly about, and eventually it crashes through the woman's window.

Should the boy who threw the football recklessly have to pay for a new window? Absolutely. How much should he have to pay? The cost of replacing the window, of course.

What if the woman was rich and did not need him to pay for it. Or she had homeowner's insurance to pay for it. Should he then be excused? The answer is no. He would not learn a lesson and other boys would not learn a lesson if he was let off the hook.

Let us say the boy was poor and could not afford to pay for the window. Should he be left off the hook then? Again, the answer is no, because then what would the lesson be for the other boys in the neighborhood?

What if the other boy was rich? Should he then have to pay the old woman more money because he is rich? No, he owes whatever it is that it costs to replace the window.

What if he were to say: That window was old anyway. Someday it would have broken. Why should I have to pay for it? That is not an excuse.

The fact that the window was old or maybe even had a crack in it and broke more easily is not an excuse. His action was the straw that broke the camel's back, so to speak.

What if the old woman had been standing at the window watching the boys play. The football went through the window, broke it, and then hit her in the eye causing damage to her eye. Should he have to pay her medical bill for her eye injury? Yes. What if he says, "No one could have ever imagined that the old woman would be standing there watching. How would I ever imagine that someone would be standing at a window watching me?" Does that let him off the hook? No. The fact is, if you recklessly are throwing a football around, someone could get hurt. The fact that you could not specifically imagine it was this woman getting hurt does not let you off the hook.

What if the woman's only pleasure in life was reading the bible. That was the only thing she did each day that gave her pleasure. And let us say when the boy's football hit her in her eye, it was her only "good" eye and she could no longer read the bible. Is it fair that he should only have to pay the medical bill for putting an eye patch on her, when so much of her life was taken away? Again, in order to make the scales properly balanced, he should have to pay for the damage to her loss of ability to enjoy reading her bible. If he were to say: "How could I possibly imagine that something like that could happen? I am just terribly unlucky. You can't punish me just because I'm unlucky."

The fact is if you are drinking beers and throwing a football around where you should not be throwing it, then all sorts of things can happen, bad, whether you imagine them or not. You should not be throwing the ball in the first place.

So, there you have it, by having a law on damages that compensates victims, we not only prevent social injustice, and, keep society "civilized," we also prevent persons from doing unsafe activities.

CHAPTER EIGHTEEN

DAMAGES – ACCORDING TO NEVADA'S JURY INSTRUCTIONS

Again, if we are looking at damages for purposes of a personal injury case, always a good starting place is the pattern jury instruction for Clark County, Nevada. The pattern jury instruction for damages states as follows:

PERSONAL INJURY DAMAGES INSTRUCTION 5PID.1: MEASURE OF DAMAGES
In determining the amount of losses, if any, suffered by the plaintiff as a [proximate] [legal] result of the accident in question, you will take into consideration the nature, extent and duration of the [injuries] [damage] you believe from the evidence plaintiff has sustained, and you will decide upon a sum of money sufficient to reasonably and fairly compensate plaintiff for the following items:
1. The reasonable medical expenses plaintiff has necessarily incurred as a result of the [accident] [incident] [and the medical expenses which you believe the plaintiff is reasonably certain to incur in the future as a result of the [accident] [incident], discounted to present value];
2. Plaintiff's loss of earnings or earning capacity from the date of the accident [incident] to the present;
3. Plaintiff's loss of earnings or earning capacity which you believe the plaintiff is reasonably certain to experience in the future as a result of the [accident] [incident], discounted to present value. [One's ability to work
may have a monetary value even though that person is not employed by another. In determining the extent to which

plaintiff's ability to work has diminished, you should balance on one hand the amount which the plaintiff was capable of earning before the injury against what [he] [she] is capable of earning hereafter. In other words, the damages should be properly estimated on the injured person's ability to earn money before the injury as against [his] [her] ability to earn money thereafter. Also, include the reasonable value of services performed by another in doing things for the plaintiff, which, except for the injury, plaintiff would ordinarily have performed.];

4. The physical and mental pain, suffering, anguish and disability endured by the plaintiff from the date of the [accident] [incident] to the present; and

5. The physical and mental pain, suffering, anguish and disability which you believe plaintiff is reasonably certain to experience in the future as a result of the [accident] [incident], discounted to present value.

A couple other "pattern" jury instructions that relate to damages, which are read at virtually every trial I have been involved in, are the "eggshell plaintiff" instruction which states as follows:

PERSONAL INJURY DAMAGES INSTRUCTION 5PID.3: PAIN AND SUFFERING: AGGRAVATION OF PRE-EXISTING CONDITION

A person who has a condition or disability at the time of an injury is not entitled to recover damages therefor. However, [he] [she] is entitled to recover damages for any aggravation of such preexisting condition or disability [proximately] [legally] resulting from the injury.

This is true even if the person's condition or disability made [him] [her] more susceptible to the possibility of ill effects than a normally healthy person would have been, and even if a normally healthy person probably would not have suffered any substantial injury.

Where a preexisting condition or disability is so aggravated, the damages as to such condition or disability are limited to the additional injury caused by the aggravation.

Case law also allows claims for "loss of enjoyment of life," a.k.a. "hedonic damages." See Banks v. Sunrise Hospital (a case that was an epic battle– eventually won– by our now Judge James Crockett. If he will tell you the story of this case, you are in for an inspiring treat.)

As virtually any good trial lawyer will tell young lawyers, when you are preparing a case in litigation, and thinking about what kinds of questions you want to ask in depositions, it is really a good place to start by looking at the jury instructions. If, for example, you have the jury instructions at the front of your "book" on the case (these days, usually on a computer now), it will help you to frame your questions to witnesses so that their answers will fit into the language of the jury instruction. This is particularly true when thinking about aggravation of pre-existing conditions.

Going along with these jury instructions and what damages can be awarded, we must also look at the instruction on what is our burden of proof. The "preponderance of the evidence" is a standard plaintiffs must meet. Our jury instruction on that states as follows:

BURDEN OF PROOF: PREPONDERANCE OF THE EVIDENCE

Whenever in these instructions I state that the burden, or the burden of proof, rests upon a certain party to prove a certain allegation made by [him] [her], the meaning of such an instruction is this: that unless the truth of the allegation is proved by a preponderance of the evidence, you shall find the same to be not true.

The term "preponderance of the evidence" means such evidence as, when weighed with that opposed to it, has more convincing force, and from which it appears that the greater probability of truth lies therein.

Again, when asking witnesses questions on the stand, or in depositions, if you can mimic or use the language that is in the jury instruction, you are way ahead of the game.

So then, we have our "laundry list" of what we can ask for.

These are separated into two general categories, "special damages" and "general damages." I am not sure what the history is of coming up with these terms, but they are universally applied by attorneys and claims adjusters.

The "special damages" are oftentimes referred to as "specials." These would include past medical bills, future medical bills, past lost wages, and future lost wages. In general, we talk about special damages as meaning those things that can be quantified with exact numbers.

The general damages include things such as emotional distress, pain and suffering, loss of enjoyment of life, disability. There are many excellent trial books and materials on how to explain to a jury how they might calculate general damages. I am of the school of that just telling the jury to "come up with a figure you think is fair" for general damages is NOT a good trial strategy. I heard of it working on occasion; but normally when I read a trial report where the plaintiff's lawyer does this, I know before even looking ahead to the end that the verdict will be "defense." I think if you tell a jury "just give me what you think is fair" it is tantamount to telling a jury you are ashamed of your case. If you feel ashamed of your case, then how do you expect a jury to give you money for it?

A lot of research over the last couple decades has shown that, without question, the words "pain and suffering" have taken on such a negative connotation with the general public that the thoughtful plaintiff's lawyer should probably never use them. When somebody asks to be awarded money for "pain and suffering" it is, in the public mind, tantamount to saying "give me money for nothing. This is a scam."

One of the great trial "gurus" of our time is David Ball, who is, or was, a professor at Duke University in the theatre arts. He got involved, originally, teaching lawyers how to apply theatre tactics (e.g., how to effectively write a play so it holds the interest of the audience) to trials. He thereafter got involved in trial consulting work, and he apparently has a close connection with the Duke psychology department, one of the top in the world. He was able, over time, to develop some theories which have been revolutionary in how lawyers present damages cases. His books are "must reads" for any serious trial attorney. David Ball On Damages is a classic.

Anyway, David Ball advocates using the term "harms and losses" instead of things like "pain and suffering." This is very good advice.

Trial lawyers for the last 30 plus years have also found that focus on how something effects a person's quality of life, i.e., loss of enjoyment of life, is much more effective than talking about pain and suffering. A plaintiff who is whining and crying on the stand will usually be a huge turn- off to the jury unless his/her injury is catastrophic in nature, e.g. quadriplegic, amputated legs. Whining how 'my life is ruined' and crying on the stand about, say, a rotator cuff tear or a broken ankle (both of which I have seen, unfortunately) is a major turn-off to the jury.

In other words, the plaintiff has to be very careful when talking about pain to a jury. Talking about pain is largely perceived as whining and begging for money. The more a plaintiff cries on a witness stand or similar (unless the injury is obviously, without explanation needed, very serious) the more the jury folds its arms. "Crying for dollars" might have worked in the first half of the 20th century, it does not work now with today's jurors.

Again, rather than belabor the points, I just refer you to read the David Ball book or books. The AAJ, through its jury studies done by David Wenner, Gregory Cuisimano, and others, have also developed some good thoughts on how to present damage cases in a way that resonates with the 21st century jury.

CHAPTER NINETEEN

WHAT BODILY INJURY DAMAGES MEAN TO AN AUTO INSURANCE COMPANY

Above we showed you the ultimate gauge of what is damages, i.e., the Clark County/Nevada State Jury Instruction on the subject; and, beyond that, what the jury decides.

But, we must concern ourselves also with what insurance companies consider to be damages, since the reality is most automobile cases are settled before trial takes place.

Insurance companies' concepts of damages are, ultimately, determined by the question: What can we get away with? But, since insurance companies do not hide the fact that they are about making profits, the "what can we get away with" standard is not illogical, nor even immoral; but it is amoral.

We start first with medical bills. Do insurance companies owe medical bills? If it is caused by the fault of another in the collision, the answer is basically: yes. But, insurance companies take the position that medical bills should not be incurred in a car accident involving minor damage to a rear bumper (other than perhaps an initial visit to a doctor or to get checked out.) They take this position because they have phony "biomechanical experts" and professional doctor witnesses who are able to sell the juries the idea that you cannot get hurt in a 'minor' rear end collision.

Ultimately, they are able to get away with it, so that, de facto, is the standard.

As to other medical bills, insurance companies are entitled, by law, to question the reasonableness of charges that seem to be too high. They think everything is too high, even though, as we all know, medical costs are very high these days. Insurance companies believe that doctors should not be allowed to charge more than Medicaid reimbursement rates; doctors, of course, strongly disagree.

Eventually, if push comes to shove, a plaintiff is entitled to what we might call "community standards" on bills, i.e., what is it most people charge for the same or similar service -- but insurance companies try to challenge even this.

Insurance companies often employ computer systems that supposedly "crunch" the numbers on medical bills to come up with 'fair' amounts. These computer programs are as phony as a three-dollar bill. They inevitably say that the bills are too high by some preset percentage amount that seems to apply to every bill submitted to the computer "shredder" machine.

Medicare rates (which are much better, usually, than Medicaid rates) for certain procedures do give us some sort of objective clue as to what things are worth, but no doctor accepts Medicare to pay for a procedure unless he has no other choice. So, Medicare rates are "fair" for Medicare patients, but doctors do not like to accept them for anything else.

As far as lost wages go, insurance companies believe we are still in the 1950's, where if you miss a day of work you need a doctor's excuse, much like getting a parent's excuse for missing a day of school. If you do not have the excuse from the doctor then they do not count the day of lost wages. That is just stupid. In this day and age people do not go to the doctors to get excuses to miss work. For one thing it is just too darn expensive and too much of a hassle. But, that is how insurance companies like to view lost wages, because it is something they can get away with.

As far as future medical bills go, insurance companies generally ignore   future medical bills claims, especially at pre- litigation stages. I recently heard an insurance lawyer tell me that "if they really needed the care they would go ahead and get it. We figure if you're not actually getting the care then why should we pay for it."

I am being somewhat hyperbolic when I say insurance companies do not pay attention to future medical bill reports. They do, but just because you have someone saying this or that, do not delude yourself into thinking that the insurance company will buy it unless they think it is a realistic threat at time of trial. Sometimes, if you really think you are entitled to future meds, the only way you are going to get it is at trial (and, the bad faith proceedings that may follow.)

As to awards for pain and suffering from an auto accident, insurance companies tend to be somewhat formulaic. They give far less value, settlement wise, for pain and suffering and other general damages than, would, say, a jury in a case that was not a "MIST" case. They value general damages (pain and suffering) much lower than, say, 20+ years ago.

They will give more for pain and suffering if you have an injury that involves solid objective proof, e.g. broken bone, torn ligament, etc. If it is just a soft tissue injury, then they will give less.

If you have a permanent injury (and by that, I mean something that is obviously permanent, as opposed to just arguably permanent), they will give a lot more for pain and suffering.

The current experience of my office (this is in 2018) is that, in Las Vegas, at least, the adjuster on auto cases will typically start out at medical bills (per their calculation of what is 'fair' for them), plus about $1500 a month for pain and suffering. On MIST (minor impact) cases, typically the first offers are less– less than the medical bills, not uncommonly. Sometimes first offers are better, sometimes they are worse than this; but, the client should keep in mind that first offers, just like first demands, do not decide what a case a worth. They are just places to start. I will say this: pre- litigation (before suit is filed) offers on automobile cases in Las Vegas have gone down quite a bit the last ten year, and the remedy for this is for more of us (plaintiff's lawyers) to take things to trial when necessary. If everyone keeps 'playing chicken' then there is little reason for insurance companies to quit this diminution of case value on automobile cases.

My own experience is that typically, the pre-litigation adjusters (at least, the ones not trying to be 'heroes') will go up about 15% above their first offers, and if that is insufficient, then they really don't care, because now the case will shift to the 'litigation adjuster,' the next step up the ladder. Sometimes the litigation adjuster can offer more right away after they see you are serious enough to file suit; I would say that this happens maybe about half the time. If the case is litigated, usually the offer will go up at some point (unless the client 'bombs' at his or her deposition, or is caught in a major discrepancy), but, whether the client wants to wait out the time for litigation to ripen, or, wants to take the risk of things going south, is something only the individual client can decide.

CHAPTER TWENTY

DAMAGES -
WHAT ARE THE "DRIVERS?

Every five years or so, it seems that there is a new batch of "cool guy" words to use when people who are normally not all that smart want to sound smart. Thankfully, the latest batch of words is coming to an end now. I refer to "feedback," "blowback," "empowerment," "tools" (as in, we are trying to educate the students so they will have the "toolset" to find jobs) "narrative," and "agenda." So, I apologize in advance for using the term "drive," as in, "what 'drives' the damages awards by juries?" What things make jurors give all the medical bills, not part of them; give all the requested general damages, not just part of them; etc.?

Insurance companies are, if nothing else, smart about collecting "mega data," so they are well aware of what the "drivers" might be, even if they typically lag behind a few years in figuring things out.

One thing that I would like all my clients to know is that an item that does NOT "drive" damages anymore is sympathy.

Permit me to tell a little story. There was a very excellent trial lawyer in Las Vegas named Randy Mainor, who was the "big gun" personal injury trial lawyer here in the nineties. He was one of the founders of the law firm that is now known as Eglet and Prince, which is a current "big" trial firm in town. Randy started out as an ordinary, in- the - trenches type personal injury lawyer, who did a lot of dog bite cases for   postal workers back in the day. He was partners with another lawyer who is now, also, deceased, named Bill Skupa. Back in the eighties, when Randy Mainor was with Skupa, he had a case that he tried that involved some pretty severe injuries, but very stretchy liability. It had something to do with a brake pedal on a Winniebago RV. He won what was, in the day, considered a big verdict; mid six figures as I recall. We were all pretty impressed by it. He followed it up with big verdict on a case involving really bad injuries at an outpatient surgical center (before we had the caps on malpractice cases.)

I remember Randy saying to me afterwards, when I had occasion to talk with him (back in those days, the small firm practitioners used to meet in the courthouse and swap stories), and he said that "just give me a plaintiff who is badly injured, and I'll get him some money."

Randy thought in those days, as did we all, that if you could get a jury feeling sorry enough for a plaintiff, they would find a way to give him some money. They would find liability for the plaintiff if the sympathy factors were bad enough, or, so we all thought.

I have heard old timey trial lawyers talk about how, especially back in places like New York City, in the fifties and sixties jurors would give money to people out of sympathy, even if their liability cases were weak.

It sure is not that way now. For whatever reason, many of my clients still think that verdicts are driven upwards by sympathy. I try to tell them the last thing I want them to do is to go on the witness stand and start crying and going on about how their lives have been ruined. Today's jurors, especially the Millennials, are totally turned off by appeal to sympathy. It is as though whatever existed in the world previously that made people feel sorry for one another, has been wiped out by modern culture. It is kind of sad, really, because I think sympathy is a fine and noble human emotion. The world was a better place when people felt sorry for one another. The day to day world is truly a much nastier to live than it was when I grew up.

The things that drives verdicts today are jurors' anger toward certain behaviors, and, their concerns about making the community a better place to live.

If you can get jurors feeling angry at the other party, then you can expect them to give you higher amounts for all the damage items. Mr. Spock, the emotionless vulcan of Star Trek, is not in the jury box. Part of doing your homework for a jury trial is finding out what 'real people' are mad about, and what they are not mad about. It is usually something quite different than what you might guess at. Just running the case past a few non-lawyer friends or relatives will yield interesting results; if the case is big enough to warrant it, formal focus groups are very valuable.

Jurors are also concerned, about safety. They know, intuitively, that what they do in the jury box will have an effect on the community's standards for safety. They are, in effect, the 'conscience of the community.' This has been made clear in many Nevada cases, most notably Gunderson v. D.R. Horton, 130 Nev Ad 9; Foster v. Costco, 231 P3d 150. The term 'conscience of the community' was expressly approved in Vinci v. LV Sands, 115 Nev 243; and probably most significantly, the recent case of Pizzaro v. Cervantes, 396 P3d 783, made clear that the court was expressly allowing plaintiffs to argue that the jury in an auto case is 'sending a message based on the evidence' to the community about the safety standards in the community. A case that concerns a big safety threat to the community at large, e.g. drunk driver, texting, is going to get bigger damages than a case concerning a singular incident not likely to be repeated by anyone else on the roadway, and not preventable by a rule, e.g. person having totally unpredictable stroke while driving.

Jurors are also more likely to award damages for things that actually "fix" a problem. If there is, say, a medical piece of equipment that health insurance will not cover, they are willing to give you money for that. If you were out of work for a while, and have the documents to prove it, and you did not

105

receive vacation or sick pay, they are willing to give money for that, to fill in the hole. David Ball has some very good discussions of this in his books.

Beyond trying to fix things that can be fixed, jurors like to award money if it will make them feel that they have done something satisfying. By this I mean if the juror is angry at the defendant's conduct, it makes them feel good to lash out, with a verdict, against the "bad guy." Also, if their verdict will bring about a change in society, something that might life a little bit safer, then it is in society' s interest to give an adequate award. Asking them to give money "even if you don't feel good about doing it, because that's the law" is not going to work.

Jurors, like voters, vote self-interest and pocketbook; they vote to favor their own "tribal" groups. Politicians and insurance companies realize this and exploit it as best they can. Some of it is done very subtly; they hire psychologists and others who send out "dog whistle" messages to jurors to appeal to their base instincts.

I once read that an insurance company exec said his favorite book was "The Selfish Gene," which basically defines all human conduct in terms of animalistic selfish instincts. Insurance companies want individual jurors to think: if I give an award, it will make my rates go up; why should I care about someone else if it hits me in my pocketbook.

106

Personally, I believe that one of the main things that holds damages down in automobile cases is that jurors do not want their own insurance rates to go up. That is a very powerful motivation for them to fold their arms and not listen to the plaintiff's side of the story. Plaintiff's lawyers have to find other motivations that are just as strong. As noted, the concepts of "sympathy" and "justice for all" do not have much, if any, traction in 2018. Some of these alternative concepts/motivations have been discussed at some length, above.

Likeability is another large factor in deciding how much damages will be awarded. I refer here to the liability of not only the plaintiff, but the plaintiff's lawyer as well.

Likeable does not mean "everyone's idea of a good friend." It basically means likeable in the sense of who people trust and want to help.

A client who is someone you did not like the first time you met him is someone the jury will not like in a case. Remember that. If your gut instinct, the first time you meet a potential client, is that you do not like this person, then by all means try to settle that case before it goes to trial.

In a similar way, lawyers are either likeable or they are not. Be honest with yourself. If you are someone who never was particularly good with people, had trouble making friends or relating to people, and so forth, you are probably not going to be very well liked in a jury courtroom, either.

Harsh words, I know, but true. True, I have seen some rather unlikeable lawyers win trials, but, they were good at putting on a demeanor in the courtroom that was at odds with their true personalities. Most people who try this fail, but a few people– very few– seem able to pull it off.

CHAPTER TWENTY-ONE

ANOTHER DAMAGES FACTOR CREDIBILITY OF THE PHYSICIANS

The fact is, the insurance companies don't believe doctors who are commonly involved in the treatment of automobile accident injuries, whether or not the doctor is a completely honest fellow.

Doctors who fool themselves (I have run across many of them) that if they do this or that "it will hurt my reputation with the insurance company" operate under the delusion that the insurance company actually ever thinks of them in positive light. If you are a doctor and you treat, frequently, people injured in automobile accidents, the insurance company considers you a piece of garbage no matter what you say or do. And again, this has nothing to do with reality. It simply is a facet of "us versus them," you cost them money, therefore you are evil.

There are certain doctors who are better witnesses than others on the witness stand. If a case gets to the point where it looks like it might go to trial, this is considered, at least, by the defense lawyers (I'm not convinced that the insurance carriers concern themselves with this, because they are trying to evaluate everything by computers and data bases that are not Las Vegas based.)

Again, if it gets to the trial stage, the same things that affect people in everyday life affect their perceptions of physician witnesses. This means that if a doctor is a temple Mormon and the juror is a temple Mormon, the juror is likely to give extra credit to the doctor's credibility. The doctor who has quit practicing medicine to testify full time for insurance companies (there are at least two in LV, and they make over a million dollars a year) is going to have less credibility than a real doctor, because people understand on a basic level that this man has given up treating sick people to make big bucks running his mouth for insurance companies.

Doctors who act like real jerks on the witness stand (and there are many -- the "God complex" thing and all that), are less well liked than the "folksy awe shucks" type doctor (there are several who put on an act of being folksy. There is one doctor the insurance company hires quite frequently to be an expert witness. This fellow is about as egotistical as they come. But he always likes to slip into his testimony the phrase "I'm just an ole country bone doctor" in every trial.)

Doctors who have a military service background typically parade it around the courtroom. Frankly if I am the attorney for someone and the treating doctor has a military background, I like to highlight it. In 2018, that is a big positive factor in doctor credibility. There are some doctors with military backgrounds who make claims about awards of medals they do not have, or make false claims about combat experience. There are websites where you can check these things out. Interestingly, I have also encountered several doctors who make false claims about college athletics, e.g. claiming they 'played ball at SC' or "was drafted by the Red Sox," when they never sniffed the field. There is a service that, for about $1500, will thoroughly check out an insurance doctor's CV. I have benefitted from them. In about 50% of the names submitted, they have found alarming misrepresentations about awards, degrees, fellowships, residencies, alleged articles published, etc. – not just picky picky, but major, flat-out lies. More than once I have encountered insurance doctors who say they are 'board certified,' and it turns out they flunked their boards. It seems that the easy big money of being an 'insurance testifying expert' attracts the kind of doctors who like to put fake stuff on their resumes. In a way, it makes sense, if you think about it.

One factor in doctor credibility that I have always found puzzling is the misleading nature of bragging about a doctor being a "clinical professor." The insurance expert doctors all like to crow about this. Unsophisticated jurors do not know that virtually any physician who gives some help to the medical school will receive the honorary title "clinical professor." It is not a "professorship" in the way in which lay people understand such things.

Jurors like doctors who do not use the big words all the time. The doctors who are effective witnesses understand this and avoid trying to show off with medical lingo. The more insecure doctors cling to using medical jargon on the stand as a kind of shield, and jurors don't like it.

Jurors do not care all that much about where people went to medical school, where they did their residencies, etc. Doctors themselves put a lot of emphasis on this, and they think that once a juror hears they went to Stanford Medical School, that should be that: game over. But, the average juror is just as impressed with a fellow that went to, say, University of Illinois Medical School, or, for that matter, an osteopathic medical school.

Back in 70's and 80's, chiropractors had a kind of, shall we say, 'funky' reputation with the public. If I went to trial then, and I had a chiropractic treating physician, the defense lawyer would sneer and say, "you're not a real doctor, are you, Mr. Smith," and then make a point of calling my witness "Mister," instead of "Doctor." Things have changes. Jurors now are totally OK with chiropractors, in general, as testifying witnesses, as long as they "stay in their lane." If the chiropractor sticks to talking about necks and backs, ok; when they venture out into giving opinions on, say, diabetes treatment, or treatment of drug addiction, etc., it can undermine credibility. Chiropractors can claim a lot of the 'high ground' these days by stating that their treatment does not involve narcotic prescriptions, and that if a person can get relief without taking opioids, that is well worth the cost.

If you have a doctor testifying who is new to the process, and is scared, and consequently wants to veer off into rambling discourses, or use a lot of medical lingo to show he is, for God's sake, a real doctor; I would recommend that you get the medical records admitted, and then go through the records (selected sections, of course, not all of them) on the Elmo, and have the doctor read this or that sentence, and then explain what this or that means. Then, also, have some props (medical illustration blow ups, plastic models of the bones, etc.) he can use.

As lawyers, we get very concerned with the physician's credentials, when the jury doesn't care very much about them; and, we are concerned about the doctor being attacked because he has been on the stand in the past for one of your cases, etc (again, I don't think jurors are all that concerned with this.) What makes jurors like, or dislike, doctors, more than anything else, is whether they can talk in language (i.e. 8th grade level, no higher) that a juror can understand, and who seem NOT to condescend to the jury (which is the impression they get from overuse of medical lingo and rambling discourses on medical topics, etc.).

CHAPTER TWENTY-TWO

DAMAGES DRIVING FACTOR TRIAL EXPERIENCE OF ATTORNEY

The lawyer is an incredibly important piece of the puzzle in determining the value of the case. I guess considering that I am the person writing this book (and I am a lawyer) that's self-serving; but it's true.

If you had asked me this question 35 years ago I would have said something differently. I would have said that the lawyers are relatively minor players in everything and that the "facts" of the case are what drive value. The facts are still more important than the lawyer, I will give you that; but I would put the lawyers' importance much higher now than I did before.

A good lawyer can sometimes lose a case, even a good case; you never know who might end up on a jury panel through luck of the draw, or, you might get a judge who is very opinionated. But it is very unusual for a bad lawyer to ever win. This is especially true on the plaintiff's side of the case, where winning a case is much more difficult than, say, the job of an insurance lawyer. (Many an insurance lawyer has thought themselves to be exceptionally good because they have won the large percentage of their trials, only to find out, when they switch to the plaintiff's side to make what they think is the "big money," they can't win even the "easy" cases. It's a lot harder on our side of the fence, trial wise. We have the burden of proof, and the public perception is not in favor of plaintiffs– e.g. the 'cash for crash' TV lawyers and billboards– at the moment.)

As far as being a good trial lawyer, I will rate experience as being the primary factor that separates the "men from the boys," or, "the women from the girls."

There's no substitute for experience, and by that, I mean being the first chair attorney on a "real" jury trial (i.e., not the "one day" jury trials that are more akin to arbitrations.)

One of my idols, law professor Irving Younger (now deceased) once said that it takes 25 civil jury trials to become competent; it takes far more trials than that to become good. I would agree with him.

Trying cases to become experienced is the most expensive school in the world. The fact is the first 25 trials that you conduct as first chair, you are going to stumble a lot. You are going to spend a lot of money on experts and so forth, and a lot of time, and a lot of heartache, just to end up with the most devastating of feelings when the jury tells you they don't like your case with a defense verdict (even very experienced lawyers get defensed. It happens if you try enough cases and are not afraid to try the tough cases.)   But, you're never going to get there unless you put on the uniform and go into the battle arena. For the vast majority of lawyers, this is too high a price to pay and they never do it. They fake their way through by claiming to have extensive trial experience when in fact they do not. My advice to a young attorney who has a good case that must go to trial is to hire a good trial attorney to try the case, and sit in there as second chair and learn. Do this a few times and then you can try being the first chair yourself, and have a decent understanding of what it takes.

You can go to all the trial colleges you want and do all the "mock trials" and one-day jury trials you want. But the fact is there is no substitute for the "live bullets" of a real trial in a real courtroom with a real jury, especially where your own personal financial well-being is on the line.

It is not pleasant going through this, but when you've done it 25 times, you will at least have the self-confidence that you've been there, done that, faced the real bullets, taken a few, and these other fellows talking tough are just posers and pretenders. You don't have to say it, you just know it. It's the difference between being real and being another one of the posers.

I have been asked sometimes: Can I get the same kind of experience trying criminal cases? That is, would trying 25 criminal trials put me in the same place as, say, the guy who has tried 25 civil jury trials?

116

My answer is not really, but it's a heck of a lot better than the guy who hasn't tried a jury case at all.

Prosecutors, in particular, get bloated notions of how good they are as because they win virtually all their cases. The fact is, winning a criminal prosecution case is like shooting fish in a barrel. The jury is on your side, the credible witnesses all want to help you, usually the facts are overwhelmingly against the defendant, and the judges bend over backwards to help you (as they are elected and do not want to see as 'soft on crime.') But, it does give you the experience of being in a trial, talking to a jury, dealing with evidentiary objections, dealing with witnesses who run the gamut from extremely smart to extremely dumb, etc.

I think the experience of being a defense lawyer in a criminal jury trial, such as being a public defender, is probably more valuable. You certainly won't get the "big head" of being someone who wins a lot if you are a public defender. You are probably going to lose the vast majority of your cases. The witnesses and the jurors basically hate you before you even open your mouth, so keeping your composure and trying to think fast on your feet and come up with something are big requirements. You oftentimes have a tiny or non-existent budget to work with as opposed to the prosecutors, who have unlimited resources, so you have to be creative. I think being a criminal defense lawyer doing jury trials is great experience for being a civil trial lawyer. Unfortunately, in today's world there are many public defenders who never go to trial because they plea bargain everything, and the only cases they get to try are involving "nut job" clients who insist on their innocence even though there is video film of them doing the crime. But, any public defender who hangs in there long enough is going to get in his 25 jury trials, and I would say that they have a big leg up on the typical attorney who gets out of law school and never tries a jury case as first chair.

There are a number of lawyers I know who get their experience trying cases in civil jury trials as insurance defense lawyers, and then switch sides. Frankly, many of the very best plaintiff's trial lawyers have this experience pattern in their background. The most famous example would be Gerry Spence. In Las Vegas, we can look at Bob Eglet and Dennis Prince, both of whom were fearsome insurance lawyers who switched sides (and who now acknowledge how unseemly the defense side of the bar can be in its tactics.), or Bob Vannah, or my partner, Mike Koning (who at one time won over 80 jury trials in a row on the defense side), who all tried scores of cases as insurance trial lawyers. (As a side note, there are a couple lawyers who advertise and brag how they used to work for insurance companies and know the playbook. Some of these guys never tried a case to the best of my knowledge. The 'real deals' like Eglet, Prince, Vannah, and Koning, do not advertise in such a manner.)

As much as I dislike insurance companies and their attorneys, I will acknowledge that if you are a lawyer looking to get civil trial experience, this may be the route you have to go to get it. You hold your nose, do 25 trials on the defense side, and then break free of the shackles and the lies and get to pick and choose your cases and put our own money and your own time on the line.

To readers of this book who have never had the experience of being first chair in a real jury trial, I can tell you it's a real thrill. Personally, I am exhausted by it more now than I was 25 years ago, but I l still like it a great deal; it's a real 'rush,' to use 70's venacular, and I can now do many parts of the trial much more easily than before, based on experience. But, the world keeps changing, and the law keeps changing.

CHAPTER TWENTY-THREE

DO CAR DAMAGE PHOTOS REALLY SHOW IF SOMEONE IS HURT?

The answer to the above question is twofold.

Can you tell by looking at a car damage photo if someone is really hurt or not? The answer in the "real world" is no.

But, can a jury tell if someone is really injured by looking at a photo, or not? The answer is: They think they can. They have a strong bias in favor of believing that not much damage in a photo = no one could be hurt.

I once employed a true expert, a professor from Marquette, on a case that involved determining whether or not someone's injuries were related to a seatbelt being absent, or not. In this particular case a taxi cab didn't have a seatbelt, and we were arguing that had one been there, the injuries would have been prevented. Anyway, this particular fellow was the real deal, unlike the vast majority of the "biomechanical" experts. He was qualified both as a physician and as an engineer, and his specialty was "real" world biomechanics for institutions that needed true data. Most of his work was actually done for the military. The military doesn't care about lies from the witness stand, it just wants to know if someone is really hurt or not, if something really works or not, etc. I asked this fellow: can you tell from the deformation of a car body if someone is hurt?

He told me the truth: that just looking at deformation or damage to a vehicle doesn't really tell you much, if anything useful, about what kind of injuries occurred. For example, soldiers in the Middle East experienced horrible brain injuries from concussion effects of roadside bombs that, while causing major concussive effect, sometimes caused relatively little damage to the vehicle occupied by the soldier.

Soldiers whose helmets were not deformed suffered major brain injuries because the force of trauma can oftentimes be transmitted without deforming protective coverings.

I recall he told me of a simple lesson in physics which applies in the everyday world of car accidents, except that, when it comes to jury trials, it doesn't apply when biomechanical experts are allowed to testify about the results of 'studies' conducted by auto insurance companies.

Let's say you are on a giant roller skate that got hit by a high velocity object in the rear. You would shoot forward in this hypothetical roller skate, going from a stop position to a very high velocity position instantly. If the roller skate was, say, on an ice rink, to make the example even more clear, it would shoot forward at great velocity when impacted, yet, the roller skate itself would have no deformation on it. The energy would be absorbed by the sudden acceleration on the ice, vs. deformation of the back of the roller skate. And, the sudden acceleration (the change in velocity, called "delta V" force) would cause injury to the person sitting on a roller skate.

But let's say that you are on the same hypothetical roller skate, and the front of it is up against a concrete wall. The skate can't move forward. The skate gets hit from the back by a high velocity object. The skate is totally crushed but doesn't move forward because it is against the wall. The occupant of that hypothetical roller skate wouldn't get hurt at all. Even though the roller skate is deformed, totaled, in fact, the change in velocity from the impact is zero.

To take this same analogy even further, modern cars are designed to absorb impact by deforming in certain ways. In a way, going against basic intuition, the more the car deforms, the more energy was absorbed, and the less energy is transmitted to the occupant.

If you are in a heavy vehicle like a full size pickup truck with a steel frame, and you are hit, there may be little damage to the truck, but the force would be transmitted through the heavy steel frame directly to the occupants. The fact that an old-fashioned truck body doesn't deform makes it more likely to transmit force to the occupants.

The people who serve as "biomechanical" experts for insurance companies know all this. But they sell themselves out for money, and argue things that actually go against the laws of physics. If you hire your own expert to argue the other side of the case, the jury oftentimes will sit with folded arms and not even listen, even though it is the truth.

I suppose if a car is totally wiped out, as in a rollover, one might presume that the occupant of that accident had a lot more force applied to his body than did the occupant of a "minor impact" rear collision. But, beyond that type of extreme example, it's very difficult if not impossible to draw any conclusions about whether or not someone was hurt, by looking at a photo in reality (but, jurors are fooled by the plastic or rubber bumper cover that just shows a 'scratch' on the outside.)

In today's world, the most effective way of countering the 'minor impact defense' is to find preexisting vulnerabilities of your client (e.g. preexisting arthritic changes) and argue how those would make the plaintiff more susceptible to injury; or, to try to tell the jury the truth about minor impacts, and hope that somehow the truth will penetrate past the lies. This, plus the 'egg carton argument' (i.e. you cannot tell if an egg is cracked by looking at the outside of the carton) are your two best arguments in a minor impact trial.

CHAPTER TWENTY-FOUR

THE 'WHO DESERVES IT' QUESTION

If we look only at the jury instructions and the "relevant facts," in order to determine whether or not a plaintiff deserves damages, and if so, how much, which is, after all, what the jury is instructed to do, we will miss a very important basic question that, subconsciously, the jury is deciding: *Does the plaintiff "deserve" to get the money, and does the defendant "deserve" to pay it?*

This is a question of basic morality that would occur even to a six-year-old. It may not, technically, be "right," but it is looming in the background of every case. The amount of damages plaintiff gets can depend on this analysis. (Note: avid "Reptile" proponents say that if the case has enough aspects that relate to community safety issues, who and what the plaintiff is becomes of little or no importance. I take my hat off to the lawyers who have won big verdicts with 'bad' plaintiffs. While I agree totally with the philosophy to focus more on the defendant, and his/her/its conduct, as opposed to the plaintiff, I still think that the 'deserve' question is relevant.)

How you might come up with answers to this question would depend largely on your own background, I suppose.

But I can tell you a few observations I have made.

Juries generally think that plaintiffs who have "worked" the system don't really "deserve" to get a windfall of money from an accident case. Therefore, if you have a client who receives public assistance, I recommend filing a motion in limine to keep that out of evidence.

Jurors dislike plaintiffs who forget to file tax returns, or, who file obviously inaccurate ones. (If you have a client with this issue, consider dropping your lost wage claim, so that you can keep tax return evidence out on a motion in limine.)

People who work in the "sex industry," even on the fringes of it (e.g. gentleman's club bartender, limo driver, the guys who flap the pamphlets on the strip) are going to be disliked by many jurors, despite our city's 'everything goes' reputation.

If you have a plaintiff who is hardworking, churchgoing, etc., you want to play up those factors in a jury trial. Military background is especially good. Those things should not, theoretically, matter when it comes to assessing harms and losses, but they do in the real world. The background of your client is important, both for better and for worse, and plays a big part in the trial even though it has nothing to do with who ran the

125

red light, or, whether the bone was broken. Insurance company lawyers have known this for decades. This is why they are so hell-bent on 'digging for dirt' on every person who was unlucky enough to have a drunk driver plow into their car.

Defendants, on the other hand, are subject to the same kind of analysis, even though everyone already knows it's not them, personally, paying; it's their insurance company. The grandma who worked hard all her life raising her children, belongs to various well thought- of charities, etc., does not "deserve" to pay for a momentary lapse in not knowing there was a red light at the intersection, in the childlike mind; but, you are going to have to deal with the "child" part of a juror's brain. We all have parts of our brain that decide things based on childish criteria and emotion. The defendant who has a felony record is going to fare less well in trial, even though the fact that he defrauded a bank thirty years ago does not really directly relate to whether he ran the red light. (Note: many prior criminal convictions, if they are more than 10 years in the past and do not involve crimes of dishonesty, can be kept out of evidence upon a motion in limine.)

(Nevada does allow, expressly, attorneys to ask jurors about whether or not they have any interest in insurance companies during voir dire. This is the Silver State case. Plaintiff's attorneys should always spend some time making sure the jurors understand that the plaintiff is very concerned about the prejudicial effects that might occur if a juror had a family member who worked for, or otherwise had some interest in insurance companies. Insurance lawyers will sometimes object that this sort of questioning will clue even the most dim witted juror into the realization that the claim is actually being paid by an insurance company, which is considered overly prejudicial by cases decided 70 years ago; but, even if this is a collateral effect of such questioning, under the Silver State case, this line of questioning is expressly allowed in order to ferret out persons connected to insurance companies, who would obviously be biased.)

I would like to finish this section by stating that I am not endorsing, by any means, the apparent practice of jurors to inject their feelings of "who deserves" the money into their decision-making process. David Ball, in his books, has some very good advice on educating the jury, early and often, that they are only to consider the 'harms and losses,' in deciding damages, and no other factors. I think this can help get the juror's attention onto what they are supposed to decide.

But, I am old school, and before I start any auto accident trial, I take out a scratch pad, and I write at the top of it: Why is my client deserving? And, then I write down stuff like, "raised 3 good kids; worked to put herself through college; never been in trouble," etc. And, I also write down: Why does the defendant deserve to pay? I put down things like, "never asked if anyone was OK at the scene. Keeps causing accidents. Been in jail for

127

not paying child support. Has a sinister looking tattoo."

As a related side bar to this: be sure, before the trial, to check out your client's social media pages, and the defendant's social media pages. Even the judge tells the jury not to do this, rest assured, some of them will, anyway. A lot of the "who deserves" information can be found on the social media pages.

But, what if your client has a lot of "warts," and you can't keep them out with motions in limine? Does that mean you are doomed before you even come out of the gate? Sometimes, yes (which means you settle the case if there is a fair offer on the table.) But, if the defendant is a real "black hat," and the facts egregious enough, you can still win. You just focus on the defendant and his conduct, and keep bringing the trial focus back to that at every opportunity, as much as you can. The "deserve" thing is a two way street.

CHAPTER TWENTY-FIVE

"OBJECTIVE" VERSUS "SUBJECTIVE" SYMPTOMS IN TERMS OF DECIDING CASE VALUE

Insurance adjusters and lawyers make a huge thing out of whether or not a patient's symptoms are "subjective" or "objective" in nature, in terms of assessing the damages value. I agree it's important, but I think they overestimate its importance, thinking that jurors will be impressed by the distinction. In my observation, jurors are confused by this and do not give it the attention that insurers think it deserves.

A "subjective" symptom is something that the patient tells the doctor, that cannot be determined for truthfulness/veracity by things that a doctor can tell simply by visual observation, or, by means other than what the patient says verbally (e.g. xrays, diagnostic testing.)

For example, I tell a doctor "I have a headache." That is a subjective symptom, because the doctor can't tell, just by looking at me, whether I have a headache or not. I tell a doctor "I am in pain," and generally speaking, he cannot tell if I am in pain or not just by looking at me.

The fact that we can talk and tell doctors where we hurt is essential to a good diagnosis. It's the difference between being a doctor and being a veterinarian. A vet cannot ask the animal "where does it hurt," he has to depend upon observation, or poking the animal to look for reactions, etc., to tell. Human doctors, on the other hand, have the great advantage in diagnosing by listening to a patient tell him what hurts, how it hurts, etc.

And "objective" signs (technically, things that are subjective are called "symptoms," and things that are objective are called "signs"), would be something that you can tell without even hearing the patient speak. For example, a doctor can look at an x-ray and tell whether a bone is broken or not. The patient doesn't have to say, "My bone is broken," the doctor can tell it by just looking at an x-ray.

Similarly, a doctor can tell you have a laceration simply by seeing the broken skin; you do not have to tell him "I got cut on my leg," for him to arrive at the diagnosis. But, if the laceration hit a nerve, the doctor would not know that unless you said, "Doctor, there where it's cut, it's numb, too, below the cut." So, to make a full diagnosis, he would need both subjective and objective data.

So, medicine is a combination of making a diagnosis from both symptoms/subjective things, and signs/objective things.

The most basic form of a doctor's office notes are called "SOAP" notes. This stands for the format of "symptoms, objective, assessment, plan."

So when the patient comes in, the doctor (at least in the old days) would actually write out the initials "SOAP," and then jot down his findings under each category. For the "S" part he would write down what the patient told him was hurting and where it was hurting and how it was hurting, etc. For the "O" part he would write down things that he might notice with his eyes (patient limping), etc., or things that he saw in an x-ray film, etc. The "assessment" is basically the "diagnosis" or, educated guess, as to what is wrong. The "P" or "plan," is the treatment the doctor plans to give.

Thus, in the case of any doctor who is not committing malpractice, the "S" part of any patient visits in arriving at a diagnosis is critical.

Yes, it's possible for a patient to "lie" about "subjective" symptoms, whereas a patient is not capable of faking "objective" signs. That, I suppose is what insurance lawyers are trying to point out when they make a big deal out of the distinction.

But this is not the same as saying that "subjective" is worthless. However, that is the position taken by many insurance companies.

The plaintiff's lawyer will point out sometime in the trial that subjective symptoms are critical to the diagnosis made by any legitimate physician for any condition. Were it not so, we would all receive the same sort of treatment that a veterinarian gives to a dog, where the cause of a problem is oftentimes guessed at, wrongly, because the animal cannot speak to give precise information.

Also, more critically I think, is that the attorney must educate himself in some basic medicine and learn which particular items in the exam are actually "objective" in nature and cannot be faked.

For example, the finding of straightening of the spine caused by muscle spasm is a common finding in many x-rays. It can also be described in different medical terms which the attorney must know. Pointing out that the x-ray proves there is muscle spasm is extremely important. A patient cannot fake this.

Doctors also have means of determining if patients are faking by a system of tests they call the "Waddell test." The Waddell system is a series of tests, usually five, which, to a non-educated person, would seem to be testing a certain body part for pain. In fact, the test is not affecting that body part. But if the client/patient says "ouch" when the doctor does the "Waddell" test on him, that tends to indicate that the patient may have psychological issues happening, although, there have been many studies showing that the Waddell tests are flawed in terms of actually determining who is telling the truth, since some of them actually can cause pain, and some patients are hypersensitive.

Doctors are also trained, after doing tens of thousands of exams, in spotting "fakers." There are thousands of "tell" signs that people give that doctors are professionally trained to recognize. I have had many doctors call me up and say, "That patient of yours, so and so. I can't really put my finger on it but there is something about that guy that just doesn't seem right." I am usually grateful to get the "heads up" like this, and then I drop the case. The doctors are too busy, and I'm too busy, to waste our time with someone who is trying to "pull the leg" on the system, or, who is a hypochondriac of some sort.

The software programs insurance companies use to evaluate auto bodily injury claims ("Colossus" and its clones) supposedly ask the claims processor to list the objective signs; and so our firm's demand letter on auto cases will list objective signs, to make the adjuster's job easier. Frankly, I don't think this makes much of a difference these days (this is being written in 2018), as I think that the claims processors do their own analysis of the medical records for 'objective' signs, and do not pay much attention to the demand letter contents in this regard.

To sum it up, insurance companies put much more importance on 'subjective' vs. 'objective' than do juries. Jurors are confused by the distinction (although jurors do put undue weight on technological evidence, such as MRI, which normally works to the plaintiff's advantage, I think.) But, this being said, in terms of arguing a cases' value for purposes of settlement, a good plaintiff's lawyer should know some basic medicine and be able to point out the 'objective' signs that are noted in most every auto accident case. These typically include: muscle spasm or hypertonicity; straightening or abnormal curvature, e.g. kyphosis, of the spine caused by spasm; MRI findings such as protruding or torn disks; swelling/edema; contusions; popping or clicking sounds; range of motion testing (if done properly); abnormal findings in EMG/NCV testing, particularly those that are deemed acute or subacute, and are relatable to injury being claimed (e.g. cervical radicular, not carpal tunnel, in a case not involving wrist trauma). Successful (even temporarily) epidural or facet injections also provide objective diagnostic data, in addition to the treatment aspect.

CHAPTER TWENTY-SIX

WHAT SPINAL MRI'S DO AND DO NOT SHOW IN A CAR ACCIDENT CASE

We are, as a society, overly impressed with technology, I think. It is true that technology has freed us from the ravages of many diseases that are now curable, and has greatly enhanced our lives, doing things that even 200 years ago would have seemed like "miracles" from the Bible.

But technology has its limits.

MRI tests are an example. This is a really incredible piece of technology, in general. It sends pulses of magnetic energy through the body which are deflected by various substances inside the body (water, muscle, bone, fascia, tendons, ligaments, etc.), and the deflections are measured, and a computer puts it all together into an image.

Among other incredible features of the MRI, the device does not use x-rays, which have been shown to be very harmful in human beings, and cumulative in their effect. Whereas a "CT scan" uses x-rays, and actually can subject the patient to a thousand x-rays over the course of a couple minutes, an MRI machine uses harmless magnetic energy (although, there are what are generally regarded as crank theorists who dispute that magnetic waves are harmless.)

The images from an MRI machine are almost 3D-like (and I am sure, within the next few years, we'll have actual 3D hologram type images put together by these machines), and they can show what x-rays cannot: soft tissue such as discs, ligaments, etc. The MRI, in terms of the spine, for example, can show whether or not a disc is in its normal shape, or not in its normal shape, whether it is in position or out of position, etc.

But -- and this is a big but -- it cannot show, by itself, how painful a given abnormality might be; and, just by itself, it cannot tell you the exact date an abnormality began (to do that, you need 'clinical correlation,' which means other data, such as the patient's symptoms and history of trauma.)

There has recently been a trend with insurance companies, who know about jurors' overreliance on technology, to hire radiology "experts" who claim that they can look at an MRI film, and determine not only if there is an abnormality shown, but can tell you exactly how old it is, whether it came from the accident, and whether it actually causes pain or not. There is one such particular expert in central California who I have seen more and more frequently being called upon by insurance companies to testify here in Nevada. They pay him upwards of $20,000 to testify in court that he can read MRI films for all sorts of data that others cannot see. Of course, these 'experts' say everything is preexisting, and, not painful. They are indeed quasi-psychic, not unlike Uri Geller, in their ability to tell exact date of origin of disc protrusion, which is always some date other than the accident itself, and whether it *truly* causes pain. (More honest radiologists will say that the film tells you a lot, but it cannot tell you, just by itself, how painful something might be; or, just by itself, the exact date when something started; for that, you have to look at other information and correlate with the MRI.)

To sum up, the MRI is a marvelous piece of technology, and it can give us a lot of useful information. It can show, precisely, if there are disk abnormalities, and where they are located. But, it cannot show whether and to what extent the abnormality is painful. It can, within very broad parameters, show if something is quite old, vs. not really old; but beyond that, it cannot, just by itself, show the exact time an abnormality started (for this, the doctor needs to have other information, which they call "clinical correlation," such as whether there was a traumatic event, and, the relevant symptoms as reported by the patient.)

CHAPTER TWENTY-SEVEN

BULGE VERSUS HERNIATION VERUS PROTRUSION

There is a subject that is more important, I think, to adjusters and attorneys than it is to members of the public that sit on juries. It has to do with whether or not a disc shape abnormality shown in an MRI is a "bulge," or a "herniation," or a "protrusion."

Twenty years ago, discs were classified as either "bulges" or "herniations" by radiologists. A "bulge" was usually smaller in size than a "herniation" and generally was perceived to be non-surgical or something caused by the effects of aging. A "herniation" was assumed to be more surgical in nature and more likely to have been caused by trauma.

I am personally aware of a situation some 25 years ago where a workman's compensation insurance company was offering large financial incentives to a radiology firm to refrain from ever using the word "herniated" in describing a disc in its reports.

I have a radiologist friend who told me that, years ago, at a medical conference, this subject came up during one of the presentations. The speaker remarked "if you use the word herniated, you just handed a lawyer $50,000." This comment was meant to discourage the attending radiologists from using the term, since they generally have resentments towards lawyers (as do most doctors, in general.)

In order to relieve radiologists of the perceived role of helping lawyers, or getting entangled into legal matters, radiologists started using the much more general word "protrusion" instead of "herniation. " The large majority of the time a "protrusion" described in a report it is what used to be called a "herniation." It is a disc that has an unusual shape that is possibly traumatic in origin, and could be a pain generator. A "bulge" is a mis-shape, what a lay person would call a protrusion, but generally speaking, a mis-shape milder curvatures in the mis-shaped portion. A bulge could cause pain and could be surgical, but is much less likely to be so than is a "protrusion." Both a bulge and a protrusion can cause pain. A protrusion, generally, has a more acute angle to the mis-shape portion, and the 'bulge' has a less sharp angle to its mis-shape portion. The distinction between "bulge" and "protrusion" is a continuum, with plenty of shades of grey.

Under older workman's compensation guidelines and older AMA Permanent Partial Disability guidelines, the word 'herniation' was kind of a magic term that meant more benefits to be paid on a work comp claim, vs. the word 'bulge.' This semantic distinction, all important in work comp 30+ years ago, got carried over into personal injury work; but, today, even the work comp people don't

139

make a big distinction between 'protrusion,' and 'herniation,' because, medically, the terms are more or less indistinguishable as presently used, and the younger radiologists don't ever use the term "herniation" in their reports.

The fact that "protrusions" are not described as "herniations" these days is more the result of political correctness and outside non-medical interests, as opposed to medical accuracy, and in my opinion, in the year 2018, it does no longer matter if a disc is called 'protruded' vs. being called 'herniated' in so far as legal matters are concerned.

But, to take matters a step further, it does not mean that a disk is a pain generator, or surgical, simply because it is protruding. It might be both, but the word "protrusion," by itself, does not indicate either of these things. As per the above discussion re MRI results, "clinical correlation" is needed to determine whether it is surgical.

As a general rule of thumb, if a disk protrusion is over 5 mm, it is probably surgical. Under that size, it may be, depending on its location and whether it is a pain generator.

A disk protrusion that is shown to impinge on a nerve, or, cause stenosis (closing off of an opening through which a nerve or the spinal cord travels) is more serious, generally, than a disk that is not shown to be doing these things.

A disk protrusion that is causing stenosis of the spinal canal, or, that is touching the spinal cord, is a major danger, and a high chance of being surgical. This can only occur in the cervical (neck) or thoracic (mid back) spine, as the spinal canal and spinal cord ends at the lumbar level (approximately level of the 'belly button'). At the lumbar level, the spinal cord ends, and there is, in place, a cascading bundle of nerves called the "cauda equina," Latin for "horse's tail," so called because it looks like a horse's tail. A disk pushing on the "horse's tail" will cause pain and likely, pain down the leg (sciatica); this is serious, but not on the same level with spinal cord impingement. Whether a protrusion is impinging on a nerve, or the spinal cord, is usually shown and described in an MRI report. Whether the nerve or cord is impinged by the protrusion depends not only on the size of the protrusion, but also, its location.

A pre-accident protrusion that was previously close to, but not touching, a nerve, can be shifted or enlarged so that it does touch, which means it goes from asymptomatic (causing no problems) to being symptomatic (causing pain) as a result of the accident. This is a common phenomenon in persons who are older (e.g. over age 40), who have 'bulges" or small protrusions before a car accident, and then, afterwards, have much worse (or new) problems caused by the disk.

CHAPTER TWENTY-EIGHT

CAN YOU FIND OUT WHAT A CASE IS WORTH USING THE INTERNET?

A couple years ago, I was shocked when a client came in to tell me that he had gone on the internet, and had put in the "facts" of his case into the system of several programs that were designed to tell him what his case value was.

I went on the internet and tried it out myself. Indeed, there were several websites that claim to tell you how much your case was worth by filling in a simple form.

These things were real jokes. Plug in a couple variables such as type of accident and amount of medical bills, and then it would tell you that your case was worth such and such. Generally speaking they were just multiplying the medical bills by certain factors and were coming up with numbers that were, in my judgment, much greater than what the case value actually was in Las Vegas.

The unsurprising kicker was that once you ran your case through the system, a pop-up would come up on the screen saying, "if your current lawyer is telling you your case is worth less than this, you need to contact a new lawyer." And then it had the name of a different Las Vegas law firm than my own.

Let me first of all say the law firms who ascribe to this "scam" system of advertising should be ashamed and perhaps penalized by the Bar. Talk about bottom feeders!

Trying to look up similar cases to your own on the internet is not worth your while, and will give you misleading results. It is a joke among lawyers about how their clients look on the internet and see that someone had a case "just like mine" and it was worth seven or eight figures. Again, do I really need to tell people that the internet is not an accurate source for information, and that trying to compare your case with someone else's is even less accurate than trying to diagnose your own condition using the diagrams on "WebMD"?

Clients will also ask me, oft times, "isn't there a formula you guys all go by?" Virtually everyone over a certain age has heard "they just multiply the medical bills by three." Or sometimes "they multiply by it two."

As the prior chapters make clear, insurance companies don't do this (although, 40 years ago, they did. But, again, that was *40 YEARS AGO*.)

Auto insurance companies these days do use a computer software type system now involving complicated algorithms that take into account over

100 factors, not just one or two. These computer programs are "tweaked" on a regular basis so that even "experts" outside the system who try to guess at what are the "value drivers" on the computers are wrong. It's kind of like Google. Once someone figures out a part of the Google algorithm that yields results in increasing a person's Google rating, Google sees this, and then changes the algorithm. It's the same with systems used by auto insurers.

There are available, for a price, some computer data bases that ask for several dozen pieces of information, and then can give a range of what the case might be worth before a jury, and, the chances of success v. failure. A company called "Jury Verdict Research" offers this service. (I believe they were purchased by Lexis or Westlaw or something similar, but they still exist.) It costs about $175 to run your case through, last time I checked. I have found that they generally come up with odds and numbers that are within the bounds of what the common wisdom of experienced practitioners would be, but, they cannot take into account unusual or unique circumstances (e.g. the case has received publicity, this or that party is especially likeable or dislikeable, etc.) Their reports do not tell me things I do not already know; but, they can be useful to show to clients who think their case is worth a lot more than it is, and who think you are downgrading the value because you are lazy or whatever. This shows the client that a national data base computer system came to the same conclusion that you did. I do not think these

144

reports are useful to show to adjusters, who have their own similar services they consult on their own, or, who think they know it all, anyway.

Is it worth it to keep track of small expense items for increasing damages?

I have occasionally had clients who make spreadsheets showing all sorts of different items such as charges for gas going to and from the doctor's office, mileage charges, wear and tear on the cars, costs of Advil pills, etc. These are legitimate items, and, frankly, they are the sort of stuff that an insurance adjuster might reimburse.

But ultimately these things add up to "peanuts" in the larger picture. If we start focusing in on these items, i.e., the nickels and dimes instead of the dollars, it tends to make the whole discussion of how much the case is worth diminish into a fight over smalls items. It plays right into the adjuster's hand, i.e. focus on small details. A very bad strategy, altogether, for the plaintiff in a pi case.

Jurors on the other hand hate stuff like this. It is boring, and not only makes them go to sleep, but makes them dislike the plaintiff. (Note: in a catastrophic injury case, with a life care planner calculating costs for care over a lifetime, these small charges do have to be taken into account, and, are not so small when calculated over a lifetime of years. But for the typical car accident case, the charges for things like gas to and from the doctor's office are very small, and make the focus

145

of the case on small items, instead of the more important items.) I have encountered this problem even with my own clients who get mad when I give them an accounting of my out of pocket costs (which I am required to do, to the penny, by the State Bar Association. I do not do it because I am cheap, I do it because if I'm going to charge costs, the State Bar requires me to account for everything down to the penny.)

CHAPTER TWENTY-NINE

EFFECT OF THE MCDONALD'S COFFEE CASE, AND HOW TO COUNTER THEM

This was discussed briefly above. It is a cloud hanging over every personal injury trial. Virtually every juror over the age of 30 (not as much now that the case is over 10 years old and demographics are such that younger people never heard of it), hears the story of the McDonald's coffee case. The folklore -- and it is that, folklore -- is that a woman spilled hot coffee on her leg, got a "boo-boo" and got millions and millions of dollars.

There is a documentary about the real facts of the case on HBO, called "Hot Coffee." Please watch it. You can stream it from HBO or Amazon Prime Video.

The real story is that McDonald's was told repeatedly by the government that there is a regulation that coffee cannot be kept over a certain temperature. However, profits were increased if the coffee was kept over the temperature. McDonald's did this on purpose. The woman in question received third degree burns to her vaginal area and had to receive skin graft surgery to her vaginal area. The jury was asked to award her the amount of profits McDonald's made in one day from coffee sales. Put in that context the verdict makes sense, but the "spin job" put out by the US Chamber of Commerce and the "then" version of Fox News was the urban folklore version of "crazy money" and "frivolous lawsuits" that is now cemented in the public consciousness.

Today's plaintiff's lawyer has to accept that no matter what he does, jurors will not be convinced that McDonald's coffee was anything other than the folklore story that persists. The McDonald's coffee legend has brought down verdict amounts by, probably, billions of dollars over the years. It was the greatest single piece of "fake news" ever generated by the corporate and Chamber of Commerce deception machines. But, it is a 'perception reality' in today's world. The plaintiff's lawyer who now goes into court has to acknowledge to jurors that there are "frivolous cases" and "unjustified awards," or else the jurors will not trust him. There may well have been frivolous cases and unjustified awards over the years, but McDonald's coffee was not one of them. There have also been numerous publications and stories floated over the years about other "crazy" lawsuits.

I oftentimes listen to a local sports radio show on a local channel. For a while, the people running this show had a segment that they thought was humorous and a break from the usual sports handicapping chatter, where they would read newsfeeds from some news service they subscribed to. The news service was, to me at least, obviously something run by insurance companies to put out fake news about "real cases.".

The one announcer (who is a fellow I respect as a sports handicapper, meaning that he is not stupid), read one story to the effect that there was somebody driving an RV on the freeway who felt the urge to go to the bathroom, got up from the driver's wheel, and walked to the back of the RV to go to the bathroom, leaving the RV to steer itself on the freeway. The RV crashed and the man sued the RV manufacturer and received millions of dollars.

On its face this story is totally absurd. You don't have to go to some sort of fact checker to know that this is crazy. This is beyond saying Obama was born in Africa crazy; this is the Holocaust never happened crazy.

I remember the guy who read this story chuckling and saying, "I didn't make this up folks. This is the truth. You can't make stuff like this up."

All I can say is that in today's world, I hope everyone has learned that people generate false stories all the time to help their political and financial interests. Everyone who reads or hears something these days that doesn't sound right should probably assume that it isn't right.

Unfortunately, as lawyers we have to deal with the reality that most people have heard stories like

McDonald's coffee, or the driverless RV, and even if they don't believe them completely, believe them enough, so that before you even open your mouth to say the first words to the jury, they are suspicious of you and your client. It's unfair, but that's today's world.

Score one for the insurance company publicity machine.

Let's put this into the context of trying an automobile auto case. You may assume that the majority of the jurors, before you open your mouth, assume that you and your client are trying to scam the system. The insurance lawyer doesn't need to sell the jury on that concept; they already have it before they have heard a word.

In terms of auto accident cases, the McDonald's coffee effect is that the jurors think that your client only had a 'boo boo,' and you are trying to puff up the boo boo and trick the jury into giving big money for it.

There are two main things you can do to counteract this attitude. One is to focus on the defendant, and his conduct, and how the tort system is meant to enforce safety rules. (See the "dime store" example in the Damages Overview section above.) One good thing about the McDonald's coffee story, if you want to call it 'good,' is that the urban folklore left out the part of the case– the main part of the case– that was the plaintiff's lawyer emphasizing how McDonald's brazenly ignored the rules and the warnings. If you emphasize that aspect in your auto case, i.e. defendant conduct and safety rules, no one in the jury panel will recognize that you are actually doing what the McDonald's lawyer did (in reality.)

The other 'antidote' is to acknowledge, in voir dire, that there are plenty of frivolous lawsuits and crazy lawyers, but that you are not going to lie to them, and will they at least give you the chance to show that you are the exception to the rule? (Don Keenan has developed this very effectively, and I have used it ever since I heard it.) Then– and this is very important– you have to dial back the "lawyer schtick" so that you do not come off as a phoney salesman or TV lawyer, etc. There is more to this latter part than I can address in this book; a lot more. Again, I suggest that you access some of the widely available modern trial lawyer practice materials and seminars mentioned in prior chapters.

To the extent you do have "objective" signs of injury in your case, especially, MRI or xray findings, emphasizing these goes a long way to getting around the McDonald's coffee stigma. You can take your MRI film and have a place like High Impact Graphics (in Colorado) make a dynamite demonstrative exhibit from it; or, if it is a little case, you can a local vendor blow up an xray or MRI film onto a chart at a very low cost, and then, have your testifying medical expert do a show and tell with the chart, pointing out the disks, straightened spine, etc. This is the opposite of what jurors think about when they think about the McDonald's coffee 'boo boo.'

Think twice about making a big deal out of small bruise or cut as part of your case in chief, as this fits right into the McDonald's coffee 'boo boo' frame of reference. Showing a photo of tiny bruise is likely counterproductive, unless you need it to prove there was direct trauma to some body part or other (e.g. knee in a 'dashboard knee' case.)

CHAPTER THIRTY

EFFECT OF TASTELESS ADVERTISING ON REAL TRIAL LAWYERS

I am old school. I came from a time when lawyer advertising was not allowed, and people like me thought it was horrible in terms of the image of the profession. Back in the 80's, the U.S. Supreme Court decided it was a form of protected speech and the floodgates were open. There was no turning back after that. So, the message to people like me (i.e., older lawyers) is: Get over it. It is what it is.

Does it have a negative effect on jury perceptions of personal injury cases? Absolutely. The typical value of a verdict went down drastically when the lawyer advertisements, particularly on television, got going. Insurance companies getting defense verdicts (where the plaintiff gets zero), especially on auto accident cases, went up dramatically when attorney advertising came into full force. How could it not? You have attorneys going on TV saying, "Cash for Crash," and "in a wreck get a check." We've even had attorneys dressing up like leprechauns, fairies, or comic book heroes for TV commercials in LV.

This being said, what can attorneys do about it? I have tried asking jurors in voir dire "who hates lawyer advertising?" and usually about half the people will admit to really disliking it. So, if you have that information, what do you do with it? It's something you knew before you asked. There is nothing you can do about it, it's out there and you can't turn it back.

I would say this: If you are injured in an accident and you go to one of the "clown" TV advertisers, you are doing yourself a major disservice. Jurors really don't like these guys at all, in my opinion. That is why most of these law firms will have other law firms do trials for them, so their name can be hidden from the jurors.

On the bright side, if you want to call it that, the younger generation, millennials and even younger, have grown up with TV attorney advertising and it doesn't have the same negative impact on them that it did on older generations. But, it has the overall effect of making them cynical about everything involved in auto cases. Very cynical. They tend to believe all injury cases are scams because they have grown up seeing scammy ads.

If you are an attorney like me who does not advertise on television, I think it is good for you to make clear to the jury in voir dire you don't like it and are not part of it. There is no downside to doing this, and upside with probably at least half the panel.

I have seen some attorney ads on TV that are basically honest and, show some class. I have seen such ads in Las Vegas from the Benson and Bertoldo office, and, back in the day, Crockett and Myers. The Greenman, Goldberg and Raby firm also have TV ads that take the high road. These attorneys are in the minority of advertisers, unfortunately. But, such attorneys do not have to be so afraid of jury backlash when they go to trial. If you are a young attorney and you are considering advertising on TV, ask yourself: am I now, or in the future, planning to be 'real' trial lawyer? If the answer is 'yes,' then you need to consider seriously whether you want to have an outrageous or comic ad, or, do you want to take the high road, even if, in the short run, it does not bring in the daytime TV viewers? If you do not plan on going to trial, and just want to 'churn and burn,' then by all means, pump iron, wear a tank top, and go on the air showing off your 'bod' and talk tough like in an old Bruce Willis movie. As a 'joke' maybe weave in a sexual innuendo, or a cartoon, to grab attention. Yeah man, that's the stuff!

CHAPTER THIRTY-ONE

EFFECT OF "OPIOID CRISIS" ON PERSONAL INJURY DAMAGES

I am writing this in May of 2018. At this time, there is an avalanche of news coverage on the "opioid crisis." The crisis is very real. By "opioid crisis" I am referring specifically to prescription opioids being given to persons in large quantities, who become addicted and who eventually end up having their lives controlled by getting narcotic pills.

I have heard it said that if you give even a rabbit enough opioid medications, it will become addicted. So, it is not a question of "willpower" or even moral character. Simply put, if you take enough opioids long enough you will become addicted, and once that monkey is on your back, it is extremely hard to shake it loose.

There is also an even seedier side to the "crisis." There has developed a "black market" for the sale of these pills, and many people supplement their income by getting prescriptions, selling the pills, and they become so reliant on this "extra income" that they cannot stand to be cut off.

There are many people who legitimately need the medication, and who, realistically, are going to have to take a lot of it for the rest of their life unless they get professional help for the addiction part, and, can learn to live with the pain through non-narcotic means.

But the narrow focus of this particular section of the book on this particular aspect is: Does the perceived overuse of opioid medications negatively affect the damages that can be awarded or given to a plaintiff who was used these pills? The answer is a definite yes.

Right now, jurors are extremely sensitive to this issue. If it looks like the plaintiff is taking a lot of narcotic medications, no matter how legitimate it is, it makes the plaintiff look bad and drags down the value of the case. I have clients who think: If the jury sees how many of these pills I have to take, they will know how bad my pain is and give me more money. Sorry, but the exact opposite is true. The more of these pills you are taking, the more the value of your case is dragged down.

Jurors have no trouble accepting that a person will need these pills for a month or two following an accident or following a surgery. But when it starts to get into months and months, or years and years, of use, and the sheer number of pills escalates higher and higher, again, no matter how legitimate the use is, jurors hate this and it drags the value of the case down. Insurance company lawyers figured this out long ago and tend to make this a real focus of their pre-trial discovery. They want to find every pill prescription that was every received by the plaintiff for pain pills, no matter how old. They want to get the printouts from the State DEA Task Force that show every time you've had a prescription for controlled substances made. They want to be able to infer that you were "doctor shopping" for pills, double dipping: getting pills from two different doctors at the same time, etc.

If there is evidence of doctor shopping, double dipping, etc., it is poison to a case. It could possibly literally ruin what would otherwise be a good case.

If you are a personal injury victim, and you are reading this book, I hope you will get the message loud and clear that taking these opioid pills should be limited by you as much as possible. If you are hooked on them, try to get off. You will need professional help, as you cannot safely quit narcotics 'cold turkey' without major side effects. But, this week Congress just passed a raft of new laws mandating that opioid treatment be required as a benefit on every health insurance plan. I applaud, loudly, anyone who has been addicted to these pills and gets off them. It is never an easy fight, but one well worth the effort.

At the time of writing this book, there are two LV physicians I know who specialize in treating persons addicted to opioids: Dr. Michael Levy, and Dr. Mel Pohl. They have different approaches, but they are both legit, both sincere, well trained, and not interested in quick buck recovery schemes. But, unfortunately, they are not free, but what is worth more than getting back your life?

There is one silver lining to all of this and it is that jurors are very forgiving of persons who recognize they have a problem, seek help and correct it. If I have a client who gets addicted to opioids, and enters a treatment program, and then goes "pill free" for some time prior to the trial, the jurors love that. Again, I emphasize "pill free." Jurors are like everyone else who has a family member addicted. If the claim is "I cut way down on the pills and I'm really watching it now" this is viewed with skepticism, especially if the actual number of pills filled at the pharmacy is essentially the same.
Jurors also are not particularly forgiving of persons who switch from oxycodone, to morphine Yes this is "treatment" in a sense, but the plaintiff is still viewed in a negative light.

I can hear voices of people reading this to the effect: This guy's got no heart. There are a lot of people who legitimately need these pills! He should be taking the side of these people, not criticizing them!

I'm not criticizing people who get addicted to opioids on a morality basis. As I said, anyone who takes these pills for more than a few weeks gets addicted. It's a matter of chemistry, not willpower. And once you're addicted, as a matter of biochemistry, not character, it is very difficult to get off them without professional help. And, as I said above, *there are a lot of people who legitimately need these meds*, and will have to take them for the rest of their life, for example persons who have had multiple spine surgeries with broken hardware inside them.   But, persons who have injuries that are not obviously serious to most lay persons will be suspected, often unfairly so, by most jurors, of negative character defects if they take narcotics in quantity for a long time.

I am just pointing out what is a fact: Jurors are not forgiving of this, they view it with an extremely negative bias, and a victim of an accident who is taking a lot of these pills for a long time is going to be criticized for doing so by the insurance lawyer (*unless* it is a catastrophic or extremely serious injury situation.)   This is yet another of those things I am pointing out that isn't 'right,' but it 'is what it is.'

CHAPTER THIRTY-TWO

RECENT MEDIA STORIES AGAINST AUTO INSURERS

As noted above, for the last 25 plus years, the insurance industry, auto manufacturers, big pharma, and the Chamber of Commerce have been successful in mounting an avalanche of negative publicity about plaintiff's lawyers, frivolous lawsuits, etc. And, to be fair, a lot of the avalanche against damages awards has been self-inflicted, the best example of this being creepy television advertising by attorneys.

The "opioid crisis" (actually I shouldn't put quotes around it, it's real) has also helped to throw a damper on damage awards. Jurors think that people who claim chronic back pain are using it to get narcotic pain pills, if in fact they are getting large quantities of pain pills.

However, there are a few "bright spots," if you want to call them that, in the media.

There has been a lot of recent publicity underlining that people get very serious brain injuries from what were previously thought to be "mild concussions." This has been particularly demonstrated by football players who, later in life, suffer horribly; and the soldiers coming back from

Afghanistan who suffered "mild concussions" from IEDs, and who turn out to have suffered major brain injuries (and these are not just excuses for psychologically inappropriate behavior. These are things that show up on the more precise MRI machines we have now that can detect these things.) So, if you have a brain injury case, you are probably in a better position now to get fair compensation than you were even two years ago.

Insurance companies have also suffered self-inflicted wounds by having exposure of the level of their corruption and greed to the public. I think it is pretty well known that the financial crisis of 2008 (the "Great Recession,") was caused, in major part, by the greed of the insurance company AIG, who succeeded in getting the US taxpayer to cover their losses (AIG is a major commercial and, through subsidiaries with different names, motor vehicle liability insurer.)   There was, not too long ago, an expose by one of the news magazines (I think it was Dateline) about a scheme an auto insurer used to have college students fill out fake "medical reports" on claimants, which reports were signed in masse by a greedy surgeon in the San Diego area. This same surgeon was hired by a local auto insurance company to be their main expert, and they continued to use him as a 'biomechanical' expert even after the televised expose!   (Check out Google on "Operation Ace," re State Farm.) Allstate was exposed by the Wall Street Journal a few years ago as they hired members of the Church of Scientology to use Scientology "tech" to help develop "get tough" systems (I know that sounds bizarre, but check it out.) There was also a recent expose on a network news magazine about how certain insurance company allies were helping to fund   lavish vacation get -a -ways for state officials charged with regulating auto insurers.   A recent biography of Warren Buffett shows how used the "float" from Geico insurance to make, presumably, billions of dollars (legal, I suppose, but not seemly.)   Other media sources have revealed that Progressive Auto Insurance is owned, in large part, by George Soros, the   East   European/former   Communist   bloc billionaire, and that he uses his profits to help fund many causes that are divisive to the American fabric.   Farmers is owned by Zurich, a Swiss company that controls major portions of the European financial scene; frankly, Switzerland could care less about the United States and its citizens, except how much money they represent.

In summation, at least some– at this point, still a minority– of the American media is willing to take on the auto insurance companies to expose their dirty little secrets to the American public.   With time, Americans will realize that it is not the trial lawyers who are the ones fooling the public.

CHAPTER THIRTY-THREE

MEDICAL TREATMENT OF NECK INJURIES

The stereotypical injury from a car accident is "whiplash." The term has achieved a negative connotation in American culture. Most people are not old enough to remember the movie "The Fortune Cookie," starring Jack Lemmon and Walter Matthau. The movie was actually very funny, but it concerned a fake "whiplash" case being handled by Walter Matthau, the attorney, on behalf of his comically neurotic client, Jack Lemmon.

In today's courtroom, attorneys that represent victims do not want to use the word "whiplash" because it has such negative connotation.

But "whiplash" is very real. The fact is, your head is like a 12-pound bowling ball balanced on top of a skinny column of bones held together in place by muscles, tendons and ligaments. A sudden force, such as is generated by a 6,000 pound object traveling even at a relatively slow speed, can cause severe injury. Our bodies were not designed by the Almighty to travel in automobiles. We weren't designed to withstand the forces that happen even in milder automobile accidents.

This being said, if you suffer a "whiplash" to your neck, how should you go about getting it treated?

The first step is generally an urgent care center or emergency room. It is extremely rational and logical for persons involved in car accidents to decline an ambulance and go to an urgent care center on their own. However, insurance lawyers will always make a big deal out of the fact that someone declined an ambulance, as though that means they were not really hurt.

It is very commonplace that injuries to the neck don't become symptomatic until the next day, or even later. The tissues take some time to swell up. Anyone who has played sports knows that you don't hurt that much in a game when the injury occurs; it's the next day or the day after that when it really starts to bother you. It takes tissue a certain amount of time to swell. We now understand, that with disk injuries, the disk will slowly over time leak fluid that has a slow, corrosive effect on surrounding tissue, in particular, the nerves. Also, generally, people 'take it easy' following a car accident, and will take medications, either prescribed, or, over the counter (such as Motrin.) The lack of activity plus medications/anti inflammatories also delay recognition of the full extent of injury until such time as normal activities are resumed and medications ceased.

With neck injuries, there is the possibility of a small tear in the disc. We are finding out through the use in more and more cases of MRI's that this

165

happens a lot more frequently than we thought. A small tear in a disc will cause spinal cerebral fluid to leak out. This has a corrosive, slow eroding effect on the soft tissue nearby. Again, this is something we are only learning about over the last several years. This is why neck injuries can, slowly over the course of the time, get worse instead of better (contrary to what all the insurance doctors say.)

Normally, in this day and age, if you call up your family physician and say I was just in a car accident, I want to come in to see the doctor, the doctor's receptionist is instructed to tell you, "Doctor doesn't treat car accident patients. Go to a chiropractor or a doctor that takes accident cases." Regular family physicians don't want to get hassled with all the paperwork of a car accident case. Insurance companies, in particular, disability insurers, and med pay insurers, can bombard them with requests for reports. Insurance attorneys later subject the treating doctors to grueling, extremely annoying, depositions. The insurance lawyers treat these doctors as if they were something you need to pick up with two sticks, simply because they had the gall to say that their patient seemed genuinely injured. If I were a regular family doctor, I would not take car accident cases, either.

Typically, patients are directed to a chiropractor by either the woman who sits at the front desk of the family doctor's office, the urgent care clinic, or, an attorney. (Chiropractors will not even see a patient unless they have an attorney, since otherwise they will probably not get paid when the case is settled.)

The fact that people are referred to chiropractors by attorneys should not be held against them. In today's medical marketplace, at least in Las Vegas, the "regular" family doctors who work under health insurance want nothing to do with a car accident case.

Chiropractic care has come a long way in the last 30 years. Their education is much more like a regular doctor now than before. The care that they give is generally more like a physical therapist than like someone who "cracks bones."

And, the majority of chiropractors in Las Vegas, in the year 2018, will usually have the patient also see a medical doctor as well as a chiropractor, in order that they can be diagnosed and treated from both perspectives. (Often, the medical doctors will prescribe a muscle relaxer. Chiropractors are not allowed to prescribe medicines in Nevada.)

Some patients also go to internists or family practitioners who don't mind taking accident cases, in particular, soft tissue neck injuries. These doctors will usually direct the patient to go to a physical therapist or a chiropractor for physical therapy.

If the therapy and muscle relaxers don't do the job, after a couple months, then typically an MRI is ordered. This test can tell whether there is something serious going on in the neck other than just the "soft tissue" (this term, used in this sense, basically refers to the muscles and ligaments.)

Typically, if the MRI shows something suspicious, the chiropractor, and/or general practitioner, will refer the patient to a pain management specialist for consultation, or a neurologist for EMG/NCV testing (to see if a nerve is pinched), or both.

The pain management doctors are, generally speaking, anesthesiologists who have gone to a special fellowship in pain management treatment. A legitimate pain management specialist may first see if there is some other kind of physical therapy that can be used, and if that is not needed, try injections into the affected area. These injections are done under a fluoroscope, so the danger of having the needle go in the wrong place is very, very small.

As a matter of fact, I have never had a client who has had the needle "go in the wrong place" during one of these injections. I have heard of it happening, and it always involves someone who is doing an injection without a fluoroscope, or, is a doctor that is really not trained as a pain management specialist, but is not properly certified. The injections are almost always done under short-acting anesthesia so there is no pain involved in the injection itself (unless the doctor tries to do it without injection, which is like a dentist doing a filling without novacaine. There is one such doctor in LV, who does, to my knowledge, only work comp cases, and he does the shots without anesthesia. I would hate to be one of his patients, but the people sent to him generally have no choice in the matter, since under work comp you have to go where the insurance company sends you in most cases.)

The injections are usually done in a series of three, one month apart. Typically, the injections work for a while and wear off. Sometimes they give lasting relief. But if the third injection doesn't give lasting relief the patient is typically told to either "live with" the problem or to get a consultation with a spine surgeon, or, to get a radio frequency ablation (rhizotomy, or 'nerve burn,') procedure.

Very, very few of the whiplash cases end up going for a spine surgery. Everyone who gets in a car accident is afraid this will be the outcome, but it's extremely rare.

There are many different levels of spine surgery. They go from making tiny incisions and cutting out a tiny piece of bone or a disc, to putting in screws and rods in a "fusion" procedure. In my own experience, none of my clients who ended up getting neck surgery were doing it to "make money." Everyone I have represented that ended up in that position did not want the surgery, but were in such severe pain, or in such danger of being paralyzed, they had no choice.

We have all heard that neck surgeries sometimes end up making people worse.

My own experience is that a lot depends on who the surgeon is. I am not going to throw names around, but I'd have to say there is a group of spine surgeons, I would say, about one-third of them, who almost always make the patient better, and about a third of them seem to usually make people worse.

That's my observation. I'm sure if you ask the medical community they would disagree. I'm just telling you what I see as someone with no "dog in the race." There are a lot of reasons for this; some have better training, some are more talented, more careful, some practice surgery at hospitals that have better OR's and post-surgical care and infection prevention, better staff, and some are a lot pickier about who they choose to operate upon. Bottom line, from my perspective, is that if you go to one of the 'good' surgeons, spine surgery is not nearly as risky as common wisdom would have you believe.

There is one other form of treatment I didn't describe in detail above, and that is "RFA." This stands for "radiofrequency ablation." It is also called "rhizotomy." This is where the pain management specialist inserts not a needle shooting out "juice" but rather, a needle that "shoots out" radiofrequency electromagnetic energy pulses. These will affect the nerve endings and disable the nerve for a period of approximately 6 to 12 months. The nerve ending then grows back and the procedure has to be repeated. This is an effective way to control pain without using narcotics and can give good results in relieving pain for up to 12 months, which is an attractive alternative to narcotics.   It's not a cure but it's a real lifesaver for people who want to avoid surgery, quit taking narcotics, and have a way to live with the pain. Unfortunately, RFA does not work on every type of neck pain generator, but if you are candidate for it, and, you are not at risk of paralysis absent surgery, it is certainly worth considering. The procedure itself is done under short term anesthesia, so no pain is involved, and the risks are small if done by a board-certified pain management specialist with fluoroscope.

CHAPTER THIRTY-FOUR

MEDICAL TREATMENT OF LOW BACK INJURIES

The low back, or "lumbar" spine, is where all of the "axial loads" are centered, spine-wise. In other words, that's at the bottom of the spine, at the bottom of a column of bones called vertebrae, and just by the law of physics, is the part of the spine that has most of the vertical force applied to it. This is why the bones in the low back are a lot bigger and stronger than the bones in the neck. The forces they have to endure is simply much more. This is also why, typically, if people have spinal problems, it's usually in the low back, since that's where the greatest loads, physically, are located.

The good news, if you want to call it that, for people who suffer low back injuries in a car accident is that, medically speaking, the anatomy of the low back is a lot easier to work with than that in the neck. The bones are bigger. The spaces are bigger. There's a lot more "room" to maneuver about, medical treatment wise.

As was described above for the neck, typically the treatment goes: ER or urgent care, then (if needed) chiropractor or general physician, then (if needed) physical therapy, then (if needed) pain management doctor; then (*rarely*) spinal surgeon.

Read the above section on neck injuries. The sequence of treatment is basically the same for low backs.

Low back surgeries tend to be much more common than neck surgeries. I suppose this is probably because there are more low back problems out there than neck problems, but another reason might be because it's a lot less risky to operate on a low back than it is a neck. By "risky" I mean not in terms of having a good result versus bad result, but in terms of not risking paralysis, having more room in which to operate, not having to navigate around tiny structures, etc.

Again, if a condition ends up in surgery, the surgeon you choose makes all the difference in the world. In my estimation, probably one-third of the back surgeons in Las Vegas almost always have good results.

A lot of the factors in whether the surgery turns out well or not depend on factors outside the control of the surgeon. Patients who are older, for example, heal less well than patients who are younger. Unfortunately, people who are old drive cars just as much as people who are young. If your low back is "completely blown out" in a car accident, and you are older, you might (rarely) have no choice about it. You might have to get a surgery or else risk some very scary future problems (look up "cauda equina syndrome" on Google and you'll see what I mean.)

People who are diabetic heal from surgery less well than people who are not. Again, a person who is diabetic does not choose to be in a car accident. Insurance lawyers who try to "blame" them in trial for having a bad result from back surgery because they are diabetic should be ashamed of themselves.

The nerves that come out of the low back go down the legs. When a disc is injured in the low back it often shows up as a pain that runs down the person's leg. This is called "sciatica." It has been said oftentimes that sciatica can be the most intense pain of all pains, even worse than child birthing pains. Persons who have severe sciatica really have no choice, they have to get surgery to relieve the pain. In my own experience, a person who has severe disc trouble in the low back following an accident, and who has *severe* sciatica, and who does not get significantly better within 90 days following the accident, is not going to get well unless he has the surgery. He or she is either going to have to live with the pain or get the surgery. Just "hope" won't do it.

The worst sort of solution to chronic sciatica is taking narcotic pain pills as opposed to getting the surgery, or, other forms of treatment that do not involve narcotics. Taking narcotic pain pills in large amounts for months or even years in order to avoid surgery is a "bargain with the devil." I feel very sorry for people, including my clients, who get caught up in this horrible downward spiral. The more pain pills you take, the more pain pills you need just to do the same job. You get hooked on

174

them, and you have to take more and more. The doctor tells you that your only choice is to get a back surgery, but you've heard so many bad things about it, you're scared to death, so you just keep taking the pain pills "one more day." The "tomorrow day" when you might get off the pain pills and get the surgery, never happens.

Don't kid yourself, the above scenario could happen to anyone. Everyone is frightened about back surgery, and everyone will get addicted to opioids if they take them long enough. It is a horrible predicament to be put in; and if it is the result of a negligent car driver, they should offer help and real sympathy, instead of attacking an innocent victim, as though they are the 'bad guy.' The 'bad guy' is the one who caused the collision. Do not forget that fact when, as a lawyer, you are litigating a car accident case. Don't let the other side suck you in to making the case all about your client's treatment, etc. Remember, and let the jury know, "we wouldn't even here in court today if the defendant had just been careful and obeyed the law."

CHAPTER THIRTY-FIVE

MEDICAL TREATMENT OF SHOULDER INJURIES

Typically, necks and backs are the most commonly injured body parts in a car accident. The manner in which physical forces are applied to the body in a typical car accident explain this. But there are a fair amount of knee and shoulder injuries in car accidents, as well.

The first question that might occur is: what are the forces involved in creating, say, a shoulder injury, in a car accident?

This is easy enough to understand in a very severe accident, such as a rollover, where the shoulder is directly impacted. Or, in an accident involving side to side forces, wherein the body goes side to side, and the shoulder (e.g., the left shoulder for a driver) suffers direct trauma to itself by hitting the door.

It is important to note that seatbelts are designed to stop motion forward of the torso. They offer no help in side to side movement.

Most modern automobiles have airbags that are now on the side doors as well as the steering wheel. Either a steering wheel/dashboard, or, side door, airbag can hit the shoulder. If one of these explodes and hits the shoulder, the forces involved are tremendous, and although it could prevent fatal injury, it could easily cause shoulder injury.

Less clear is how do people injure their shoulders in an accident involving, say, rear end damage or frontend damage, and no air bag contact?

The main culprit in these injuries is the shoulder seatbelt strap. However, the way in which it causes injury is not always obvious on the surface, but, if you think it through, it becomes clear.

Of course, it would be obvious if one ran the front of a car into the side of another car (T-bone accident), in which case the initial action of the body is to go forward. (In physics, there is an equal and *opposite* reaction to the force applied, so in a frontend impact, the 'opposite reaction' is for the torso to go forward.) The seatbelt strap, if it's working correctly, will activate, and snag the shoulder area as it tries to go forward. The area of direct trauma from the strap would be, for the driver, the left shoulder area, for the passenger, the right shoulder. The area "snagged" is one of the most vulnerable parts of this area of the body, i.e., the area where the collarbone meets the shoulder joint, called the acromioclavicular process, or, AC joint.

This can result in a separation of the collarbone from the shoulder, called "separated shoulder," which can be extremely painful. It can also exert force on the rotator cuff area, as well as the supraspinatus tendon (which runs along the top of the collarbone.)

But a less obvious part of the forces involved in causing shoulder injuries is as follows. If the body is subjected to forces, sometimes front to back, but more typically, front to back, as in a rear end collision, but at an angle– however slight– of some kind, the seatbelt shoulder strap can still "catch" the part of the shoulder moving forward, sometimes at an angle. This would be the left shoulder for a driver. But at the same time that it "catches" the left shoulder, this forces the back of the right shoulder (in this case the right shoulder blade area) back into the wing of the seatback. Again, the *opposite and equal reaction* in physics. As one portion of the torso moves forward and is stopped rapidly, it causes a pivoting type action to force the other shoulder portion, forcing it back into the seatback. This can cause tremendous tearing or shearing type forces on the soft tissues in that area. (Jurors, and the lay public, in general, learn about "opposite but equal reaction" in high school science class, but, it does not seem to stick, and they commonly assume the reverse to be true, i.e. that the body reacts in the same line of force as that applied to the car. So, this will probably need to be explained to a jury, if a case proceeds to trial.)

Also, another situation is that when a driver anticipates being hit (i.e., sees car coming in the rearview mirror, or, one in front of him), the urge is to straighten out the arms and "brace" against the steering wheel or the dashboard. When the force occurs, the bracing action might "save" oneself from going through the front windshield, but it puts tremendous force on the rotator cuff and AC joint area of the shoulder, much as if one were falling, stuck out the arms directly to brace the fall, and then, as a result of the fall, suffers injury to the rotator cuff. This is the classic mechanism for injury to a rotator cuff.

Typical injuries to the shoulder region include rotator cuff tears (the rotator cuff is actually not one particular muscle or ligament, but is a very complicated anatomical group of numerous muscles and ligaments, any one of which can be torn and be called a "rotator cuff" tear); or tear of the tendons that run across the top of the collarbone connecting the shoulder (supraspinatus tendon tears), and injuries to the AC joint (e.g. separated shoulder.)

Typical treatment would include an MRI, first, to identify the tear area; physical therapy to see if strengthening the affected areas will solve the problem; oftentimes, cortisone shots, which can provide some temporary relief by reducing the swelling in the area; and most recently, the use of a technique used by athletes for decades, called platelet rich injections, or "PRP" injections, where the patient's own blood is withdrawn, spun to separate red blood cells, then reinjected into the area (the red blood cells, that is) to help speed up the healing process.

More recently, athletes are using stem cell injections for shoulder injuries, and it is only a matter of time until that treatment becomes available to the public.

If non-surgical measures fail, then the next step is surgery, almost always, these days, done arthroscopically (a small tube is inserted through which surgical instruments can be used to scrape, cut and stitch. A separate tube of fiber optics is inserted to allow the surgeon to see what is going on through a television camera.)

Shoulder surgeries are, generally speaking, without risk of any significant kind insofar as making the patient worse through the surgery itself (as opposed to the risks present from anesthesia in every surgery.) There just aren't a lot of 'danger' areas to accidentally cut inside a shoulder. In my own observations of clients getting shoulder surgeries over the years, the success rate of making them at least somewhat better is very high. The only negative results I have seen is with patients who get in trouble during the anesthesia due to pre-existing health issues.

In the context of automobile accident cases, the doctors hired by the insurance companies to write reports do not usually claim that the shoulder abnormalities do not exist, since they are proven to exist by the MRI, and by the video snapshots generated during the surgery. Instead, no matter how obvious the mechanism of injury and so forth, the insurance doctors will invariably say that the shoulder problem was pre-existing, but that the patient simply didn't notice it until, coincidentally, the car accident happened. The ridiculous lengths to which some of these guys will go to say these things with a straight face, in return for a $20,000 paycheck, is funny in a way, but ultimately, kind of sickening when you consider these people took the Hippocratic oath to help persons, and not try to harm them simply because the pay is so good.

CHAPTER THIRTY-SIX

MEDICAL TREATMENT OF KNEE INJURIES

Insofar as knee injuries occur, the most common mechanism of injury is hitting the knee on the underneath of the dashboard or the steering wheel column.

Oftentimes I am asked: If you're wearing a seatbelt across your lap, how can you hit your knee? This can be answered quite simply if one goes to one's own car and sits in the seat, and "simulates" the movement of a body in a collision type scenario. If you make your torso go backwards, as it would in a rear ender situation (remember, the reaction in physics is "opposite," so the torso first goes backwards, then, typically, bounces off the seatback and goes forward. Victims typically only remember that second, last part of the reaction) so that your back hits the back of the seat, you will notice that your butt slides forward. The seatbelt does not stop this "butt sliding" action. As your butt slides forward, your knee slides into the area underneath the dashboard or steering wheel column. The "leverage" pivoting effect of your back hitting the back of the seatbelt increases the force of the reaction causing the 'butt slide, 'as, again, using physics, levers always increase the speed of action (e.g. a golf club goes much faster than the golfer's arms when swung) using the physics principle of "leverage" multiplying a force.

Another common thing to cause knee injuries is that the person involved in the accident will stomp on the brake, with the leg held in a straightened type position, and then, the collision force is applied to rigid, locked knee. This action alone can injure the knee, but more commonly, once the knee is placed in this locked, rigid position against the brake, it is subjected to tremendous force when the collision actually occurs. The 'ball' on the end of the 'calf bone' (fibular condyle) is pushed hard into the meniscus (disc), and the meniscus is pushed hard up against the knob on the end of the thigh bone (femoral condyle). This can cause the condyle's cartilaginous coating to be damaged, as well as the meniscus disk. The back of the knee cap (patella) can also have pieces of cartilaginous coating damaged.

There is one particular doctor who works for insurance companies in Las Vegas and is their "hired gun" to testify at knee trials. In virtually every case involving an auto accident with a knee injury, this fellow is employed. I am told that he quit practicing medicine some time ago and does testifying for insurance companies on a full-time basis now, making a handsome seven figure income doing so. His story, which sells well to juries, is that "if they really hurt their knee in this accident, they would be on the ground, rolling about, howling in pain, on the pavement. The fact that they weren't doing this proves that their knee

183

problem wasn't from the accident but was from pre-existing issues."

Virtually any legitimate knee surgeon, or at least, one not being paid millions of dollars to tell stories, would say that most knee injuries do not involve people rolling around howling on the pavement in pain when they occur. Even the most casual sports fan will know that it is quite commonplace to watch a player do something that appears to "tweak" his knee during the game. The player finishes out the game, and then the next day you hear the MRI report that the player tore some cartilage. There are exceptions, of course, where players are howling on the ground and it turns out they tore a ligament. But, this is the exception, not the rule.

There are generally two kinds of knee injuries: cartilage injury, and ligament injury.

A ligament injury is most commonly the anterior cruciate ligament. If you tear the ACL, you either live with it or you get surgery. There are people that choose to live with it, although if I were anywhere under the age of 70, I would not make that choice. The knee lacks stability without the ACL, and it can suddenly give out, causing you to fall unexpectedly.

An ACL surgery is commonplace these days, but it involves months of recovery, wearing a knee brace and so forth.

A cartilage injury (meniscus tear) on the other hand can be corrected with a surgery that will allow the person to resume normal activities within a week or two after the surgery, commonly. Oftentimes people with cartilage repairs are able to walk (slowly) the next day after the surgery, although they must be cautious.

The "dirty little secret" about cartilage injuries is that although they are easily repaired with modern surgery, each time a surgery is done, and more cartilage is removed, it makes the knee more and more susceptible to possible total knee replacement when the patient gets old. This is by no means a certainty, but, my clients who have to get cartilage surgery after a car accident do not appreciate having this heaped onto an already pretty full plate of things caused by the accident.

"Total knee replacement" can be the result of cartilage injury (hitting the knee on a dashboard the most common cause) in a car accident. Despite the name, the knee is not "totally" replaced, but rather, an "artificial knee cap" is put into place. These operations have become commonplace and although painful, are usefully successful. But, the "dirty little secret" about total knee replacements is that the actual mechanical devices used wear out after 10-15 years or so, and at that point the patient may have to have it redone again, or just "live with it" as the case may be. For this reason, doctors are hesitant to do total knee replacements in persons who have not reached an advanced age where the lifespan of the device is not as relevant.

It is very commonplace in car accident situations to cause injury to people who have some degree of pre-existing changes in their knee (we all have them as we get older) that make the patient more susceptible, or vulnerable, to getting injured in a car accident. The law calls such people "eggshell plaintiffs," the "eggshell" referring to the vulnerability of their body part caused by the aging process.

Despite the fact that the jury instructions say that a person who is more vulnerable to injury because of age is still entitled to collect compensation, insurance companies hire doctors who will, typically for fees ranging from $15,000 to $35,000, testify at trial that everything that went wrong with the patient's knee is pre-existing, and the patient somehow failed to mention any knee problems to doctors until after the car accident happened, in an obvious attempt to fool everyone. The fact that the patient was not howling on the ground immediately after the car accident "proves" that everything was pre-existing. (I know you're thinking "when you put it that way, how does any jury believe this doctor?" But, people buy into it, and the insurance companies pay $20,000 and up for doctors who can successfully 'story' the jury for two hours and get away with it.)

CHAPTER THIRTY-SEVEN

MEDICAL TREATMENT OF HEAD INJURIES

It is very commonplace for people to have head injuries in car accidents. What is not known, generally, however, is that oftentimes the head injury is not caused by direct trauma to the head, but rather, by what is called a "contre coup" effect , wherein when the head is shaken rapidly, as happens in a "whiplash" scenario or similar, and the brain, which is something similar to the yoke of an egg floating inside the skull, shakes rapidly inside side to side, and bangs up against the inside of the skull, which is not smooth and round, as you would think, but rather, covered with various ridges, which can be quite nasty to the soft grey matter.

We are just now uncovering, as stated in previous parts of this book, the severe potential of 'mild' head trauma.

Unfortunately, there is very little you can do to treat a head injury other than let time heal it as best it can. For reasons not completely understood by medical science, most (not all) people with concussions (at least, people who have not had previous concussions, which changes the percentage exponentially, in terms of recovery time, and percentage of recovery anticipated), will recover from "mild" concussions within six to 12 months. Most agree that after 12 months go by, if symptoms still persist, they will be permanent.

There is one form of treatment that has been shown to have some curative effect on traumatic brain injuries, and that is having the patient go into a hyperbaric chamber on a regular basis for a period of, typically, several weeks. The hyperbaric chamber can accelerate the brain's own healing function, and, frankly, were it me suffering a head injury, I would pay the money to get the hyperbaric treatment even if its effects were only to give marginal "boost" to the healing process.

There are no, to my knowledge, effective drugs for treating brain trauma, other than ones to dampen or relieve the symptoms. The main "cure," if it may be called that, is mother nature and time, up to a year. That's about the size of it. Then, if you are left with deficits from the head trauma, you learn coping strategies. For example, if you can't remember things, then you carry about a recording device to make notes. If you can no longer add and subtract in your head, you have a calculator on your watch. This, of course, oversimplifies things. Oftentimes the effects are so drastic that coping mechanisms can only "cure" the most minor aspects.

We are getting much better on the technical, diagnostic end of things for TBI, or "traumatic brain injury," and MTBI, or, "mild traumatic brain injury," which is "mild" only in the sense that lymphoma is a 'milder' cancer than eye cancer, i.e. it's still pretty bad for the person who has it. The MRI and PET scanning machines of today are much more powerful, and the software is so much more powerful, that we can now detect the damage from trauma even if it is relatively microscopic. Even so, there is still a lot of brain injury that cannot be seen on current MRI scans. The neuropsychological testing that is available to assess brain trauma is greatly subject to the skills of the person interpreting the data, and so is not as trustworthy to many jurors as, say, the various scanning technologies.

If you have a motor vehicle accident, and you are thinking about making a claim for TBI, you need to know in advance that, legally, by doing so, you have now opened up your entire life, and all intimate details of it, to scrutiny by insurance hired psychologists 'digging for dirt.'

Jurors are receptive to the growing mountain of evidence that traumatic brain injuries from non-catastrophic head injuries are very real. Although jurors are overly skeptical these days about spinal injury claims, I would say the opposite is true about brain injuries, in particular, ones that show up on MRI machines that are specially designed to test brains.

CHAPTER THIRTY-EIGHT

THE LEGAL EFFECTS OF "PRE-EXISTING" CONDITIONS

Like most every state, Nevada has adopted "eggshell plaintiff" rule. This means that simply because your client has pre-existing conditions that make him or her more vulnerable to the effects of injury, this does not mean that they are not allowed to collect.

The "eggshell plaintiff" rule in Nevada is set forth in the pattern jury instruction as follows:

PAIN AND SUFFERING: AGGRAVATION OF PRE-EXISTING CONDITION

A person who has a condition or disability at the time of an injury is not entitled to recover damages therefor. However, [he] [she] is entitled to recover damages for any aggravation of such preexisting condition or disability [proximately] [legally] resulting from the injury.

This is true even if the person's condition or disability made [him] [her] more susceptible to the possibility of ill effects than a normally healthy person would have been, and even if a normally healthy person probably would not have suffered any substantial injury.

Where a preexisting condition or disability is so aggravated, the damages as to such condition or disability are limited to the additional injury caused by the aggravation.

As noted above, the phrase "eggshell plaintiff rule" comes from the law school example taught to every law student in tort class. The example is, what if, hypothetically, there was a man with a skull that was as thin as an eggshell. Assuming he was born that way. Someone comes up to him and hits him with, say, a tennis ball that they throw at the man for a "joke." Instead of just bouncing off the man's skull causing him pain, it crushes his skull and the man dies. The person throwing the tennis ball says, "I had no idea he had a skull like that, how can you make me have to pay for killing him?" The law states that "you take your plaintiff as you find him," meaning that after you injure someone you can't later on complain that "if he had been healthier this wouldn't have happened."

In closing arguments sometimes, the example is given of an intersection collision where a farmer hauling a truck full of eggs is hit by someone running a red light. All the eggs are broken. The farmer says, "I want to be paid for all the eggs that were broken. There were 5,000 of them." If the other driver were to say, "Why should I pay for all those broken eggs? If your truck had been full of tennis balls nothing would have happened." Again, you "take your plaintiff as you find him," and you can't complain that the truck was full of eggs instead of full of tennis balls. (Note to practitioner: I've used this argument in closing argument a couple of times. If you use it in the initial closing argument, the defense lawyers will invariably come up and say afterwards, "The eggs were already broken before we hit the truck." They always think they are very clever when they think of this. So, if you're going to use this argument, save it for the rebuttal part of close, when the other attorney can't come up, smirking, and use the "eggs were already broken" line.) The story about the truck full of eggs versus tennis balls is something that I "stole" from the great attorney Randy Mainor, who was the "top gun" PI trial lawyer in Las Vegas for many years prior to his death. I am sure he got it from someone else. That's what we do as PI lawyers, we steal good lines from each other.

The "eggshell plaintiff rule" is, in my opinion, one of the plaintiff's lawyer greatest friend. So often we get dragged into the argument of whether or not an injury is "new" or "pre-existing."

Our clients sometimes compound the problems by "forgetting" that they had prior neck or back or whatever issues before the injury. I try to impress on these clients if they just said, "I had some problems before, now it's a lot worse" we don't have to deal with the credibility issues that otherwise occur.

You can win a case with "bad before, worse after." You can't win a case with "no problems before," and then get blasted by defense counsel showing that there were indeed problems before.

Doctors are much more comfortable saying "yes, there was pre-existing arthritic changes shown on the x-ray, but that just made the patient more susceptible." Having the doctor say, "there was nothing wrong with this person" when obviously there was, just makes him out to be a liar. (And as a practical matter, what honest doctor is going to say that, anyway?)

The eggshell plaintiff rule is particularly useful in a situation involving alleged minor impact. Although minor impacts are in reality not minor, as shown above in this book, it's sometimes easier just to "go with the flow" and acknowledge that the impact was apparently minor, but that your client had pre-existing issues that made them more susceptible to the effects of a minor collision. Probably, this is true in the case of most anyone over a certain age.

Everyone over the age of 40 has some degree osteoarthritis, also known as "degenerative arthritis," or, in the spine, "degenerative disk disease." (These all sound much worse than they are.) Insurance companies like to exploit this by having their doctors really emphasize that "this patient had pre-existing degenerative arthritis!" preying on the jury's misunderstanding of the word "arthritis," or "degenerative disk disease," which does not mean gnarly hands and so forth, as in rheumatoid arthritis (a completely different animal, medically, as compared to osteoarthritis), but medically, simply means "inflammation of the joint," which is almost universal in every person over a certain age. The practitioner must educate jurors early on that "degenerative arthritic disease" merely refers to the normal aging process, which is usually without any pain or symptoms (i.e. is "asymptomatic"), but, which does make the person more susceptible to being injured from a minor force.

Biomechanical engineers are not medically trained. They can only cite to studies about the effects of certain amounts of 'g' force on normal, healthy bodies. They will admit that these studies do not apply to persons with susceptibility from arthritic, aging processes. This, I believe, should disqualify them from offering testimony in any case involving a plaintiff with pre-existing arthritic conditions, as they cannot say whether that person would be injured or not by this or that amount of 'g' force.

CHAPTER THIRTY-NINE

THE PRE-LITIGATION CLAIMS PROCESS

In most every law office handling auto collision cases, there are two main "departments." One is for "pre-litigation," and the other is "litigation."

Basically, "pre-litigation" means: *before* the lawsuit is filed. There are some "law offices" in town that do only pre-litigation. When they can't settle the case without going to court, they refer it out to another law firm and take a percentage "associate counsel fee." On the positive side, at least they know their limits.

From the viewpoint of a real law office, the pre-litigation part of the case is, generally speaking, easier than the "litigation" part. This is why, typically, fee agreements (such as the ones in my office) charge a lower fee percentage if the matter can be settled before a lawsuit is filed.

The claims process has changed considerably in my time as an attorney. It used to be, 40 years ago, that most claims adjusters were highly trained professionals who, typically, had a lot of experience and knowledge about what was going on. They knew laws, they knew basic medicine, they knew who the players were in the local legal and medical scene, etc. Some of them were better than others, but most of the time, talking to them on the phone wasn't a waste of your time if you were an attorney.

Now, claims adjusters are oft times what the insurance companies call 'processors' who fill out forms on computers, and the computer tells them what to do. Oftentimes they are made to work out of their homes, and read scripted speeches or follow scripts given to them by insurance companies for "negotiation." In my opinion, it's typically a waste of time talking to these people. I predict that within the next 10 years such "claims adjusting" functions will be transferred to India, Pakistan, etc., where people can input computers just as well as they can here.

Many clients buy into the television commercials that portray insurance companies as having real people who give a darn about their job or their insureds the truth is, most people who work for insurance companies end up hating them as much as I do. They not only treat claimants like dirt, they treat the people who work for the company like dirt. The insurance company is not interested in your wellbeing or 'justice.' They are interested in a computer that tells them how much profit they made at the end of each quarter. That's it, start and finish.

I have clients who think that the pre litigation adjusters are actually sitting back considering their cases seriously, and plotting various devious long term strategies to go against them. They think that a delay in evaluating the case is part of a plot or strategy. They think that a low evaluation is part of a negotiating ploy being done by a clever adjuster, like you might see on the TV series "Suits." I have to tell my clients, and I'm telling the readers of this book, adjusters don't care if you get a lot or a little, they just care if the boxes are checked on the computer form and that at the end of the year, when their job performance review comes up, the computer doesn't penalize them for whatever criteria the company is using that year to evaluate "claims processors." You are not an actual person to the insurance company. You are a set of ones and zeros on a computer, and in the auto insurance claims world, pre-litigation, it is a computer algorithm ("Colossus" is the name of the one most commonly used) that is actually dealing with you. The human is only the mouthpiece for the computer.

So, pre litigation, the claims processors sit back and wait for the demand package from the plaintiff's attorney. Then, the demand package is scanned into a computer system. The processor helps the computer to crunch the essential data. The computer tells the processor what to do, and they obey the computer, basically. They give us the numbers in a scripted process. I can predict, almost to the word, what they will say.

Here is the standard script. Them: "We received your demand package. Unfortunately, we can't pay the amount you're demanding. We've had the medical records reviewed, and it appears that your client only had very mild symptoms that should have resolved within 4 weeks. We also are not able to allow all the medical bills. But we are willing to offer $x dollars" Me: "but $x is less than the medical bills!" Them: "well, that's not true. It's more than the amount we allowed for the medical bills."

Script for second conversation. Me: "My client has authorized a counter demand for $x." Them: "I'm sorry, that's more than I'm authorized. But, I'm willing to consider new information. Do you have any new information?" Me: "I already gave you all the information that exists on this case. Do you have any new information to give me?" Them: "Do you have new information to give me? I will certainly consider new information." Me: "Look, just give me your best number and I'll take it to my client." Them: "My top authority is $x. That's our evaluation. We feel that's fair for a mild soft tissue injury." (Note: everything, including ruptured disks, and fractured ribs, is described as a "mild soft tissue injury" by these people. Also, they truly believe that they have the power to "allow" medical charges, as if they are the IRS or something allowing a tax deduction.)

They are really smug about the phony line: do you have any new information, I'll certainly consider it. Like that really flipped things around, aha, gotcha! I used to get mad at it, until I realized these "processors" are hardly paid a living wage, and they are just reading from a script they learned in their training course, and they are telling me numbers that the computer says to tell me. It's like getting mad at a telemarketer; what good does it do? In Trump's America 2018, kids coming out of college have to take any legit sounding job they can get, no matter how de-humanizing, so you can't blame these youngsters for taking these glorified telemarketing jobs.

That is 'negotiation' on auto claims in 2018. If we don't like what the computer says, we file a lawsuit. Thank Goodness, the litigation process involves real humans who are not reading scripts.

CHAPTER FORTY

SHOULD I GIVE A RECORDED STATEMENT?

Unless you have to, the answer is **no.** If it is your own insurance company requesting the statement, then you are probably obligated by contract to give it. But if it is the opposing party, there is no possible upside to your giving a recorded statement. It can only be used against you, it can never be used in your favor.

I am shocked by the naivety of people who think that if they don't hire a lawyer and give a recorded statement, that the insurance company will reward them by giving them a good settlement. I will say it straight out: People who think this are need to 'wake up and smell the coffee.'

I have even come across lawyers who allow their clients to give recorded statements to opposing party This is typically done lawyers or legal assistants with very little real experience, who think that by acting friendly and cooperative with opposing adjusters they will get better results. Oh, were that only so! Maybe in the bizarro rule where Kirk and Spock wear slashes. (OK, if you're not old, that last one went totally past you, I admit.)

When an adjuster says, per their script, "We just want to find out what really happened," you can say (if you are an attorney) you can find out what really happened without recording. The fact that they refuse to do this and want it recorded should tell you all you need to know about the legitimacy of their statement that they "need to record the statement to find out what really happened."

If it is your own insurance company, legally, you may have to give a recorded statement. Normally if this happens, I or another lawyer from my office will be part of the process, and will be there with you when the statement is given. There will be some "kid" reading off questions from a computer, not really caring what the answer is, just going through the list. But, every once in a while you get an adjuster who has watched television shows featuring attorneys and wants to act as though she or he is one. They use the recorded statement as a means to try to "get" whoever they're recording (stupidly, even if it is their own insured, since by attacking their own insured, they are actually weakening their own position.) It would be funny were it not so common. These adjusters trying to pretend they are attorneys are like comedians in a sitcom portraying a courtroom scene, e.g., Jerry Seinfeld in a "dream sequence" pretending to be a lawyer cross-examining Kramer.

In the worst of these "adjuster pretending to be lawyer" situations I will instruct my client not to answer the questions, and then tell the insurance adjuster that they need to put someone else on the phone to ask the questions.

(As a somewhat humorous aside, I once had an adjuster taking a statement identify himself as "Alpha." I said that wasn't sufficient, I needed to have a real name. The adjuster refused to give his real name stating that all I needed to know was his codename, "Alpha." He was part of the division in the insurance company called the "special investigative unit," which in theory is supposed to investigate highly questionable claims, but in my experience, is used oft times not to investigate, but rather, to simply hassle people the insurance company doesn't like.)

CHAPTER FORTY-ONE

DECISION OF FAULT THROUGH INTER-COMPANY ARBITRATION

Insurance companies oftentimes claim against each other to retrieve money. If your own insurance company pays to fix your car, they will get their money back from the at fault party's insurance company through a process known as "subrogation," and, more specifically, "inter-company subrogation."

Because insurance companies like to argue with each other, if they do not agree on percentage of fault, they will submit the matter to "intercompany arbitration." Each adjuster will submit, typically, the transcript of a recorded statement given by their own insured, to an adjuster for an unrelated insurance company, and that adjuster will then decide percentages of fault.

There are some insurance companies who take the position that they will contest fault on every case, in order to get at least some relief from the "intercompany arbitration," under the belief that if you protest fault, the intercompany arbitration person will give you at least 10 percent as a "token." This unfortunate practice has the effect of sometimes making people's insurance rates go up for no reason.

The process itself is highly flawed and susceptible to "just give them 10 percent as a token" type decisions.
The worst part about it is that the intercompany arbitration decision will sometimes be viewed by adjusters as deciding what should be the actual percentages of fault for purposes of the bodily injury claim. I will have adjusters tell me "I can't offer you more than 90 percent because the intercompany arbitration found your client 10 percent at fault."

Legally, the intercompany arbitration cannot be used in court against you, but in reality, insurance companies will try to use it against you if they can. I would give this advice to readers of this book who have had their insurance rates increased because "intercompany arbitration found that you were partially at fault." You can protest decisions of that nature. It's sometimes difficult, but if you make enough noise, and complain enough, it is quite possible to get raises based on bad intercompany arbitration decisions reversed, especially the token 10% fault decisions.

CHAPTER FORTY-TWO

"SETTING RESERVES" ON AUTO CASES

Insurance companies are required by law to "set a reserve" for claims, so that they can have enough money on hand to pay all the claims. Were this not the law, then insurance companies could be undercapitalized, and then just file bankruptcy when all the claims came due.

There are occasionally insurance companies that are "scam" type operations, where reserves are set very low, and after many premiums are taken in, and the claims can't be paid, file for bankruptcy. I would say on the average, I see one such auto insurer flame out every year and a half, or so. They're almost always insurance companies specializing in high risk auto insurance, giving insurance to people who otherwise cannot get it from legitimate companies. People with DUI's on their records, or, more typically, illegal immigrants who, until recently, could not get driver's licenses, but needed to get insurance to register their cars, are examples of the 'target' market. It is the job of the Nevada Insurance Commissioner's office to guard against companies of this sort. It is a matter of opinion as to how good they have done this job.

The problem, from the plaintiff's perspective, with "reserves" in legit companies is that they are set initially with only a scant amount of information, and if they are set too low, then later on, if it is apparent that the claim is worth a lot more than the initial "reserve" amount, it can be extremely difficult, depending on the level of bureaucracy at the particular insurance company, to get an adequate settlement paid because it is "more than reserve."

So it's important for plaintiff's counsel to try to get reserves set high enough initially that it won't be a problem later on. This is problematic since you can only spend so much of your time arguing about the value of your case when the accident is only three or four weeks old. I f you say, right from the get go, that your client looks like she is going to need back surgery, then you are painting a target on your back for the 'special investigations unit.' So, the goal is to get the reserve set as high as possible, but, without being overly speculative to the point that credibility is strained.

My own experience is that, since the high value cases never get settled without litigation, absent a policy limits situation, one should not spend too much time worrying about 'setting reserves,' since the insurance lawyer will be obtaining information and the litigation department at the insurance company will be re-setting reserves, anyway. There are, however, some very good lawyers who disagree with my viewpoint, and who believe that pre-lit reserves remain carved in stone until something like a mediation takes place, when the adjusters are properly educated about the facts of the case outside of the cheer-leader reports some hourly defense firms, tend. My own practice, to guard against 'cheer leader' defense lawyers keeping the reserves down with 'we're kickin' tail and taking names' status reports, is to, at the start of litigation, give the defense lawyer a full picture of the claimed damages. That way, the defense lawyer is required to take these things into account when evaluating the case, at the very start, and cannot claim to be unaware, later on, if things blow up.

The main problem I encounter regarding reserves issues are with clients who try to represent themselves for the first month or so and then wakeup, smell the coffee, and see that they are being manipulated, and then come to a lawyer.

Such clients oftentimes think that they will favorably impress the insurance adjusters by claiming that "there is a little crick in my neck, I don't think it hurts that bad but I'm going to go get it checked out by a doctor." They feel that by underplaying their injury and so forth to the adjuster, the adjuster will congratulate them for honesty and pay them even more later on because the adjuster will be able to tell "they're not the kind of people who like to sue."

The fact is the adjuster hears the information, inputs it into the computer, and the computer will set an absurdly low "reserve" on the case. Then later on when you try to get a fair settlement, you can't, because the "reserve" has been set so low. Again, people unfortunately buy into the television advertisements that show insurance claims representatives as being good ole down to earth folks who understand real Americans. They find out the truth eventually.

CHAPTER FORTY-THREE

THE "ISO SEARCH"

There is an organization known as "ISO." This stands for Insurance Services Organization (owned by Verisk.) This should not be confused with an international organization of the same name (International Standards Organization.)

For the first 20 years or so when I practiced law, when insurance companies would consult a computer program to find whether claimants had made previous claims, they called it the "index bureau." As far as I can tell, the "ISO" is the same thing as "index bureau."

Of course, back in the "stone ages" insurance companies had to actually wait for the index bureau, or ISO, results to be mailed (later, faxed). Now, it's a matter of a few mouse strokes, and the information is instantly available.

The very first thing that an insurance adjuster wants to do when taking in a new claim is to get the information necessary to run the "ISO" search on the claimant. If you try to handle a claim by yourself, you will find that the insurance adjuster is obsessive about trying to get from you the information about your birthdate, social security number, and the last couple addresses where you have lived. This is because they are told that the most important thing to do initially is to get the ISO information.

Insurance companies treat the ISO printouts as though they were scripture directly from God. They have adopted the jargon of crime shows on television when talking about them. When the printout comes in, any sort of prior claim by a claimant (even something like claiming a broken water heater flood damage on a homeowners policy) is classified as a "prior" (as in 'prior arrest.') Any sort of prior claim is called a "hit" and I have actually heard some adjusters refer to the ISO printout as the "the sheet" taking the crime show jargon all the way. People who have "priors" and "hits" on the ISO printout are viewed as "the bad guys." (It is funny to see how the "SIU" investigators at insurance companies try to imitate the television detectives, right down to the jargon, hairstyles, clothing and equipment. The "Sipowitz" character on NYPD Blue was a common icon for them back in the 90's. Before that, they wanted to be like the Jack Webb character on "Dragnet" right down to the flat top haircut.)

The unfortunate aspect here is that the ISO printout is almost always full of errors. If you ever Googled your own name on a computer, you know that, no matter how unusual your name, there are dozens of other persons with your same name. (Same thing comes into play on Facebook.) There are probably people with your very same name in your very near geographical area.

210

The ISO computer is extremely good at mixing up people. It may show several claims that appear to have been made by you, but were actually made by a person with your same name.

They also search claims history by addresses. Let's say that 10 years ago, the house in which you live was occupied by a large family, and several of those family members over the years had various sorts of claims, be it for broken windows or cracked windshields on their cars, car accident injuries, or claims *against them* for causing the injuries. All those pop up on the ISO screen as "priors" by individuals "living in the household."

Of course, someone with a practiced eye and some level of experience and intelligence could go through the sheet and sort out which claims are actually you and actually involve personal injuries. But, such people are rare at insurance companies, where the processors, hoping for the rare "atta boy," are eager to find 'hits' by the 'perp' on the 'sheet.' The people employed as claims processors these days are oftentimes youngsters just out of college, anxious to play the role of the bright, but eccentric, young helper who knows how to use computers, like the characters on the CSI or NCIS type shows who pull up the dirty secrets being hidden by the 'perp.'

The initial claims file may be, quite inaccurately, documented to the effect that you are someone who has made "lots of claims," or lives in a household of presumed scam artists making lots of claims. Once the computer has you pegged as a "perp" with lots of "priors" it's very difficult to settle your claim.

This phenomena is particularly troublesome to persons whose names are relatively common (e.g. Jose Garcia , Robert Jones, etc.).

I have had clients over the years who forget prior claims that they made several years previously. If it was an accident that happened 20+ years ago, I tend to believe them; if it was a claim that occurred only 2 or 3 years ago, it is hard to believe they have no memory of it, frankly. I tell them before any depositions or answering interrogatory sets that it is critical for them to reveal any prior claims. I tell them over and over the insurance company already knows, you are handing them the gift that keeps on giving if you "forget" a prior claim. I tell them we can usually keep it out of evidence as being irrelevant as long as you disclose it first. If it is not disclosed, then it becomes proof of "lack of credibility" and may come into evidence not on the basis of its relevance to the case, but as evidence that the client is a liar.

CHAPTER FORTY-FOUR

SIGNING RELEASE AUTHORIZATIONS

If you had an automobile accident case , and are trying to handle the case on your own, one of the very first things that the adjuster will ask you to do is to sign a release authorization for records. They will act as if this is routine, and if you have nothing to hide, why would you not sign this paper? Of course, the form, if read closely, gives the adjuster carte blanche access to virtually any kind of record you might have, and waives your privacy rights with anyone and anything.

Keep in mind that the insurance adjuster is not on your side. He is not paid to look after your interests. Why would you not expect the adjuster, or the insurance lawyer, to use such a carte blanche release to their maximum advantage (which means 'digging for dirt' on you) ?

The biggest issue in any personal injury case is the credibility and integrity of the plaintiff. For the insurance company, it is almost like searching for the holy grail : going after "dirt" on the plaintiff (even though their insured is the 'guilty' one who caused the accident, they try to put you on trial.)

Of course, you expect them to use a release authorization to get medical records that are involved with your case. But what else might a not particularly nice (and none of them are nice) adjuster or insurance lawyer use this to get? Hmm, let's see. They can access the national computer data system for health insurance companies, and get a printout of every doctor and diagnostic code you have had since, probably, the time you were born to the present. They can get your social security records and see how much you have earned your entire working life. They can access credit reports, and see if you are hard up for money, and not able to hold out for long in a protracted battle. They can look at the health insurance printouts and see if you have ever seen any counselors for issues such as, substance abuse etc., and request those records. They can ask for your old school records or military records. They can get records from the unemployment board to see if an employer ever said nasty things about you when you filed an unemployment claim. They can use it to gain access to social media accounts you might have. (Of course, they can probably use illegal tactics to get a lot of this information without your consent, but by giving your consent you legitimize their search so they do not have to "cover their tracks" later on.) They can get your DMV records, and they can inquire with the state to get the printout showing whenever you have received a prescription for controlled substance medications, going back from the present time to 20 years back or more. They can access records to see if you have had any legal fights with other people in the past such as relatives, ex-spouses, child custody disputes, etc. The records at family court that normally are sealed from public view are now open to the insurance company because you signed a carte blanche release. They may call ex-spouses to see if they can find any dirt on you, such as that arrest 30 years ago for drug possession when you were hanging out with the wrong crowd, that you thought was 'sealed.' They can get your employment files (and your employers will feel hassled by requests for your complete files. The insurance company will especially want any records that pertain to any disputes or reports of bad job performance.) They can request any records from any jail you were ever at (including records related to old trespassing charges, DUIs, domestic quarrels, etc.)

The thing is, under the law, the insurance company is not entitled to dig into your (irrelevant) past simply because you had the misfortune to be the victim of an accident UNLESS you sign a carte blanche release. When you think about it, the actual "bad guy" in the collision is not you, but the person or company that caused you harm. But, they try to turn the tables, and make it out that you are the bad guy, and the "target" of an investigation, when in fact the opposite should be the case. But if you sign the carte blanche release, you are opening the door to people who have malicious intent and are digging for dirt.

We have a case in Nevada, Schlatter v. Eighth Judicial District Court, that does not allow insurance companies to get medical records unrelated to your accident, except under extraordinary circumstances (such as being recent in time, or related to the same body part.) They are not allowed to get your tax returns or employment records unless you are making a large loss wage claim of more than a small amount. They are not allowed to go on a 'fishing expedition' to uncover dirt just to smear your name. All of this can be enforced UNLESS you sign a carte blanch release authorization.

Once a lawsuit is filed, the law requires that the insurance company be given release authorizations, but only for certain *limited* purposes, and, *limited, relevant*, documents. If you are an attorney representing an injured person, you should not have them sign the insurance company's form carte blanche release for medical, or other, records. Do not let them slip in a carte blanche release for Compex, or one of the other similar investigation companies. Use your own limited releases whenever possible.

In our office we will give the insurance company *our* release forms that are limited to certain providers, certain timeframes, and certain records, only. (The discovery commissioner has upheld us on this. Unfortunately, in our court annexed arbitration program, there are a few arbitrators who either do not know the rules, or, who are biased toward the defense side, who require us to sign the carte blanche "hippa's" (as younger defense lawyers call them.)

I have been told by some insurance company lawyers that "a lot of the plaintiff firms give us a carte blanche release. It makes our job easier." I strongly disagree with this tactic, and suspect it is usually the result of legal assistants, who do not know their jobs well enough, doing it without the lawyer's knowledge.

I did hear one argument in favor of giving the carte blanche release to insurance companies, which, I think, was more of an ex post facto excuse. The argument is that if you give them the carte blanch release, then it blunts, later on, arguments by defense counsel at trial that you or your client was trying to hide anything (in the event that the client 'forgets' to disclose an important fact during deposition or interrogatories.) I think most clients would not appreciate this argument if and when their privacy expectations were invaded by insurance lawyers digging in to their credit history, family court records, etc.

CHAPTER FORTY-FIVE

SOCIAL MEDIA SEARCHES BY INSURANCE COMPANIES

As noted above, a big effect on how much compensation you will get in a case depends not just on what happened to you, but "who" you are. The more "deserving" the plaintiff might appear to a jury, the more money, in general, that person will get in a jury trial, or from an insurance company by way of settlement.

Insurance companies have always, in the course of my career, been "digging for dirt" on all my clients. The lengths to which they will go is really disgusting, at times. For example, soliciting "dirt" from an ex-spouse whose name they found in the family court records, or finding out names of estranged boyfriends or girlfriends, are particularly favorite methods for the SIU crowd to dig for dirt.

The advent of social media, in particular Facebook, has made the insurance companies' job a lot easier. Although, allegedly, Facebook is now tightening privacy safeguards in light of the scandals following the 2016 election cycles, as it sits now, pushing the privacy setting options on your Facebook account is akin to pushing a dummy button for 'close doors' on an elevator– it doesn't do any good, really, except make you feel a little better.

Typically, one of the first things that an insurance company might do when the claim comes in, other than running your name through the "ISO" computer, is to have various "specialists" review your social media accounts. (Even if this is not done right away, if your case goes to a trial, you can rest assured it will be done during the discovery process in litigation.)

Even if you hit some kind of "privacy" button on your account, it is easy for these "specialists" to defeat the privacy settings and to get into your Facebook and similar accounts without restriction.

If you have posted embarrassing type materials, the insurance company will have it eventually. By "embarrassing" I mean stuff like posting photos displaying recreational drug use (bongs and the like); making remarks that are racially insensitive; making jokes about "partying," etc.; making "jokes" about "now I'm going to get a big settlement and buy your jet ski," etc.

I know one major law office in town that has a full-time person assigned to monitoring the social media accounts of their clients, to make sure people are not posting stupid items.

If you have a claim against an insurance company, you should be very careful, in particular, anything

about the claim itself. Any mention of the case,
even if vague, will be twisted out of context by an
insurance lawyer. It's best just not to mention it at
all on Facebook or similar sites.

CHAPTER FORTY-SIX

COMPUTERIZED DATABASE SEARCHES REGARDING YOUR BACKGROUND

In addition to running the "ISO" about prior claims, and running and printing out your social media accounts, insurance companies will regularly also run a public database search on you (with or without your release authorization. The release auth allows expansion of the search, but there is a lot out there available publicly.) Some of these programs are extremely impressive. I have seen one, in particular, that is the "civilian" version of the same program that the FBI uses. It shows where you've lived, different phone numbers you've had over the years, jobs you've had, any criminal convictions, and many other things.

Publicly available data bases will show your credit rating and overdue bills that you have. It will show cars you have owned since you owned your first car. As mentioned above, the "ISO" data base will show any insurance claims you have ever made, and any work comp claims you might have made.

Although insurance companies are not supposed to access the health insurance company computer system without your authority, I am pretty sure (certain, actually) that some go ahead and do it anyway. There is a database that health insurance and life insurance companies use that gives health insurance use to check out your medical history. Anytime you went to a doctor, it ended up in a bill to an insurance company with a diagnostic code attached to it. Every doctor visit from the time you were a kid is probably inputted in this system. Every time you complained of something of something to a doctor or clinic it ended up in a diagnostic code that ended up on a bill that ends up in a national database computer. Therefore, insurance companies can check out your health history going back, literally, to when you were born. Therefore, when you are being deposed by insurance lawyers and they ask about your health history, do not think that you are being clever by "not remembering" things from years ago. They already probably know about it. Sometimes they simply want to find a way to expose it without getting caught for accessing databases where they shouldn't be going, or, to get you to deny something they can later 'discover' and then accuse you of lying.

The lack of privacy should be disturbing to every American. Frankly, most people have little idea what an unscrupulous insurance company can do finding out about a person's background. Not to be paranoid: rarely are they going to go past the legally available stuff in a simple whiplash case. But what is easily available with public records and computer insurance database systems is quite tempting, and will almost certainly be looked into if it is a case of significance.

The point is, if you make an insurance claim for an injury, you must be prepared to acknowledge, honestly and openly, things in your background that pertain to the case. There is little "hiding" any information, anymore. If you try to hide something, and it is found out, then that is pure poison to your case. Every trial lawyer has a story about a client who 'forgot' to mention some important fact, only to have that fact revealed at trial in devastating fashion.

I have sometimes argued with insurance lawyers who say, "Well, your client's the one who made the claim. They were asking for it. If they didn't want me to go after them they shouldn't have filed a claim." I point out it was their client that was drunk driving, or speeding, whatever, and my client certainly didn't want to get hit by a negligent driver. I said, "How does filing a claim make my client the bad guy? Why does the fact that she got hurt make it so that you can probe into every facet of her life, like she's a criminal or something?" Insurance lawyers just scoff at such remarks. The feeling is that since my client filed a claim for injury she is no longer entitled to the rudiments of human decency and compassion, and is now a "target" upon whom "shooting practice" is somehow justified. Things that they would never tolerate were it done to their own family member (e.g. grilling a elderly person about their deceased spouse for hours in a deposition) are now OK to do since it is "just part of my job."

CHAPTER FORTY-SEVEN

HANDLING THE PROPERTY DAMAGE ASPECTS

There are two main "forks in the road" initially when it comes to dealing with car (property) damage: one fork , if your car is repairable: and a second 'fork' if it is declared a total loss.

We will deal first with the situation: repairable.

SHOULD I EXPECT MY LAWYER TO HELP WITH THE CAR REPAIR ISSUES?

In a word, yes. You are paying your attorney's office what most people would think is very good money to handle your personal injury case.

At the very least, for this kind of money they should be helping you with car repair issues when help is needed. That's how I see it.

I have heard of several attorney firms, typically the ones who advertise heavily on television, who say that it is your job to take care of the car repairs, as they are being paid only to handle the injury part of the case. In my opinion, this is being cheap and lazy, and you might consider looking for another law firm if you get treated this way . Although there is no direct profit to be made out of helping with the car damage, it is part of the service you are entitled to expect to receive.

HOW DO THEY TELL IF MY CAR IS REPAIRABLE OR IF IT IS A TOTAL?

State law in Nevada states that if the value of the repairs exceeds 65 percent of the fair market value of your car, then the car must be declared a total loss. This means it will not be fixed, but will go the route of a "total," described below.

TOW TRUCKS AND TOW YARDS

Generally speaking, every couple years or so the city or county will have a contract with one or two tow companies to service all the calls for accidents that come from the police. The bright side of this is that we don't get a situation where various tow trucks from different companies are showing up competing at a scene for the business, which could turn quite nasty. The bad part is it turns into a "monopoly" type situation where you have no choice but to deal with a particular company.

There are fixed rates for how much they can charge for the tows, which are not cheap. If your car must be towed from the scene (e.g., you are taken from the scene in an ambulance), then one of these assigned companies will come and take your car to the tow yard.

The tow yards are located in extremely inconvenient places. Virtually no accommodation

225

is made for you. You must appear on a day and time that is convenient for the tow company, and generally speaking they will only allow one visit, at certain hours, to your car without charge, although there are some companies that charge for every time you visit your car.

I would advise anyone who has valuables in the car such as tools, cell phones, etc., to get them out of the car as soon as possible, or else they may disappear quickly.

There are unscrupulous lawyers and law firms who pay tow truck drivers and tow company employees to refer cases to them. These are like fungus growing in a garden. Every time you stomp out one patch, a new patch appears. It is my observation that frequently these "bottom feeders" are lawyers who come here from other states where the practice is so commonplace that it's more or less accepted. The tow truck drivers are more than happy to take a payoff of a couple to refer clients to a lawyer. There have even been alleged situations where the tow company's owners will be involved and will direct the drivers to deal only with certain law firms. A few years ago, one law firm was even permitted to set up an office inside the tow company's building, so they could have instant access to anyone who came in, kind of like vultures roosting over a barnyard.

Needless to say, anyone who goes to an attorney referenced to them by a tow truck driver or tow company yard employee is taking a huge chance.

If you are going to an attorney who pays off a tow truck driver, what can you expect?

(As an aside, there are occasionally "cappers," also called "runners," who go about the valley with police scanners, going up to accident scenes and trying to get there before the police come. They harass the various people at the accident scene to call and "hook up with" their attorney immediately. These sorts of things seem to come in waves. You won't hear about it for a couple years and then you hear about a lot of it going on. It is illegal. Any attorney who is using people like this should be disbarred immediately, in my opinion.

PAYING THE TOW BILL

Once your car has been towed, someone has to pay the tow bill to get it out of the tow yard, whether you think it's fair or not. The tow bill will likely shock you. They are not cheap. The daily storage fees are outrageous, costing more than what you would pay for a motel room in Las Vegas off the strip.

The easiest way to handle the tow charges is to let the repair shop pay for it. Normally speaking, when you choose a repair shop (and you have the right to choose -- not the insurance company), the repair shop will send over its own tow truck to get your vehicle out of the tow yard, and they will pay off the tow bill. (They are later paid back by the insurance company. But this way, they get the

227

business for the repair job, so it is a "win win" situation for you and the repair shop.)

If the car is totaled, the insurance company who is paying for the total (assuming the at fault driver has insurance, and/or you have collision coverage) will contact a scrap yard (these days, usually CoParts) and the scrap yard will send over a tow truck, and the scrap yard will pay the tow bill (and later deduct it from what it pays for the salvage value.)

WHICH REPAIR SHOP SHOULD I USE?

The insurance companies will almost always say, "We have repair shops that we guarantee and you should go there." Or, words to that effect.

The fact that the "work is guaranteed" really doesn't mean much. Any legitimate repair shop will make sure that its work is done properly.

The main thing insurance companies are looking for with contracted repair shops is first of all, that they will charge lower prices, and make themselves readily available to the persons from the insurance company that wish to inspect the vehicles. And secondly, and more sinister, is that these "recommended repair shops" are oftentimes working with the insurance company "biomechanical experts" and will allow your vehicles to be measured and photographed and so forth so that this "evidence" can be used against you later on to prove you were not really hurt.

228

There are a couple insurance companies and repair shops that are notorious for this, and if you have an attorney who does a lot of car accident cases, he will know who they are.

Frankly, among the larger repair shops, there isn't much difference in how the work is handled basically. The same group of people who do body repair work tend to float around from one shop to another, so the people actually doing the work tend to be the same people no matter which shop you go to. They are paid on commission basis, which means that the faster they get the work done then the more money they can make, overall.

The main difference may come in terms of who is managing the repair shop. There are certain places that take forever because the managers are just not very good. They are oftentimes people who "like to party" and they and the workers they hire are "feelin' good."

There is one dealership in town, in particular, where I have noticed this sort of atmosphere for many years. They get their business by offering various incentives to insurance companies to keep using them, whether it be really cheap prices or, I suspect, gratuities offered to those who make the referrals. Again, I'm not going to name names, but you need to go to an attorney who knows who is doing what in order to avoid these sorts of shops.

As the owner of the car you don't really care how much it costs to fix the car, you just want it fixed right. The fact that a repair shop has good a good reputation for many years is sometimes of no matter. People sell their repair shops and new management comes in, so year to year, a shop that might have been good one year is now no longer good the next year

I have sometimes had clients ask me: Do the lawyers get kickbacks from recommended certain repair shops? I can say that in my own experience and observation, the answer is no. The main thing I want from a repair shop is just to have them do the job right so I don't get calls later on from my client complaining that it took too long, or the job wasn't done right, or the paint didn't match, etc.

SHOULD I GO TO THE DEALERSHIP FOR REPAIR ON MY CAR?

First of all, if your car is more than seven years old , the dealership does not want to repair your car. There are various reasons for this, but obtaining parts for cars that are more than seven years old is a big "hassle," and dealerships don't want to deal with it.

Many dealerships do not have their own auto body departments. As a matter of fact, most of them, these days, do not. The fact that they recommend a certain shop is meaningless. Generally speaking there are kickbacks involved in the process of which shop a dealership recommends, so take their recommendations with a grain of salt.

But if your car is less than seven years old, and if the dealership does have an auto body repair shop, then you may want to consider going there, especially if your car is still some under some kind of warranty. This way, they will not be able to claim your warranty was violated by repair work or that such and such an item failed because it was in the accident. You simply can say: "Look, your own auto body shop looked at the car and nothing was said about such and such item. So, it's under the warranty."

In general dealership auto body repair shops do mediocre work, not good, but not bad. If you have a fairly new vehicle, especially if it's still under warranty, it's probably best to go to the dealership that services that make and model. For older vehicles, then you have to rely on advice from knowledgeable persons, who are *not* getting kickbacks or have some hidden interest (like repair shops chosen by insurance companies that cooperate with biomechanical engineers to "document" your vehicle's lack of injury causing damage) to make adequate decisions for your repair choice.

Dealing with very small mom and pop shops is oftentimes a bad idea because they oftentimes lack credit and cannot purchase the parts necessary to repair your vehicle in a timely manner, and it ends up taking way too long for the repairs to take place (and you get stuck with rental car bills.)

Although it is not particularly easy to find out this information, any auto body repair shop that is in financial trouble that has been put on a "COD" basis with the people who supply the parts is a bad choice. Such facilities are "robbing Peter to pay Paul" and your car can be sitting there for a long time waiting for them to get the money to pay for the part that is needed to fix your car. If you are in a business that has access to credit reports, checking out the credit score of the repair shop that you are intending to use is probably as good an indicator as any as to whether or not you can expect a fast result or a "foot dragging effort.

PHOTOS OF CAR DAMAGE

The availability of photos of car damage has changed dramatically over the last eight years or so, by the advent of the smartphone. Just about everyone has a smartphone these days, and the smartphones take really excellent photographs. It's easy as pie to whip out the smartphone and take photos of the accident scene, of the cars, and to easily share these photos via emailing them to whoever wants them. (If your lawyer needs the photos you took, you can actually send them as an attachment to a text message to the lawyer's email address.)

As explained above, insurance companies have exploited the fact that modern automobiles rarely show much damage when they are hit in the parts of the car protected by rubber/plastic coverings, e.g., the rear bumper. In these cases, photographs of the exterior of the car are misleading because it looks as though there is very little or no damage, when in fact the collision force was significant.

But, let's say there is significant damage to your car, or, to the other person's car who was involved in the accident. What to do about taking the photographs at the accident scene?

First of all, if you are in an accident and able to get out of the car and walk about and so forth, the humane first thing to do is to go to the other person in the accident and ask them if they are okay and if they need help, medically. Even if the other person is at fault, they deserve to have you show them compassion. They should also ask you if you are okay. This is the first thing to do in a car accident, i.e., check on your passengers, check on the other driver, take care of the medical needs of the people at the scene.

If you whip out your phone and start taking photos right away, without even checking on the other party, it will be used against you in court. They will suggest that you were planning to "work" an accident claim from the first, as evidenced by the fact that the very first thing you did was to take out a phone and start taking pictures. I know that all the insurance company advertisements and so forth say you should take out your phone and start taking pictures right away at the accident scene, but I'm telling you from the perspective of a trial lawyer, if you do it right away, or make too big an issue of it, it will be used against you in court as "proof" that you were thinking of "working" a claim right from the start.

After you've checked on the wellbeing of the other persons in the accident, and done what you need to do to get situated, initially, such as calling 911, then you can take pictures. Don't make a big deal out of it. If you walk around snapping numerous photos, acting as though you're a professional photographer and so forth, it can be used to make you look bad later on. Virtually every cell phone photography apparatus has a zoom feature so you can very easily stand in one place, and if need be, zoom in and out to take pictures. Don't stand there trying to take the "perfect" picture as, again, if you make too big a deal out of it, it will make you look bad later on.

It is a good idea, however, to take photos at the scene, just don't make a "show" out of doing it.

If you are taken away in an ambulance before the photographs are taken, and your car is towed, it's probably worthwhile for you to go to the tow yard (or send someone else on your behalf) to take some photos of your car at the tow yard. The insurance company, if they are at fault, will take really lousy photos of your car, sometimes with an old-fashioned polaroid camera, that intentionally minimize the look of the amount of damage to your car. If you depend on the insurance company's body shop (the one they directed you to go to) to take photos, again, they will take the worst possible photos, like polaroid shots taken from 25 feet back, to make it hard to even tell where the damage is on your car. It's worthwhile to go down to the repair shop and take a couple of your own photos, with your smartphone, if you don't otherwise have photos from the tow yard or accident scene.

If you were hit in the rear by another vehicle, and the other car shows significant damage in front, yet, the plastic-rubber bumper covering on your car only has a scratch, it's sometimes worthwhile for you (through your lawyer, more than likely) to pay a repair shop to take off the bumper and photograph the parts underneath the bumper that were damaged. Repair shops will charge roughly $100 to remove the bumper.

Knowing what to look for when taking car photos is oftentimes important. If you just rely on an insurance adjuster or repair shop to do it for you, they will skip some of the more important photographic evidence showing the impact force, particularly in rear end collisions.

Oftentimes the gap on one side of a bumper will be different than the gap on another side, showing it was shoved. With pickup trucks you will oftentimes find there is damage between the front leading edge of the bed, and the rear area of the cab, showing how the bed got shoved up against the cab.

Frequently bumpers will be bent upward or downward at an angle because of the impact. This is more evident than otherwise would be the case if you look at the gaps between the bumper and the rear quarter panel. If on one side it's a quarter inch, and the other side is flush, then that shows it got moved quite a bit. There's probably damage underneath the bumper if you remove it to look. (Insurance companies will not remove the bumpers to look because they don't want to see what's there. You're going to have to pay for it to be done most of the time.)

CAN THEY USE OLD PARTS TO FIX MY CAR?

At first, we must distinguish between using "parts" to fix the outside body, versus parts to fix mechanical things in the engine and so forth.

Generally speaking, if the accident was bad enough to have affected the engine on your car, your car will probably be declared a total loss. So the issue of using "new" or "old" parts to fix the engine rarely comes up in reality, because the cars are totaled if the damage reached into the engine.

When fixing mechanical parts of your car, the focus is not so much on whether they are using "new" or "old" parts, but, when it comes to the engine, the discussion is on whether they are using factory made parts, or "after-market" parts (facsimile engine parts made, typically, in China.)

Most of the time people are never even made aware of the "old switcharoo" practice by insurance

236

companies in the body shops with whom they work in regard to using after-market parts. Especially if you have a newer car, and there is engine damage, you should insist, as is your right, that the damaged parts be replaced with factory-made parts, and not cheap "knockoffs" from China.

As to body damage, there is no absolute right to insist on a body shop replacing damaged fenders and so forth with "new" fenders. But there are boundaries. If you had a new car, say, five years old or newer, and they have to replace a fender, you can and should insist on a new fender. But if the car is, say, seven years old or older, you're not going to get a new fender. In such cases the body shop will find fenders, over the internet, from places like "Coparts" (scrap yards). Frankly, in an older car, there is nothing wrong with replacing an old fender with a fender off a car in a scrapyard, as long as everything matches and so forth. If you had a new car, and they had to replace a body part, I would insist, were I you, on a new fender. And I would also insist on it being factory-made, not a "knockoff" aftermarket copy from China.

Is there a dividing line between when you can insist on "new" and have to accept "old"? I am unaware of anything established by regulation that makes that division; but I would say as a rule of thumb, if your car is five years old or less, you can insist on new. If it's seven years old or older, you cannot insist on new. (Cars that are five or six years old, are kind of in the "gray" zone.)

237

If a mechanical part is damaged, you are not required to accept "knockoffs" replacement parts, although, many times, it really doesn't make a difference. It's not worth getting into a battle over "knockoff" versus "factory-made" unless it really makes a difference. But I can say for sure that I have never seen a "knockoff" part that was superior to the "factory-made" part. It simply doesn't work that way. The knockoffs are cheaper for a reason.

If an insurance company tells you to go to a certain repair shop after the accident because that's our "preferred shop," you can almost be sure that they are going to require that shop to use knockoff parts for replacement. Again, it's not worth making a fight out of it if it's a part that really doesn't matter much one way or the other. But, if you have a fairly new car, or a mechanical issue, again, you are not required to accept knockoff parts. But, don't get into fights over parts that don't matter, e.g the light bulb for your glove box being knock off vs. factory made (not important), vs. the entire radiator assembly (important.)

The people who own the garages want to please the insurance companies more than they want to please you because the insurance companies are the ones who are sending the business to them, by and large. At least, this is the case of the shops who are recipients of being "preferred shops" to whom insurance companies direct cars. So these guys are not going to help you make sure you get factory-made parts. As a matter of fact, if you ask them they will probably say "you're required to accept the knockoff parts." This is because they are not really on your side.

Again, I would tell people to make sure they pick their spots and pick their fights on these issues. Getting worked up about knockoff parts is not worth it for parts that "don't matter" in the final scheme.

CAN THEY FORCE ME TO TOTAL MY CAR?

Nevada has a strict regulation that says that if you have damage, the cost of which is 65 percent or more of the fair market value of the car, then it has to be declared a total.

It is usually to the insurance company's advantage to total a car in the case of any doubt. Otherwise they might get stuck for repair items that weren't apparent at first inspection, or lengthy rental car bills, etc. And if they total the car, they can get back part of their money by selling the car for "scrap" to the tow yard.

Many times, people do not want their cars totaled. The car has been paid for, and they have kept good care of it. They will not be able to secure a comparable replacement vehicle for the amount offered by the insurance company. This is understandable.

In such cases people are allowed to keep their vehicles, if they let the company subtract the "salvage value" from the car (salvage value is what

239

the scrap yard would pay for it. This sum can be determined by calling the local scrap yard. In Las Vegas, currently, the main scrap yard is Copart's.) But if this is done, the car will have its title changed to "salvage title," by the State of Nevada DMV, and you'll be required to get the car inspected every year to make sure it is roadworthy, and, its resale value will be very little.

If the car is declared a total loss, then they must pay the fair market value. If you go to Kelly Blue Book, select: used cars, private seller, rate your car as "good" and go through the menu of options, you can probably come up with a very fair approximation of what your car is worth. They also have to pay sales tax in addition to the car value. If you have a loan on your car, that has to be paid first before you are paid. If you are "upside down" on a car, then hopefully you have GAP insurance. If you do not, then all the money will go to the car lender/finance company, and you will be "stuck" with the difference.

It was commonplace 10 plus years ago for people to be upside down on car loans. Because finance companies have become more sophisticated, they usually require GAP insurance if cars are being sold on a basis where they possibly might be worth less than what is owed later on. The "GAP insurance" is typically not insurance per say, it's just a promise by the finance company to waive any extra charges in case the car is worth less than what is owed on it.

Normally speaking, it is rare to see people upside down on cars these days, other than people that buy cars for inflated prices from used car lots, or, people who get car loans on very bad terms because they are loading up past car debt onto a 'new' car loan in order to get the car financed.

In a situation where an insurance company is seriously undervaluing your car, you do not have to sign a release in order to collect the check. You can take the check for the undisputed value, and then fight the insurance company later on. Nevada insurance regulations require insurance companies to pay undisputed values without requiring a release to be signed. This is how many cases I have handled over the years are resolved when the insurance company offers less than what the car is worth, and we want to get the victim out of the rental car. The insurance company pays what they think the car is worth, and we do not have to sign the release. Later on we fight about the car value. In these cases I have found it helpful to hire a professional car appraisal service to write a report on the car's value. I have used Spring Mountain Auto Appraisers for this purpose successfully for many years and highly recommend them. Frankly, his reputation is so good that when he writes a report I have found insurance companies will 9 out of 10 times just agree with it and pay what he says the car is worth. The reports are well-documented and very honest.

It used to be a common practice for insurance companies to try to rip-off people on total values by using phony- baloney computer programs that would take things such as nifty nickel ads, auto auction sales, and so forth to establish a value of a car. Nowadays, everyone has access to things like Kelly Blue Book and so forth, so it is very difficult for an insurance company to try to "fool" someone about the value of his car.

By the same token, I've had many clients who feel that their car is worth more than say, Blue Book, because they took particularly good care of the car and so forth. Unfortunately, cars are, in the end, fungible goods, and they are worth what they are worth. Even if you polish the car every week and give it a special nickname and so forth, it does not make the car worth more than what it is worth on the open market. There are some improvements to a car that can add value, such as new tires, new transmission, etc. They probably do not add as much value as you think they might. Generally speaking, unless you have a receipt for the upgrades, you're not going to get much value for them.

If you do have a car that is obviously a total loss, and it's at the tow yard, you need to get it out of there as quickly as possible in order to avoid storage charges that are excessive and potentially charged to you for waiting too long. Usually insurance companies will get the car out of the tow yard for you, unless liability is disputed, or,it's one of the 'substandard' carriers who are oft times underfunded any given week. These days, the carriers will call up Coparts, and Coparts will send over a tow truck. The Coparts tow truck pays off the tow yard bill, and takes it back to Coparts scrap yard. Eventually Coparts buys the vehicle for salvage value, typically $200 to $700 depending on the value of the car's parts when 'chopped,' and then subtracts the tow yard reimbursement amount from the salvage price.

In cases where you are hit by an uninsured motorist and you don't have collision coverage, you probably need to get a hold of Coparts or similar ASAP to get the car out of the tow yard yourself. If you have an attorney who knows what he is doing, this can be done for you. But just leaving the car in the tow yard for two or three weeks because "it's not my fault, someone else has to deal with it" is not a good strategy. The tow yards charges huge amounts for storage fees every day.

CHAPTER FORTY-EIGHT

SELECTING THE RIGHT MEDICAL PROVIDER FOR SPINAL INJURIES

Let us say you are in a car accident, and, you think there may be an insurance claim involved against someone for causing the injury to happen. Who or what is the best kind of doctor to see for this case?

Although, in a perfect world the only concern should be "who is the best doctor to treat me and make me well"; the reality is, when legal aspects get involved, you have to consider : "who is the best doctor to treat me *and* who will get involved with a car accident case?"

The reality is there are lots of good doctors and therapists out there who could all treat you equally well, it is not just "one" who is the best. They pretty much do the same types of treatments. While there are certainly some who are marginally better than others , let us say that on the basis of just finding someone who is competent, capable and skillful enough to treat your injuries, we can probably rule out about 50 percent of the practitioners as being "below average" and the other 50 percent as being capable and competent, all things considered.

Of the 50 percent who are above average, treatment-wise, how do you narrow it down further?

Well, if there are legal aspects, they will "do it for you, " by and large. I would say the majority of M.D. Primary Care doctor offices, were you to call them up and say, "Hey, I need treatment on my neck or back, but there may be a lawsuit involved somewhere down the line," they will say, "Doctor will not see you. Go to someone else." This is because doctors who are not involved a lot in litigation detest it, and do not like lawyers taking their depositions, asking them to fill out reports, picking at their every word, asking them opinions on things that, while having a lot to do with the legal case, have nothing to do with the patient's medical treatment. These doctors feel as though they just do not need the hassle. Then ,to make matters worse, there are new interpretations that have come out regarding Medicare, that many doctors read to mean that if it is an accident case, Medicare will not pay them. The doctors are afraid that if it is an accident case, and they treat you , and if you have a governmental form of health insurance (which is most Americans these days), then they will be financially penalized in some fashion for treating you.

So, we have excluded the bottom 50 percent of practitioners, and, of the other 50 percent, the majority of them will not even see you if you have possible litigation involved with your case.

So now we are down to, maybe, 15 to 20 percent of the available M.D. pool to treat your injuries (I would point out that probably 95 percent of all chiropractic physicians are available to treat accident victims, more about that later. For now I am talking about M.D.'s or D.O.'s.)

A competent attorney who is will help you to choose the right doctor. Contrary to what the public might think, many attorneys (myself included), when faced with this issue (i.e., making recommendations to a client) will think about who is the best doctor, treatment-wise; and who has the best location and hours for this particular patient.

Las Vegas valley is now huge. There is a long distance between people that live out on Ann Road and people that live out in Southern Highlands. A doctor in Southern Highlands is not going to be convenient for a patient who lives up by Centennial Hills.

So location is a huge factor in selecting the right doctor. An experienced attorney who has the trust of the medical community (i.e., has a track record of making sure they get paid) will be able to have dozens of choices throughout the valley of doctors to see his or her patients, provided that the attorney vouches it is a good case and they will get paid.

In dealing with a neck or back injury, there are several stages of treatment. The first is the urgent care or emergency care part of it. If you go the way of an ambulance from the scene, realistically you do not have a choice of which hospital to go to. If you are driving yourself to an emergency room, I would say the most important thing to consider is to go to a hospital that accepts your type of health insurance. You are oftentimes better off going to an urgent care clinic as opposed to an ER at first (if you are not bleeding, etc.) because you will not be waiting for three hours and then given terrible service, which is typical for most ER's. (If you had any sort of head injury; if the air bags went off; if there is any blood; if there are any areas of numbness; any hand injuries; I would recommend ER over urgent care. If you are ambulatory, drove yourself home from the scene, and none of the above exceptions apply, then an Urgent Care is probably appropriate.)

I think it is important to go to the ER or urgent care asap if at all possible. Sometimes clients feel they are unable to do this because they have no health insurance, or they are worried that the health insurance will not pay if they have an auto accident case (which, believe it or not, used to not be true, but is now turning out to be partially true, at least in terms of Medicare/Medicaid and LV hospitals, who are now legally permitted not to bill Medicare on car accidents.)

After the initial medical treatment, then the patient needs to go to a doctor who can do the initial examination and so forth, and prescribe, typically, some sort of therapy and, perhaps, light medications (such as Flexeril for muscle relaxant, Ultram or similar for pain, etc.) These days, doctors are reluctant to prescribe opioids, especially right off the bat.

Chiropractors, who enjoyed a somewhat checkered reputation, in my experience, for the majority of my legal career, have now undergone sort of a renaissance in terms of public perception. The most prestigious medical magazine, the Journal of American Medical Association, recently finished a long study on treatment of neck and back problems in the United States. The study was done by the University of Oregon health science department. The study found that, dollar for dollar, chiropractic care was the most effective means to treat "soft tissue" neck and back problems. This is something that was not paid for by the chiropractic association, but was indeed the findings of the American Medical Association. A recent issue of Consumer Reports on treatment for neck and back conditions also found that chiropractic was probably the best way to go for "soft tissue" type complaints not involving disk problems or other significant problems requiring care beyond therapy and exercise. ('Soft tissue ' basically means that it did not involve a broken bone or a disc, or some other surgical type condition.)

These days, what a chiropractor does and what a physical therapist does for the initial two months of treatment are very similar . So if you go to a "regular doctor" (i.e., GP) at first, and he prescribes therapy, it can usually be done by a chiropractor or a therapist usually equally well.

If the therapy does not work, then usually diagnostic tests are ordered. Typically, an MRI is the next step. MRI's are generally risk free, health wise (unless you have something metal inside you), and an amazing amount of information can be gleaned from one MRI report. Other than the cost of an MRI, I see no downside, legally, to getting an MRI done if someone is still hurting after a couple months.

If the MRI shows something, and/or the patient has radicular findings (i.e., pains going down their arms, or legs, from nerves being pinched in their neck or back, respectively), then oftentimes a referral to a neurologist, and/or pain management physician , is the next step.

A neurologist does an electromyograph/nerve conduction velocity test (EMG/NCV) to see whether and if there is any serious interruption of the 'electricity' going from your spine down the nerves that service you extremities (upper extremities, i.e. arms, may have nerves pinched from the neck; lower extremities, i.e. legs, may have nerves pinched from the lower back. The middle back – thoracic– can have nerves pinched that go to your chest and shoulders, and sometimes, the upper extremities.)

In Las Vegas, the pain management physicians really run the gauntlet from incompetent to remarkably good and ethical people. Personally, I do not know all of them, but I do know the few at the extreme ends of the reputation spectrum.

Generally speaking, the pain management people will recommend a series of three shots done one month apart. These shots are, in my observation, relatively low risk procedures. The main danger is that they will not work and you have spent money for temporary results. But as far as hitting a non-targeted nerve area accidentally and causing injury, in the hands of a competent pain management doctor who is using a fluoroscope, the risk is very slight.

Because of the anatomy of the human body, shots that are done in the low back are extremely low risk. Shots done in the neck are somewhat higher risk than the low back. Shots done in the thoracic spine are very dangerous because of the proximity to the lungs, and most pain management doctors will not do shots in the thoracic (mid) spine.

If the shots work but wear off, the next thing that is suggested, if appropriate, is what is called radiofrequency ablation, RFA, rhizotomy, or "nerve burn." The pain management doctor, instead of shooting the affected area with "juice" (mixture of Celestone/Cortisone and Marcaine/Lidocaine), will instead use a needle that "zaps" the affected area with radiofrequencies that "burn" the nerve and disable it for a period of six to 12 months. This is not a cure but can provide a lot of pain relief for the patient without surgery.

Pain management physicians also prescribe opioid medications. Some of them are more reluctant to do so than others. Suffice it to say that in my opinion opioids are bad news and must be avoided whenever possible. I understand there are some people who have to have them and have no choice. But if there is any way at all to avoid getting hooked on escalating amounts of opioids, this should be the path taken instead of taking a lot of these pills for a long time. If you are taking these pills every day, and it is going on for more than three months' time , you are likely to get "hooked" on the pills. It has nothing to do with willpower or moral character; it is physiologic; you can give a monkey or a rabbit opioid medications for three months and they would be hooked, also. Trying to get off them is do-able, but depending on how much you are taking, and for how long, it can be very difficult to do.

I would like to make a couple recommendations here. We have two local physicians who specialize in getting people off opioid addiction, and I think well of both them. They are Dr Mel Pohl, and Dr Michael Levy. They employ different methodology, so you might wish to check that out if you are looking for treatment; also, both have differing prices and health insurance acceptance. Until recently, most health insurers would not pay, or would pay very little, for opioid withdrawal treatment, and persons ended up going to treatment that wasn't always top notch. If you go to Pohl or Levy, you will be getting top notch, in my opinion.

If the pain management shots and RFA's do not work then the next step is surgery, IF you so desire to go down that road. No one can force you to get surgery. There are many levels to surgery, some of them much more complex than others.

Despite the common public perception that spine surgery commonly makes people worse, my own experience is that IF you are going to one of this area's really talented and good spinal surgeons, the chances that you will come out worse, not better, are very small.

Notable exceptions to this are patients who are not good candidates for surgery in the first place. The same factors that make surgery risky for anything else make surgery risky for people with: e.g. serious psychiatric issues. Of course, sometimes people who have prior health issues get good results from surgery, anyway; but the odds of success are much higher if you choose a really good spine surgeon ahead of time.

How do you find a really good spine surgeon? Not so easy as it sounds. If you are lucky enough to know a nurse who works in orthopaedics, or works as a surgical nurse, they are good sources. They know who is sloppy and who is not. Lawyers who do significant medical malpractice work know who the 'bad guys' are.

I can tell you that in my mind there are probably only a handful of surgeons in Las Vegas I would let operate on my back if I ever needed a back operation.

Sometimes I am asked: Is it better to go to an orthopedic spine surgeon or go to a neurosurgeon who specializes in spinal surgery?

Really, this is basically a "six of one half a dozen of the other" type question. Either specialty is capable of doing a good job on spinal surgeries.

I would say this: Just because someone is a neurosurgeon does not mean automatically that he can do a good job on your back. Sometimes people think "well if he is a brain surgeon, then he must be top of the line, able to do a great job on my back." Not true; not even close.

Or they will think, "the neurosurgeons will go in there and just cut out little small pieces whereas the orthopedic surgeon will use a hammer and take out big pieces," etc. Again, not true. Orthopedic surgeons can do microsurgeries, and neurosurgeons can do fusions.

Years ago, the micro surgery vs. macro surgery distinction used to be valid, but these days, ortho spin surgeons do micro surgeries as needed, and neurosurgeons do 'macro' fusion surgeries, as needed.

I think a lot of what makes surgeons good or bad, at least when it comes to spines, depends on, at least at the higher levels (if we rule out the fellows who try to do rush jobs) whether or not the person has the God-given skill to do this kind of surgery. Everyone can do the "book learning" part of it and get the training, but do they have the talent with their hands to make precise cuts; do they have that inner talent or skill that allows them to see trouble before it happens? When it comes to surgery, you are either born with "good hands" or you are not. You cannot teach someone at medical school to have "good hands" or fine motor control. Not everyone who becomes a surgeon has good hands.

Ultimately, the proof is in the pudding. A fellow who repeatedly has bad results is probably just not that good. A guy who rarely has bad results is probably pretty good.

Your own doctor might be able to make good recommendations, but unfortunately, doctors are human beings and like to refer people to their friends and people who belong to the same country club, or go to the same church, as opposed to who is the best in town. And quite frankly, family doctors are not well situated to hear or see much in the way of spine surgery results. A physical therapist, or nurse who works in orthopaedics (or in the Operating Room recently) would have a better take on who is good and who is not.

A lot of the success rate on back and neck surgeries has to do with the hospital or, these days, outpatient surgical center (a lot of the less complicated spine stuff is done outpatient, nowadays, although, if it were me, I think I would still prefer the hospital if given the choice). This is because it is actually the hospital, not the surgeon, who controls the infection risks; and it is the hospital who has, or doesn't have, the most up to date surgical equipment and anesthesia gear. I think that local's kind of have a decent feel for which hospitals are the best and which are not.

UMC and the Valley Health System hospitals are 'teaching hospitals' that allow medical school residents to work on patients under various levels of physician supervision. I know that these residents have to learn somewhere, but, if you are asked to sign a form that allows residents to 'assist' during your spine surgery, I would refuse to sign such a form. Although it may be coincidence, some of the worst surgical outcomes I have seen, in general, take place on cases where residents are assisting during a surgery. The hospital is supposed to give you a specific form to sign allowing residents before the surgery. But, if you are going to a Valley Health System hospital, or UMC, I would ask in advance to be sure. The other hospitals in LV do not allow residents to 'assist.' This is not, by the way, a knock on the hospitals. In many ways, having residents in the hospital will improve the quality of your care. They are going to make more thorough notes, and, could be a 'plus' in paying attention to things outside the OR. I just would not want one of them 'practicing' with surgical instruments on me, even if it is supposedly something easy. Nothing is easy the first time you do it.

CHAPTER FORTY-NINE

PROVIDER AND HOSPITAL LIENS ON P.I. CASES – AN OVERVIEW

In an automobile insurance case, there is almost always the possibility of doing treatment on a "lien" basis. So to begin, what is a "lien" in the context of paying a medical bill on a personal injury case?

Most people are familiar with the concept of "lien" as it applies to real estate. That is, in order to make sure a bill is paid, certain kinds of creditors are allowed to assert "liens" on real estate, for example, personal residences. The "lien" is a legal document of some kind that is filed at the county recorder's office, and it gives (theoretically) notice to everyone that if this house is ever sold, this bill must be paid from the proceeds. If the bill underlying the lien is paid off, then documents are filed showing the lien has been 'extinguished.'

Recently, in the news in Las Vegas, have been articles showing how the local garbage pickup company, Republic Services, is allowed to file "liens" on a home to secure payment of overdue garbage pickup bills. We also have seen a lot of news coverage about "liens" being filed by homeowner's associations for unpaid homeowner's dues. If a new home is being constructed, the subcontractors who are working on the home can file "liens" to make sure they are paid for their services (in case the general contractor welches on the bill during construction.)

In the context of auto repairs, mechanics have been allowed to put "liens" on the automobiles they work on in order to secure payment for the repairs that they made to the car. (This means they don't have to give you the keys to the car until you pay the repair bill.)

There are loan liens available for car titles, aircraft titles, boat titles s, all matters of property rights, etc. And, alas, we have developed the doctrine of "liens" on personal injury settlements. That is, the lien is a right for a creditor to get paid from the proceeds of a personal injury settlement.

In most other states, they have similar programs, but instead of calling them "liens," the attorney issues what is called a "letter of protection," which allows the doctor, hospital, etc., to be assured that if there is a settlement, they will get paid. The attorney sends out the "letter of protection" and basically puts his own word on the line that the bill is going to get paid later on when the case is settled.

In Nevada, the practice involved is not a "letter of protection," but rather the patient will sign a document ("lien") promising to pay the doctor, hospital, etc., from the personal injury settlement, and generally speaking, the medical provider will then send a copy of the "lien" to the attorney, who must sign to acknowledge receipt of it.

Our Supreme Court has come up with several cases to define the rights of these personal injury case lienholders. In general, they enforce the rights of the lienholders to be considered before all the money from the settlement is disbursed.

Hospitals are given a special right to put liens for ER treatment on personal injury cases in Nevada, by operation of statutory law, whether or not the patient agrees to it. Various hospital chains have, over the years, tried various ways to manipulate this right to extraordinarily greedy extremes.

For example, in Las Vegas, for a while, the county hospital, UMC, was filing liens on citizen's and taxpayer's houses automatically whenever a personal injury case was suspected to be the cause of a hospitalization emergency room or trauma room treatment. (They seem to forget that the property taxes paid by these citizens is what pays their salaries in the first place!) These liens, oftentimes filed even when the patient had plenty of health insurance, would sometimes cause people's credit ratings to plummet, for no good reason, or would cause people to lose their chance to get financing to buy a family home. Many h of these abuses with hospital liens were curtailed by a statute passed years ago, largely at the behest of Barbara Buckley, a consumer-oriented state legislature who, unfortunately, ran out of term limits. As I dictate this in 2018, I must unfortunately report that on October, 2017, the "Buckley" law was largely undone, and now ER's can ignore Medicare and Medicaid and lien the case (they still must bill private health insurance, however.) They still, however, are not allowed to automatically file liens on people's homes, although, I have recently seen one hospital chain, who uses an out of state lawyer for the purpose, start to file these liens as a matter of course.

Many of the hospitals contract without out of state vendors (collection agencies, really) to prosecute their liens. I have a cease and desist order from the Nevada State Bar that says that in many, if not most, of these instances these vendors are practicing law without a license. Many of the vendors work on contingent fee basis where they get paid percentage of what they collect, and they in turn farm out the "lien" work to various persons working out of their homes on computers, typically in economically depressed areas of the country. This racket is a real cash cow, and companies such as Xerox have jumped into the business with both feet. Recently, one of these vendors filed a lien on my client's home, even though the client had health insurance to pay the bill. I was able to get a local court to remove the lien and punish the out of state vendor for abusive behavior. Hopefully other lawyers who are reading this book will be similarly inspired to take these fake lawyers to task. They are always from out of state, and they could give a darn about the people of Nevada; they just want "theirs" and the patients be damned. I predict it will not be long before the hospitals start using vendors based in India to file and record liens on people's houses to strong arm payments (even though, with the existing statute, it is quite unnecessary to file liens on person's homes to enforce the right in 99% of the cases. This is just being mean, for no good reason, exposing the fact that, these days, the companies that own the hospitals are all about making money, first, last, and always, and if the patient's home is threatened in the process, well, too bad.)

CHAPTER FIFTY

TREATING ON LIEN VERSUS PRIVATE HEALTH INSURANCE

As noted above, in many auto insurance situations you may not have a choice as to whether or not to go on health insurance or lien, because your primary care physician refuses to see you on an auto accident case. But, sometimes there is a choice. Whether you want to treat on a lien or not involves weighing various pro's and con's. Here's a general list.

"Pro's" of treating on health insurance.
---It gets paid-for even if you lose the case.
--- Cost is generally cheaper since doctors are on contracts that require them to write-off charges.

That's pretty much it for the "pros."

Con's are as follows.
--- Your choice of healthcare providers may be greatly limited if you can only see people on your plan.
---Treatment may be limited to a handful of office visits wherein pain pills, anti inflammatories, and muscle relaxers are prescribed as a cheap form of treatment.

---Doctors resent having to fill out paperwork for auto insurance companies since they already feel underpaid by the health insurance, and may not do so unless forced. Doctors resent and drag feet on filling out any forms for employers such FMLA; or disability insurance forms.

– you do have to pay back the health insurance from the settlement

Treating on a lien has pros and cons.

The pros are :

---a greater selection of doctors and, more importantly, a selection of doctors who don't mind the extra paperwork and hassle involved with auto insurance cases.

--- Usually, treatment is better

The con's are :

---the doctors' charges are ultimately more under liens than they would get paid by health insurance, since they are charging "retail" instead of the discounted "volume" price given to health insurance.

---if you lose your case, you could get stuck with the bill (so you should not treat on a lien unless you are pretty darn sure you're going to win your case.)

— at a trial, insurance lawyer may be allowed to accuse the lien doctor of bias if lien does not allow recourse against you should you lose case

CHAPTER FIFTY-ONE

TREATING ON LIEN VERSUS WORKMAN'S COMPENSATION

Sometimes, automobile accidents happen while people are on the job. Most commonly in Las Vegas, this involves cab drivers. If you are in a car accident, and you're on the job, should you do your treatment on a lien or under workman's compensation?

If it is a serious injury, there's really not a contest here. Factors greatly favor you going under work comp for serious injuries. Serious would include anything requiring surgery, broken bones, etc. But for the more common "whiplash" soft tissue type injuries, there is a choice, and a rational argument to be made to favor going lien rather than work comp.

The "pros" of going work comp are as follows.
---Guarantee they will pay for your medical bills.
---Lost wages paid at the rate of two-thirds if you are out for more than five days.
--- Permanent partial disability rating award at end of case.
---Theoretical lifetime reopening rights (I say "theoretical" because it is hard to reopen the case in reality.)

Negatives of treating under work comp are as follows.

--- You have to pay the money back when you settle your PI case (at least, most of it. Discounts are available.)

---The employer can force you to go to the doctors they choose, and the doctors they choose are looking out for the interests of the employer, because that is who gives them referrals in the future

--- The attitude of the primary care doctors and staff who do only work comp, as well as work comp doctors of physical medicine (physiatrists) toward you will be, at best, condescending, and more likely, rude (along with the suspicion that you are lying)

--- And, even if you get to choose your own specialist, if the specialist gives you an opinion that is favorable (i.e. you are not faking or exaggerating), the employer's insurer has the right to force you to go to their 'own doctor' for a second opinion (the second opinion is almost always that you are faking or exaggerating.)

The pros of treating on a lien for workman's compensation are as follows.

The pro's are:

---many employers, although it is illegal to penalize employees for making work comp claims, do so anyway on the sly, since claims makes their rates go higher. In particular, cab drivers who make work comp claims are oftentimes labeled as pariahs by their employers and are given less favorable shifts, cars, etc.

---Lien doctors are truthful about your condition, and are not hired guns for the benefit of the employer's insurance company. They do not have incentives, such as the hired gun work comp doctors, to write derogatory comments about you in the file.

---The treatment will be by a better selection of physicians, and diagnostic tests will not be denied (in workman's compensation cases, sometimes diagnostic tests are delayed because, among other things, they don't want to have proof in their files that you are seriously hurt.)

Negatives of treating on a lien basis are

---: that lien prices are generally higher than work comp prices for care.

--- If you lose your case, you will owe the money for the medical bills.

--- If it turned out that you needed something like a surgery, and did not go through the work comp doctors, you might not be able to get back on the work comp system to get the surgeries, since the work comp insurers do not have to take the word of "your" physicians, but only have to listen to the ones that they hire.

Every case is different and if you are on the job, and in a car accident, you need a reputable lawyer who is looking out for your interests, first, to advise you which choice is the best. In general, there is a sliding scale: serious injury, work comp only; mild whiplash, mostly lien. Sometimes, there can be a 'hybrid' of care between the two extremes: work comp for ER; then back to work comp if it turns out to be more serious than first suspected.

CHAPTER FIFTY-TWO

TREATING ON LIEN VERSUS MEDICARE

Contrary to urban folk lore, most of the time, Medicare will pay for bills related to auto accidents. However, there are some exceptions, and many medical providers will simply refuse to bill Medicare when they find out an accident is involved, as they are fearful of nonpayment.

Until recently, emergency rooms in Las Vegas were required, by state law, to bill Medicare (for those patients who were on Medicare) on automobile accidents. That law has now been changed and the hospitals no longer have to bill Medicare, although they can if they so choose. Normally, emergency rooms prefer to go after the car insurance directly, as Medicare reimbursement rates can be small compared to what they can get through a statutory lien.

Doctors and physical therapists can bill Medicare for automobile accidents, although there are rumors that this, too, may be changing(I am writing this in 2018. Many doctors' offices will tell patients that Medicare will not pay them for car accidents. At the present time of writing this book, that is not true, and most of the doctors who say this do so because they don't want to treat automobile cases. All I can say is I have handled thousands of cases over the years involving patients who have Medicare, and automobile accidents, and Medicare did pay on the bills , although they still do not pay chiropractors to my knowledge.) However, people who I trust say that there is a growing push in the Trump administration to change interpretation of the rules regarding this subject, so stay tuned.

For purposes of this discussion we will assume that Medicare still pays doctors and therapists. Should a Medicare patient treat under the Medicare or under a lien?

The fact is, doctors don't get paid that well under Medicare, so they resent it if they are treating a patient for an auto case, where they perceive that the patient is going to get a "big" settlement and they get the "crumbs." That's just human nature. The bad attitude can be carried into the doctor's records, which may negatively reflect on the patient who "forced " the doctor to bill Medicare.

Again, this isn't right, but it's human nature.

In a broad general sense, I will tell my clients who have Medicare that if we are talking about care that isn't, in a relative sense, terribly expensive, they might be better off going on a lien rather than Medicare in order to not risk raising the anger of the physician, which later shows up in refusal to cooperate with legal matters; but it can be considered for other things.

There are exceptions to every rule and these are just general guidelines. For example, sometimes the client will require a surgery that Medicare will not cover, because it is a new procedure not on their approved list (which generally lags 5 years behind the times.)   I have actually had Medicare refuse to pay for surgeries that are much less involved than traditional type surgeries, simply on the basis "that's new and we aren't covering it yet."

These days, most of the people on Medicare are signed up with "Medicare Advantage" plans, which are essentially HMO's, where their choice of physician is severely limited. Such clients are oftentimes forced to go on a lien just to get to a decent surgeon, instead of the ones that are on their HMO plan. But, just assuming it's "regular" Medicare (not Medicare Advantage) what are the pros and cons?

The pros of using Medicare are that your bill gets paid whether you win or lose the case. Even though you have to pay Medicare back, the rate is generally cheaper than the amount under a "lien." Negatives include the fact that Medicare won't pay for a lot of services, such as chiropractors, or the newer surgical techniques. Doctors who treat patients under Medicare for a car accident case , against their wishes, are oftentimes resentful and will go out of their way to avoid the extensive paperwork that is oftentimes required to complete an auto accident case, or will try to sabotage the case through 'passive aggressive' type record keeping in which the car accident is not even mentioned.

As far as treating on a lien basis, the advantages stated above in the prior chapter apply. That is, the lien doctors are usually ones who are used to the paperwork of auto insurance claims. They do not resent the patient for making an accident claim, which many doctors do. (Again, I would point out that although it may be, technically, that you could 'force' a doctor to take Medicare, in the real world there may be practical and human-nature type considerations that would make it in your interest not to force the doctor to take Medicare if he or she does not want to do so.) I also think, there actually is some "high moral ground" to take about not using Medicare. Why should the U.S. tax payer have to foot the bill to treat injuries when it's the fault of someone else? Shouldn't they have to step up and pay the bill?

Also it should be kept in mind that treating on Medicare isn't "free." The patient is required to pay back Medicare. The process of determining what is to be paid back oftentimes delays finalization of a claim, after it is settled, by several months, which is another reason why people would want to avoid Medicare on a case not involving catastrophic injury. Particularly when the client is elderly, having to wait six-plus months to settle a Medicare lien on a case could be highly undesirable.

CHAPTER FIFTY-THREE

TREATING ON LIEN VERSUS MEDICAID

The above discussion about Medicare applies equally well to Medicaid, only it is amplified, because Medicaid pays less than Medicare. Although most doctors accept Medicare, I would say that most doctors don't accept Medicaid. You are limited in your choices if you want to go through Medicaid, and if you treat through the Medicaid, you will be looking at very crowded waiting rooms, long waits, and treatment by physicians who are annoyed that you are "using the system" to pay for your medical bills caused by a car collision. All in all, there's a lot of negatives regarding treatment on Medicaid. But sometimes, particularly for serious injuries, the patient has no choice. A person on Medicaid who needs a fractured femur open reduction surgery following a car accident is going to have to use the Medicaid.

As I write this, most of the Medicaid care in Las Vegas is done through HMO groups such as HPN "Smart Choice," or Amerigroup. This is HMO style care at extreme "cost-cutting" standards. Frankly, most people who have a choice, would prefer to get their treatment outside of this system. In many cases, the care under a lien can be much better than that available under Medicaid, and "paying extra" to get the lien care is a choice I would certainly make if I were the patient, were it feasible to do.

CHAPTER FIFTY-FOUR

TREATMENT LIENS – ARE THEY ADMISSIBLE IN TRIAL?

We have above discussed the pros and cons of treating physician liens in terms of comparing them against health insurance.

But what about their pros and cons in terms of trial?

The negative is obvious. The defense will say that the doctor or treating professional only gets paid if the jury awards money for the case, and in order to accomplish this, the professional must slant his or her testimony to relating the bills to the accident, so that they will have a better chance of getting paid. In other words, the argument is the lien biases the treating physicians. (On the flip side of the coin, the counter argument is that people without health insurance have to use liens to get treatment, or at least, to get treatment that is not under an HMO setting: and that by making a lien admissible in trial, it is prejudicing the rights of financially disadvantaged persons to get equal treatment that 'rich' persons can get. Therefore, by allowing lien evidence, you prejudice the poor, and create two classes of plaintiffs, those rich enough to get non HMO health insurance and those who are not.

273

The case concerning admissibility of lien evidence is Khoury v. Seastrand. Although the insurance industry reads this case as a carte blanche permission to use lien evidence in trial to show bias, more than half of the current district court judges in Las Vegas believe that if the lien states within its terms that the patient is responsible to pay the bill should he not win his case, then that fits one of the stated exceptions in Khoury, and under such circumstances, the lien is inadmissible.

I think a further reason why a lien should not be admitted is because it creates collateral issues. If a court were, theoretically, to allow in a lien, then the plaintiff should be allowed to counter that by allowing counter evidence, e.g. that the client's own PCP would not accept auto cases, that the client had an HMO that would provide care of deficient quality, that the client had no health insurance and no choice, that the client wanted to treat near his home with facilities that had convenient hours; and, perhaps, evidence how and why the plaintiff's lawyer chose this or that particular facility over others, such as the quality of care, the location, the hours, etc. I think not allowing such counter evidence would be reversible error; but on the other hand, it would bog the trial down in all sorts of collateral issues. As a matter of judicial economy, the judge could decide that the probative value of allowing the lien in is very limited, and the prejudicial effect, and, in particular, the collateral issues raised, would not warrant allowing the lien into evidence. Although the Seastrand case decided that liens did not qualify as a "collateral source," this is an entirely different legal doctrine than "collateral evidentiary issue," and the Seastrand case did not decide the collateral issue side to things, as it was not before them.

If the practitioner finds himself in a courtroom that will allow evidence of the lien, I believe it should be stressed that the patient is responsible to pay the bill if the trial should be lost; and perhaps the reasons why the patient chose to go on a lien (most usually, because his regular physician refused to take a car accident case, thus leaving the patient with only the option of lien treatment.)

CHAPTER FIFTY-FIVE

INTERPLEADER/DECLARATORY RELIEF ACTION FOR UNCOOPERATIVE LIENHOLDERS

Sometimes the settlement is small and the liens are high, and not all the lien providers will agree to reduce their lien amounts so that everyone can get a piece of the pie. In such a case, a lawyer does not have the freedom, under our current laws, to pick and choose which provider gets paid and which provider goes home emptyhanded. (This is assuming they all have lawful liens on the case, and there is not any statutory priority for one lien vs another.)

If all the providers cannot agree how to cut up the settlement 'pie,' the attorney has no choice but to ask the court to decide how to cut up the money. This can be done by means of putting all the money with the court in a special bank account, and asking the court to cut it up. This is called an action for "interpleader." Or, the attorney can file a complaint for declaratory relief asking the court to decide how the money can be cut up (this is necessitated because sometimes the clients won't sign a release until they know how big their slice of the pie is, and the insurance company won't cut a check until it has a release from the client; therefore, in order to get the client to sign the release, a court determination must first be done.)

The good news is that I have found that in 90+% of the cases where I did have to file a dec action because one party wanted a better deal than everyone else, the recalcitrant party will call me and say "I don't have the time to fight this" and agree to the proposed split, and then, I can dismiss the suit.

I have found that people who work for me seem to think that filing such a complaint to get the case resolved is somehow a huge undertaking, and it gets put off for too long. I am not sure why there is this attitude. The complaint, itself, is form-like, and once you do one of them, then your legal assistant can simply fill in the blanks of the form and do one quickly. There is, unfortunately, the filing fee to consider, but, when a nice fee is riding on getting the thing done, it's well worth the money to file the complaint. As I said above, it's usually one obstinate lienholder gumming up the process, and 9 out of 10 times, when they get served with the lawsuit, they fold and agree to the split.

In the typical situation where I have, say, 8 lienholders, and a small settlement because the case went unexpectedly south, and I explain things to the lienholders, and 7 out of 8 of them agree, but one tries to get a bigger slice than others and won't agree to an equal discount, I will just file a dec action against the one recalcitrant lienholder, instead of an action naming every lienholder. I admit that doing it this way is not as 'full proof' as naming everyone, but, since everyone else has agreed in writing to the discount (usually), I am not concerned; and, normally, the footdragger concedes or defaults and litigation is not necessary beyond just serving the complaint. If you name everyone, you have to spend a lot on process servers, and the 'innocent' lien holders will say, "hey, I agreed to your proposal. Why are you suing me?" and become upset.

CHAPTER FIFTY-SIX

COMPELLING DELIVERY OF THE SETTLEMENT CHECK

Whenever I settle a case, quite naturally, the first thing my client asks is "how soon will the money get here?"

By regulations in our Nevada State Administrative Code, insurance companies have, basically, 30 days after the settlement to get the check in. Most of the major carriers are faster than that, and typically will only take 5 to 10 days to get the check in after they receive a signed release.

Carriers can– and do– refuse to cut a check until the Medicare lien (if any) has been finalized. For Medicare clients, this usually means an additional delay of about 45 to 60 days while Medicare goes through its steps. Medicare will not even begin the 'final' process of settling their lien until the case is settled. So, Medicare is often the biggest hang up to getting a check quickly.

Every once in a while, I will get a defendant (typically, a self-insured like a cab company, hotel, or nursing home) that will go beyond the 30 days in issuing a check. In such cases, I have found that if I file a "Motion to Enforce Settlement Agreement," asking for sanctions/attorney's fees, the check seems to appear, almost as if by magic, three days after I file the motion. I have had lawyers working under me who hesitate to file these motions because they think it "will make me look bad, like I'm desperate for money or something. The other lawyer is promising me that he's keeping on top of things, and I don't want to insult him. I have my reputation to think about." I have a lot to say about this kind of attitude (most of it, quite negative), but here's the thing: if they are taking more than 30 days to get the check to you, then they are playing you for a chump, and if anything, your "reputation" will be damaged by NOT filing such a motion. Again, it's magic: you file the motion, three days later the check comes in by fed ex. I have filed scores of these motions over the years, and I have no evidence that it created any sort of 'negative reputation' that I wasn't a 'gentleman' or whatever.

If the reader is a plaintiff's p.i. lawyer, I would say: do not hesitate to file a motion to compel settlement, on order shortening time for hearing, if the defendant takes longer than 30 days. Otherwise, they will just jerk you around for weeks because you're 'such a nice guy.' On the other hand, even if your client is really hammering you for the check, a judge is going to look sideways at you if you file such a motion before you give them the 30 days. Also, when you do the motion, you don't need to lay it on thick with all the gory details; just say we settled on day 'x,' it's now 30 days after 'x,' and all I am hearing from so and so is that, essentially, the check is in the mail. The less you get into personal attacks, the better. There is no 'official' form for such a motion. You can put together such a motion in two pages' length, or less, not including the notice. The main reason the motion works is because the adjuster (or whoever is handling the check writing) does not want to get stuck with a $1500 attorney's fee sanction.

Normally, if the check comes in a couple days after the motion is filed, I dismiss the motion voluntarily, without requiring payment of sanctions, since it's purpose was served.

CHAPTER FIFTY-SEVEN

SUBROGATION ON AUTO INSURANCE CASES – AN OVERVIEW

Generally speaking, subrogation is the right of other parties who paid for your medical bills, or, possibly, other benefits, to put a "lien" on your case to be paid back some of their expended funds when and if you get a settlement. In most cases, subrogation is created by a contract between you and the subrogating party, typically, a health insurance company or similar entity. Sometimes, subrogation rights are created by statutes or regulations (laws passed by legislatures, or, regulations written by various government agencies. This would pertain to Medicare, Medicaid, VA, work comp, and, by virtue of a special statute in Nevada, ER hospital bills.)

The laws regarding subrogation have changed drastically during the time I have been a lawyer. Forty years ago when I first started practicing law, subrogation was rarely allowed. The common law took the view that since you had already paid for benefits, either through taxes or insurance premiums, to make you pay back benefits from your settlement was, in effect, allowing your health insurance company or the government to "reap where it had not sown." Since you paid for the health insurance, why should you have to pay money back to them? This imminently reasonable line of thinking was the law until the late 1980's, when our country's legal systems started to be populated more by judges and legislators who favored commercial interests as opposed to judges who favored individuals. Who knows, the pendulum may swing back the other way someday, but for right now, the law has changed so as to allow subrogation in most (not all) circumstances.

Quite frankly, 40 years ago working with subrogation liens maybe took up two percent of my time, total, as a lawyer. Now, dealing with the liens after a case is settled probably takes up 20 percent of my and my staff's total time and resources. There are so many hands in the "till" trying to get the settlement monies that it becomes the "second case" after the "first case" is settled. The law surrounding subrogation rights has become very complicated.

People who think they can handle their cases on their own and cut out the lawyer fees are unaware that a lot of the "real fun" begins after the case is settled, when the subrogation holders try to take as much of the settlement as they can.

CHAPTER FIFTY-EIGHT

SUBROGATION BY MEDICARE

Medicare has become extremely aggressive about pursuing reimbursement/subrogation rights on cases, especially in the last six years or so. Insurance companies are paranoid that if the Medicare rights are not fully protected when they settle the case, that the insurance company will incur drastic penalties from the federal government. The federal government has insurance companies so afraid they will do something wrong that on virtually every case I handle now, typically I have to give the insurance company signed affidavits, letters from Medicare, etc., to assure them that Medicare does not have a lien, when common sense would tell you that the claimant does not (e.g. healthy 25 year old plaintiff.) When Medicare does have a lien, it can take anywhere from six weeks to three or four months to get the lien finalized, after the case is otherwise settled. Medicare uses private contractors to enforce its subrogation liens, and they switch contractors every couple years, and things are often in a chaotic state of affairs. I have one employee whose job is mostly just to deal with Medicare liens. I don't know what we would do without her as a resource; just knowing the everchanging phone numbers, fax numbers, forms, "buzz words" to use, etc., is something only a person who deals with these people on a day to day basis can keep up with. The Medicare people will commonly claim liens for payment of services that have nothing to do with the accident, and it takes weeks to get this straightened out.

Then, in addition to paying the reimbursement lien, we have additional problems with Medicare trying to assert offsets for future care, and this brings up issues concerning "Medicare set-asides." This issue is so complicated that I don't want to go into it in this particular book. Suffice it to say that if you have serious, long-term injuries, and the settlement you get is more than just a few thousand dollars in your pocket, you need to be concerned about Medicare set-aside issues. You need to have a lawyer who is competent enough to understand when Medicare set-aside is an issue, and if so, how to deal with it (or, hire people who do.)

Medicare will give discounts on liens, but it is according to an algebraic formula set forth in the Code of Federal Regulations. You can petition them to give a discount greater than that allowed by the CFR, but, this is a very difficult thing to accomplish, as it is asking a bureaucrat to make a judgment call concerning money.

These days, most Medicare recipients opt for Medicare Advantage Plans, which are HMO's that service Medicare recipients. At the time of writing this book, the most common Advantage Plans are Senior Dimensions, Humana Gold, and Caremore. By federal statute, these plans are given the same subrogation rights that Medicare has; and, they must follow the same CFR discount formula that applies to Medicare.

CHAPTER FIFTY-NINE

SUBROGATION BY MEDICAID

Medicaid is a kind of health insurance that is a hybrid between federal and state concerns. Medicaid programs are oftentimes farmed out to private companies to administer, such as United Healthcare or Amerigroup. Medicaid does have statutory subrogation rights on any settlements. It is oftentimes a nightmare to figure out who to deal with once the case is settled, since the Medicaid programs can be farmed out to different entities, and then in turn those entities farm out the subrogation claims to various vendor companies (e.g., Xerox, Optim, Conduent, etc.), and those vendor companies will change when contracts are renegotiated. It used to be that with Medicaid we could simply deal with the State Attorney General's office; that is rarely the case anymore. Again, this is another nightmarish bureaucratic tangled mess that is hard to solve unless you have a person on your legal office whose job it is to deal with Medicare and Medicaid liens on a full-time type basis. Otherwise, you don't know who to contact, where to send your fax, which agency uses which vendor, etc. A person trying to handle their auto accident case by themselves, who has had Medicaid pay some of their medical bills, would likely get caught up in this bureaucratic tangle and find it hard to get out of it.

Some of the private vendors will give discounts, some won't, claiming that the law forbids them to do so (it does not, by the way, but it sounds good to say as an excuse.) I have found that, in asking for a 'discount,' it is more effective to argue that this or that bill is not related, or, that this or that bill has to be apportioned to pre-existing conditions, as opposed to pleading that your client 'deserves' more out of a sense of justice etc., (make whole doctrine) or, complaining that you did all this work and now they are getting a free ride ('common fund doctrine'). These vendors and bureaucrats do get that if the bill is only partially related to the accident, then they only get partial reimbursement; but when you start throwing around ideas like common fund doctrine, etc. you might as well be talking to the pigeons in front of the park bench.

CHAPTER SIXTY

LIENS BY GOVERNMENT HEALTH INSURANCE PLANS

Besides Medicare and Medicaid, we now commonly will have liens asserted by other governmental agencies such as the Veteran's Administration (they will claim a lien for the value of whatever services they render); federal government insurance programs (formerly known as GEHA); the state insurance for employees, or PERS; the County of Clark's insurance plan; the City of Las Vegas' insurance plan; etc. All of these entities have subrogation rights built into their contracts, and the efficiency with which they handle these rights varies greatly from one entity to the next. With the V.A., it can sometimes take months just to obtain from them the figure they are claiming (since basically, they make up the figure as they generate no real "bills" for their services); agencies such as Tricare can farm out its subrogation services to one of several different branches of the JAG core, depending on which branch of the service the member was in originally. Some of these agencies will give discounts on the liens and some will not. The main thing is to make sure they are not putting liens on the case for services that are not related to the accident itself. The various agencies will oftentimes contract out the subrogation end of their work to civilian contractors. Again, just figuring out who is the right person to deal with, and then, getting that person to do their job, can be a very annoying and time-consuming experience. Again, this makes it difficult for people to "handle the case on their own." Insurance carriers will not give you a settlement check unless they know that the subrogation lien from a governmental agency has been handled ahead of time.

Particularly in regard to the VA, I have found that oft times, it is almost impossible to even get someone to respond to a subrogation inquiry; and then, getting a figure, and negotiating a final figure, can take months simply because no one will respond to any communications, or, they will keep referring you to different people, claiming that this or that isn't their job. Considering that you are trying to *give* the government some money, and they won't answer any communications to allow that to happen, is really frustrating. Although this may sound kind of crazy, I have found, through experience, that, if the situation gets really out of control and months go by with just nothing happening on the government's end, the way to light a fire is this: have your client figure out who is his or her local congress person. Then, have the client go into their office to complain. You can write out, very briefly, the nature of the problem, and the name and address of the person at the government currently not responding. As long as your client is a registered voter in the district, the congress person's staffer will send a brief note to the foot dragger to please get on the ball, and presto, things start happening.

You might think: why can't I, as a lawyer, and one who contributed to the congress person's campaign, just write a letter asking for help, instead of sending my client in to the office in person? The reason is because it does not work. I have tried it. They blow off letters from p.i. lawyers. But when a voter walks into the office, in the flesh, they will do something. (Having your client try to do it via email or phone call is similarly less successful. Why, I don't know; I'm just telling you from experience that if you want it done, here's how to do it.)

CHAPTER SIXTY-ONE

WORKMAN'S COMPENSATION LIENS

If you are hurt on the job while being injured in a car accident, the workman's compensation carrier who pays your medical bills and lost wages has a right to subrogate the personal injury auto liability claim. The amount to be paid back for reimbursement is controlled by a case in Nevada known as Breen v. Caesar's Palace, which sets forth a formula for discount. The rights of the workman's compensation carrier against uninsured or underinsured motorist benefits are varied and are set forth in some complicated legal cases in Nevada that define whether and to what extent the work comp carrier has a right of subrogation against the UM (uninsured) or UIM (underinsured) coverage. Even lawyers who do a lot of auto cases sometimes have a hard time understanding the work comp rights against UM and UIM coverage, since it involves various offsets (technically, an 'offset' is different than a 'credit') for the work comp benefits paid, and also vary depending on whether it is the employee's own UM policy, or, the employer's UM policy. (Generally speaking, they can subrogate against the employer's policy, but not against your own personal policy.) Suffice it to say that if you are injured on the job in a car accident and have a car insurance claim pending in addition to a work comp case claim, you need a lawyer who is very competent to understand what the subrogation rights are so that you are not paying subrogation money that you do not owe, and, the UM and UIM carriers are not taking overly generous offsets from the work comp benefits paid.

CHAPTER SIXTY-TWO

HOSPITAL SUBROGATION LIENS

By statute in Clark County, hospital ER's have a right to charge subrogation liens on auto insurance claims. This right does not extend to uninsured motorist benefits, however. Until recently the hospitals were required to bill Medicare or Medicaid first before asserting a lien. All that changed as of October 1, 2017; the new law now allows hospitals to ignore Medicare or Medicaid, and instead assert a lien against the liability insurance coverage. However, if they choose to do so the lien is limited to 55 percent of reasonable charge amounts.

It is my opinion that hospitals are still required to bill private health insurance companies for persons involved in auto accident cases. Many hospital E.R.s will try to "accidentally on purpose" not ask for health insurance cards of people who come in for a car accident, so that they can claim ignorance of health insurance and go directly after the car insurance. The hospitals have become quite adept at various tricks to avoid billing health insurance and taking health insurance discounts on car insurance cases. If you are unlucky enough to have gone in an ambulance to an ER following a car accident case, then you will probably need a lawyer to keep the hospital from taking most of the settlement from you, which they will try to do in most cases if the patient does not have a lawyer.

CHAPTER SIXTY-THREE

PRIVATE HEALTH INSURANCE LIENS

If the health insurance you have qualifies as being an "ERISA" plan (the acronym stands for a federal law that regulates most union or big group health insurance policies), then they do have health insurance subrogation rights. The extent to which their rights can be affected by state laws that put various controls on the liens varies year to year, depending on decisions by the federal courts on ERISA liens; and such decisions, made in federal courts, vary from circuit to circuit. Much of the decisions regarding enforcement and valuation of ERISA liens have been delegated to the states by various federal court circuits, and so there is a confusing blend of federal and state court opinions on ERISA liens. (In the 9th circuit, in which Nevada is located, the federal courts have mostly delegated legal decisions on ERISA liens to Nevada state courts; our Nevada Supreme Court has ruled mostly in favor of the ERISA plans on the various issues, but, such rulings may be changed in the future as the political landscape is changing.)

Various doctrines such as the "Make-Whole Doctrine," etc., have been eliminated in many ERISA situations by contract language that specifically excludes them. The current state of the law in Nevada on ERISA liens is to the effect that if the contract specifically excludes this or that, the Nevada Supreme Court will honor the exclusion; but, if the contract does not specifically exclude something, the court will not infer it.

As far as individual health insurance policies are concerned, Nevada State law still forbids subrogation. But there are very, very few individual health insurance policies any longer, so unless you purchase the individual plan under "Obamacare," this is not going to apply to you.

As of about 10 years ago, our statutes in Nevada allow group health insurers (who do not qualify as ERISA) to have subrogation rights.

CHAPTER SIXTY-FOUR

SUBROGATION BY DISABILITY INSURANCE

Although rare in this day and age, people do sometimes have disability coverage, typically through their employer. Oftentimes this is done on the basis of giving the employee a chance to take out the disability coverage as an option, and deductions are made from the paychecks to pay companies like Aflac. Typically, if these companies find out there is a car accident involved, they will try to put a subrogation lien against the personal injury case.

Probably, in many instances, these liens are invalid, and should be contested.

These private disability plans, like Aflac, are not ERISA plans, to the best of my knowledge. They are private forms of insurance coverage by for-profit companies, and do not qualify as ERISA. There is no, to my knowledge, statutory provision in Nevada that gives them a subrogation right.

The common law in Nevada says that absent statutory provisions granting subrogation rights to insurers, they do not have subrogation rights. See, for example, Maxwell v. Allstate. (While I am not so sure that if the issue was revisited with our Nevada Supreme Court in its current configuration, they would decide the same way, but as far as I know, Maxwell v. Allstate is still good law. The makeup of the court, and its leanings, like all political institutions, changes over the course of time.)

The argument of the disability carriers is that there is language in their policy that gives them subrogation rights; but again, the common law in Nevada (that is, the law created by judges as opposed to legislatures) denies subrogation rights on insurance unless there is a statute to the contrary. (The reason we have almost universal subrogation rights for health insurance now is largely because of statute, not common law decision. State statutes now grant subrogation to group health insurance plans, and ERISA gives subrogation to union plans, large employer plans, etc.)

Of course, if a lien is asserted, the practitioner risks putting himself or his client at risk by simply denying it without consent from the subrogating

300

insurer or, court order. My own experience is that I have found that when I threaten court action for declaratory relief, these disability insurers will back off; but each case must be handled on a case by case basis. My main point is simply to alert practitioners that disability insurance from private insurers probably does not have valid subrogation rights; there may be exceptions, but one should not just assume that their subrogation interest is valid simply because they send out a form letter claiming as much.

I have also encountered some of these disability insurers claiming that they are ERISA plans. Again, if this is challenged, and court action threatened, my experience is that they back off. ERISA is supposed to govern *nonprofit* health plans of large employers and unions. Because it is (allegedly) nonprofit, the health plan's efforts to subrogate and recoup benefits theoretically inures to the benefit of all the members in holding down their premiums, and so, therefore, is not morally abhorrent. In a for profit situation, such a rationalization does not apply, therefore, for non ERISA carriers (e.g. Aflac disability), subrogation is not allowed.

There may be instances in which disability benefits are provided directly by a union under an ERISA qualified health and welfare plan, and in such a case, subrogation might be allowed. 20 years ago, union provided disability benefits were common; but, I rarely see them these days.

CHAPTER SIXTY-FIVE

THE DEMAND LETTER

The settlement process typically begins with a demand letter from the attorney. The demand letters are usually not sent until the client has completed medical treatment. Many times, I have clients complain that their case is taking too long because it's "been months since my accident" or similar. I have to remind them that we cannot even begin to try to settle the case until they have completed their medical treatment, so it is unfair to start complaining about how long things take if they understand that it would be to their disadvantage to settle the case before they were done with their medical treatment.

When I first began to practice law, the demand letters were usually short, conclusory documents of two pages in length, laying out the most basic facts in a perfunctory matter, together with copies of all the relevant documents such as medical records, police reports, photos, etc.

Then, the trend was towards doing "settlement brochures" which were binders with fancy graphics, photographs, sometimes even video settlement brochures. Insurance adjusters oftentimes laughed at these efforts saying that they didn't even look at them, although I think that was overstatement on their part.

Then, the fad became doing demand letters that were supposed to "plug in" to the insurance company's software system called "Colossus." These demand letters required attorneys to list out all the various ICD-9 and, later, ICD-10 diagnostic codes, various items that were supposedly "value drivers" for Colossus, etc. These letters were long and very technical, generally. At first, when our office was using these "Colossus style" demand letters, it did seem as though they worked well. But the insurance companies figured out things well enough and soon started to more or less ignore the 'value drivers' highlighted in the "Colossus" style demand letters, and told the claims processors to do their own research in the records for the items to be inputted, and to not rely on what the plaintiff's attorney said.

Today, the demand letters our office does are still somewhat lengthy, as we oftentimes use them as reference later on for litigation, and figure: why do the same job twice ; but we no longer believe that the demand letters are used by adjusters to "plug in" to the Colossus software system.

A good demand letter should point out the factors that insurance adjusters think are important. Theoretically, these should be the same factors that a judge or jury might think are important, but typically are not , because adjusters are still taught to look at things from a 1990's perspective, in my opinion. If a demand letter is not for a typical claims processor, but, rather, for a particularly knowledgeable (higher level) adjuster or a seasoned insurance defense lawyer, it will tend to point out factors that would be impressive to a judge or jury. So, the demand letter content varies oftentimes with the audience; is it a processor just inputting a computer, is it a knowledgeable litigation adjuster, is it a young insurance lawyer, or is it a seasoned trial attorney on the other side? They will all value things differently due to their experience.

What clients need to understand is that the demand letter is simply the first shot fired in a round of negotiations. You can *ask* for anything you want. You can ask for 10 billion dollars, hypothetically; that doesn't mean your case is worth 10 billion dollars. Oftentimes I get clients who start counting their money before anything has even been offered to them, believing that just because we ask for a certain amount that is how much they are going to get.

Typically, I just ask for the "policy limits" in the demand letter, as that is the most, practically speaking, that they could tender; and it sufficiently sets up things for potential bad faith exposure in the future (or, more realistically, it should make the insurance company think twice about things if the case is worth close to the limits.)

Up until 2 years ago, when our state legislature changed the law, the insurance companies had to tell us the policy limits when we requested it pre-litigation. But today, they do not have to reveal that information until suit is filed. So, when sending out the pre litigation demand letter, oft times we do not know what the limits are; as a result of this ignorance, we can do little more, at time of the pre litigation demand letter, than demand, in effect, the "policy limits, whatever they happen to be."

One advantage of a well written demand letter is that you can "cut and paste" sections of it from your computer, to use later on as interrogatory answers. In this way, a thorough demand letter can do double duty.

CHAPTER SIXTY-SIX

SETTLEMENT EVALUATIONS

First of all, keep in mind that a settlement means that neither side is going to get everything that it wants. You are going to get less money than you think your case is worth, and the other side is going to pay more than they think the case is worth, if it is a good settlement.

Also keep in mind that you cannot make a good judgment about how much your case is worth by comparing your case to those of other persons who you know or have heard about. Every case is different. Other people will not tell you everything about their case, adding or omitting facts to make themselves sound more clever, or, more victimized, etc. than is truly the case. And, of course, in every re-telling of a story by others, the facts are twisted for dramatic or other effect.

The thought that you know somebody who was "hardly even hurt" got a large amount of money, so you should get even more since you are "actually hurt," is something I hear on a regular basis. But, the truth is that you do not know what the test results showed on the other person; perhaps he or she had a ruptured disc. You do not know the circumstance of the accident; if the other driver was drunk or texting while driving, the case is worth more than say, if someone takes their foot off the brake and rolls into a car at a stoplight.

Trying to find out how much your case is worth by going on the internet is foolish, also. There are some websites that purport to have "calculators" to help you figure out how much your case is worth. These websites are all scams. They inevitably tell you that your case is worth a lot of money, and then at the end say if your current attorney is not trying to get this much money, then you should fire him and hire the attorney whose ad appears below.

Trying to use formulas such as "three times the medical bills" is also not a valid way to determine case value. *Forty years ago*, in "whiplash" cases, when medical bills rarely exceeded $1500 on a whiplash case, insurance companies did commonly multiply medical bills by three. But, they haven't been doing it for over 30 years, at least. Insurance companies are far more sophisticated now about evaluating cases, most of them using complex computer algorithms that take into account hundreds of variables. And, over the years, some types of cases are now valued more by juries, and some types of cases are valued less. For example, jurors in today's world are much more punitive against drunk drivers than they were, say, 30 years ago. On the other hand, jurors in today's world are much more punitive towards plaintiffs who are perceived to be abusing opioid pain medications, due to all the recent bad publicity about opioid abuse. The world keeps changing and juries keep changing. Who is perceived as a "good guy" and who is perceived as a "bad guy" often depends upon the whims of public opinions that can be, and are, sometimes controlled and influenced by huge financial and political interests.

The best way to get an evaluation of your case for purposes of settlement is to have a good attorney who knows what he or she is doing. For example, I have been doing personal injury cases for close to 40 years. I have tried over 70 civil jury trials, and over a thousand arbitrations and mediations, and I have settled thousands of cases. I subscribe to and read the periodicals that show all the jury verdicts in Clark County every month. I am in regular communication through various list servers, as well as meetings at the courthouse and at seminars, with other LV attorneys comparing our notes on how much is this or that sort of injury getting on the "open market" of jury verdicts in Clark County.

There simply is no substitute for experience here. If you want to know how much your case is really worth, you need to ask a good, *experienced LV personal injury attorney.* Any other way to evaluate your case is going to be either totally a waste of time, or, close to a total waste of time.

I would like to point out one last thing. Sometimes I will hear from clients that they are suspicious that I am recommending lesser settlement amounts to them because "someone got to" me. In today's world of political corruption, bribes and payoffs, it's easy to see how people are so suspicious about this. But I can tell you that in 40 years not only has this never happened, I have never been approached in any way, shape or form about something like this. If you think about the logistics of what's involved, it really makes no sense that an insurance company would engage in this kind of behavior. We're something like that to happen, and become public, the persons involved would go to jail, and the insurance company could lose its license. The attorney involved would lose his license.

Generally speaking, I find that most people overvalue their cases, not surprisingly. It is human nature to only look at the positive side of things, and to diminish or ignore negative factors. There is no such thing as a "perfect" case. Every plaintiff's case has some detracting factors which often have nothing to do with the honesty of the parties involved. Oftentimes, a professional mediator can point out, in objective fashion, to each side, the weak points of his or her case when viewed by a jury or judge. No one is capable of being objective in viewing his or her own case. It is just human nature that, when looking at our own recollections of things, and our perceptions of things that could be viewed in different way, we will put the facts in a light most favorable to ourselves. This is what makes settlements difficult to achieve, since both sides will, as one mediator puts, "buy their own (stuff)" too much.

CHAPTER SIXTY-SEVEN

"COLOSSUS"

Automobile insurance companies, at least the big ones (the ones you have heard of) all use some version of "Colossus" to evaluate claims.

"Colossus" was originally a software program developed by General Dynamics Corporation for an Australian insurance company. Allstate insurance liked the program and had it redeveloped for use in the U.S. The program basically purports to predict the range that a jury might award on a case, given certain facts.

It used to be claims adjusters (real people) would look through a file of materials accompanying a demand letter and would make educated predictions about the case value. Colossus and its progeny now have "claims processors," typically recent college graduates, input the many questions (more than 100) asked by Colossus. I have no doubt that in the last few years insurance companies have progressed to the point where computers can probably do quite a bit of the processing without human help. The software program then predicts a case value.

Adjusters and insurance lawyers are advised that the insurance company will not tolerate their going beyond the Colossus prediction range without excellent reasons and several levels of bureaucratic appeal and approval.

Like any computer system, Colossus operates effectively when the person inputting the facts does so accurately, and works very poorly when the processor makes a poor input of information. This is known as the "garbage in, garbage out" principle. Given that many of the claims processors are persons who have no medical training whatsoever, and little, if any real, real world experience with jury trials, it is no wonder that many of the Colossus predictions come out with head scratching results. Nonetheless, the use of these algorithm systems has become a reality and a large majority of auto insurance injury claims are evaluated by these programs.

There have been numerous books and seminars written by persons who claim to have "inside information" about what Colossus -type systems value and what they do not value. When this information first came out it was mostly accurate and useful. But the insurance companies are smart enough to know when others are trying to manipulate their programs, and they make changes. It is very similar to how people allegedly figure out the algorithm Google uses to rank people on its website, and promise that they can deliver high rankings by manipulating the Google algorithm. Then Google figures out what the manipulation is, and then changes its algorithm so that sometimes the manipulation actually have a negative, rather than positive, result on the rankings. This "spy versus spy" process goes on with Google in an ongoing process, month after month. In a not dissimilar way, I think plaintiff's lawyers who fool themselves that they know how to manipulate Colossus are probably relying on algorithms that are three or more years old, which, in computer cyberworld terms, is ancient.

The main point here I am making is that laypersons who think insurance companies evaluate cases based on a "three times medical bills" formula or similar are 30 or more years behind the times.

Also, people who think that they have come up with a new system of writing medical reports or medical bills that will trigger insurance company computer systems into paying off like slot machine jackpots are also fooling themselves and, perhaps, others. Keep in mind that the insurance industry rakes in more dollars per year than the GDP of all but the superpower nations. With this much firepower, they certainly are not going to be fooled by manipulative chicanery for very long.

I have seen commercials by various attorneys, usually young, inexperienced ones, who, with a wink and a nod, imply that they are so smart they have figured out the "game" and no how to manipulate the system. People who buy into this are probably good "marks" for con artists as well. The truth is, to do well against the insurance industry, an attorney must have intelligence, experience, and good old fashioned hard work. Although I do not like "the other side," I do not underestimate them.

CHAPTER SIXTY-EIGHT

LIEN DISCOUNTS AND REDUCTIONS

Probably the biggest part of determining how much you "clear" form a settlement is dependent on whether and to what extent an attorney can reduce or obtain discount on the various liens. There are liens from the government (Medicare, Medicaid, Tricare, Social Services, etc.); liens by private health insurers (Health Plan of Nevada, Blue Cross, etc.); liens from hospitals under the statute that gives them lien rights in Nevada; liens from private health providers (doctors with whom the client has voluntarily agreed to treat on a lien basis, and some providers, such as the ambulance companies for the county and city, who refuse to bill health insurance); workman's compensation liens; child support lien; etc. I would say that it is impossible for a layperson to deal with all these lien situations on his or her own. Thirty, forty years ago a layperson could settle a simple whiplash case and not have to worry about liens; that is simply no longer the case. This was discussed in above chapters.

Liens from governmental insurers are sometimes reduced according to statutory or regulatory formulas, e.g. Medicare. Work comp liens are reduced according to case law formulas. Liens for ERISA plans can be reduced; but, the law on whether and to what extent reductions can or should be given changes on a yearly basis, it seems, and the vendors and law firms who handle these liens are oft times working on commissions, and are loathe to give reductions. So, often, the best tool for reducing ERISA liens is to challenge the relationship of the bill to the injury, and, similarly, to demand apportionment for preexisting conditions, rather than insisting on discounts per "common fund doctrine" or similar.

Liens for health care providers, e.g. chiropractor, MRIs, etc. are oft times discounted, but how much depends on a host of factors. I find that insurance companies vastly overestimate how much of a discount I get on these liens. There is no set amount for the discount.

There is one published decision from the State Bar of Nevada dealing with an ethics charge against a Reno based p.i. lawyer. In the reported facts, the lawyer, upon settling the case, requested discounts from the various providers, except for one, who (the opinion implies) had some special relationship with the attorney. The attorney was sanctioned for not asking all the lien providers for a discount; and, the opinion infers that it would be unethical for a p.i. lawyer not to request discounts from all possible discounters.

There are some lienholders that an attorney knows, from experience, will not give discounts, period, so I do not think the State Bar opinion requires fruitless effort to be undertaken; but, the lesson here is that not only is not unseemly to request discounts, it is ethically required.

There is also a State Bar published opinion to the effect that attorneys may not purchase lien rights in the background, and make money themselves off the liens. The situation addressed by the State Bar involved two attorneys who engaged in a scheme where one attorney purchased the liens on the cases of his buddy; and his buddy reciprocated. This practice was obviously quite sleazy and in conflict with the rights of the clients.

In summation, the State Bar says that p.i. attorneys are not to be involved in the business of purchasing provider liens, period. If an attorney wants to get into that business, then he or she must give up their plaintiff's practice. You can't do both.

Despite the obvious sleaziness of a p.i. lawyer buying provider liens on his own clients, about every two years or so, it seems that there is yet another lawyer in LV who thinks he has found a clever way to get around this prohibition. My warning is, to all who read this book: don't even think about going there. Many have tried this sleazy scheme before, and gone down in flames; and in my opinion, people who try this should lose their license when they are caught. (Another version of this scheme is for the lawyer to secretly own the clinic to which he refers clients, or, to get a percentage kick back of fees collected by a provider to whom he sends clients. This is all WAY OVER THE LINE. Don't do it!)

It is your right to ask your attorney, when discussing settlement figures, "after I pay you and pay all the liens, how much am I clearing?" Absolutely! You should be focused on this question before you sign the release.

Although sometimes I am not always able to give exact discount figures at the time the release is signed, because the lien discount requests are still pending, I am able to give meaningful estimates to the best of my knowledge and experience.

CHAPTER SIXTY-NINE

WHOSE DECISION IS IT TO SETTLE?

The injured victim is the person who has the right to decide whether to settle the case or not. The attorney can advise and recommend, but ultimately, without the signature of the injured person on the release, the case does not get settled.

This is the layperson's final guarantee that they will not have a settlement made that is against their wishes. (I know of some attorneys who have fine print in their retainer agreements giving them the right to make a settlement without the client's express, prior consent on cases not involving a policy limits situation. I have never done this, although, I have had cases where the client consents, and then, after I make the settlement deal, they decide to withdraw their consent, usually, after talking to some relative who is 'advising' the client. In such situations, the insurance is usually able to enforce the original settlement agreement, even if the client refuses to sign the release, on the basis that the attorney is the authorized agent for the client, and, the insurance carrier relied upon the settlement to be valid and has acted, to their detriment, in reliance upon the reasonable belief that the case was settled.)

There is somewhat of an exception to settling without prior express consent, and that would be where the at fault party tenders its policy limits, which, is the most that they can pay. Such a situation is not a settlement, but rather, more of a surrender or capitulation. In such cases, I will, on behalf of the client, accept the policy limits, because there is simply nothing more than can be paid (other than the extremely rare instance where the claim is huge and the tortfeasor wealthy and underinsured.) Occasionally I have clients complain to me that they wanted more than the policy limits, but they have to understand that as a practical matter, that is the most that you can get in 99.9% of the cases. Normal people with normal car insurance policies cannot be effectively sued for personal assets, the large majority of the time, because they can simply file bankruptcy if such a lawsuit was filed (although bankruptcy does not discharge punitive damages.) Persons and companies who are rich and can pay a lot of money for a claim are never put in that situation, as a practical matter, because , since they are rich and therefore vulnerable, they carry very large insurance policies. So as a practical matter, 99.9 percent of the time, the most that you can collect on any motor vehicle collision case is the amount of the policy limits.

I suppose that theoretically, there could be a rich man or a rich defendant corporation, and the injuries are catastrophic, and the insurance limits, although millions of dollars, are not sufficient to cover all the damages. Might, in that case, the plaintiff deserve more than the policy limits and, more to the point, be able to collect more than the limits? I suppose so; but such cases are so rare that discussing them in this book, which is intended to cover the ordinary, not extraordinary case, is not within the purview of this book's intended audience and subject matter.

CHAPTER SEVENTY

SETTLEMENT AFTER SUIT IS FILED

In many cases, the insurance company will not offer enough money to interest the client in a settlement *before* a lawsuit is filed. Many insurance companies have found that there are a lot of lawyers out there, who will settle cases for low amounts of money in order to avoid having to litigate, and so they will typically try to settle for a very low amount, without litigation. Given that there are so many "poser " type law firms who will accept whatever is offered, this is not a bad strategy to try. But, for the client with a good lawyer representing them, the amounts offered pre-litigation are quite often insufficient, and a lawsuit must be filed. I would say in my own office this happens on at least 50 percent of the motor vehicle cases we handle; 30 years ago, the percentage was probably closer to 15 percent.

Just because a lawsuit is filed, it does not mean that the case will not be settled. As a matter of fact, the great majority of the cases upon which litigation is

324

filed do end up getting settled. Sometimes this is after an arbitration hearing is held; sometimes just filing the lawsuit will make the insurance company "serious" and offer a fair amount; sometimes a professional mediator, or a settlement judge is involved.

A major drawback to the litigation process is that it takes a long time. Smaller cases can be litigated to trial with in less than a year, and often within six months. But the bigger cases, let us say, cases involving damages of over $100,000 or more, will typically take over 18 months to 24 months (currently in Las Vegas, year 2018) to get to a trial after the lawsuit is filed. Very oftentimes on the bigger cases, especially, the insurance company will not make a fair offer until a couple weeks before trial is to begin

People need to understand that the more money a case is worth, typically the longer it is going to take to get fair value in a settlement. On the bigger cases, the insurance companies like to sit on their money as long as they can. I recently saw a documentary about Warren Buffet, who until recently was the richest man in the world. His hedge fund owns Geico insurance company. The movie talks about how Buffet was able to become the richest man in the world in large part by investing the "float" from Geico, i.e., the money that they had collected, but had not yet paid out in claims.

When a client's complain to me that things are taking too long, I tell them "well, you can cut it very short by just taking the settlement offer they made before we filed suit and settle it right now. If that's what you want to do we can settle this thing today. But if you want to get the money that you are hoping to get, then you're going to have to wait and let the litigation process play out more. The insurance company knows that people are anxious and they count on you losing patience and taking the cheaper amount. Again, if you want to do that, that is your business. You can do it if you wish. But if you want to get more money you have to wait. There is no magic wand I can wave to force them evaluate the case the same way that you do."

People sometimes think that insurance companies fear bad publicity if they go to court and lose a case, or that they fear 'exposure' on social media, etc., as being "unfair" to injured persons. My own experience is that insurance companies do not care about bad publicity threats. Media outlets are not interested in stories about insurance companies not offering fair settlements; and the internet is so full of complaints about everything and everyone that another complaining person is just another drop in the storm. The only thing the insurance company cares about is money. They do not care about you, or, truth be told, their own insured; it's all just dollars and cents, and most decisions are driven by computer algorithms and heartless bean counters handicapping how much it will cost them to do 'x' vs. doing 'y.' Sometimes they predict very inaccurately, but, they are not unintelligent about their guesswork, and they know that many plaintiffs are unwilling to wait them out.

In the bigger cases (six figures and up) that are litigated, frequently the cases are settled in a formal mediation process that typically occurs about a month before the trial date. The mediators– typically retired judges– will go back and forth to each side pointing out the various pro's and con's of the case, and trying to get each side to be more objective. One of the more popular mediators in Las Vegas, former county DA and judge Stuart Bell, always says, when starting out each mediation, that "the main problem that keeps people from settling is that both sides start believing in their own BS. My job is to give you an outsider view of what is going to be believed, and what's going to be questioned, by a judge or jury, and you probably won't like a lot of what I'm going to say." Another popular mediator, former chief judge Gene Porter, usually starts out by saying, "I believe what you're telling me. But what I believe isn't what matters. It's what those 8 people sitting on a civil jury believe, and you never know who is going to be picked to show up for the jury that day. "He then says, "when you were coming to my office building today, you drove by that pawn store where they make the TV show 'Pawn Stars,' and you saw about 50 or more people standing in line outside, just to go inside and look at the pawn store. I want you to think about what those people standing in line looked like, because those are basically the same people who are going to be sitting on your jury, judging you. They're going to be deciding the case mostly on how much they like you or don't like you, from seeing you testify for an hour or two on the stand, or how you look sitting at counsel's table." He stresses that jury trials are basically a coin flip, and if you like gambling so much, take your settlement, go to the Golden Nugget, and put your money on "black" and spin the wheel, because that's what can happen with a jury.

Now, of course, both Stu Bell and Gene Porter say these things for effect, to get people to move towards a settlement frame of mind, and hyperbole is involved; but, there is a lot there to consider for a person who thinks a trial is like something they saw in a movie or TV. Real trials are much more boring than TV, take a lot longer, and, juries can be really smart and attentive, or, they can be the opposite; so much depends in 'luck of the draw' in who is selected by the court's computer system to be subpoenaed to jury duty that day.

If you think that the jury is going to have a lot of people on it who are a lot like you, guess again. Chances are that maybe one of the eight people on the jury will be 'kind of' like you, and the other seven will be from different generations, different races and religions, and will not necessarily see things the same way you see things.

So, usually (not always), when suit is filed on a case, the case will still probably settle someday, although 'someday' may take a while. The smaller the case, the quicker the "while;" the bigger the case, usually, the longer the 'while.'

CHAPTER SEVENTY-ONE

BREAKDOWN SHEETS

When our office settles a case, we give the client what we call a "breakdown sheet." Other offices call it "disbursement instructions." It is a sheet of paper that shows exactly how much everyone is getting from the settlement. It contains, as an attachment, a printout of all our out of pocket costs, it shows the fees we are charging, the amounts being paid to the lienholders, the amount that the client is getting, etc On many occasions we cannot give exact figures in the breakdown sheet at the time the release is signed, because various lien discounts are still pending, but we give estimates as closely as we can in such situations.

Sometimes, problems arise when parties, other than your client, want to see a copy of the proposed breakdown before a settlement has been reached. For example, let's say that there is a settlement proposal on the table for $100,000. Your client says: I would accept that, but only if can clear "x." You tell your client: " I think I can clear "x" for you, but I'm not sure. I will first need to see if the lien holders will come down enough to get to that number for you. " The client says: "well, make sure you can do it; I'm not signing the release until I'm sure." So, you have your assistant contact the lienholders, telephonically, to ask if they will discount whatever it is you need to get the deal done. Say, three say OK, but the fourth says: "I am not agreeing to anything until you send me a copy of the breakdown sheet. I want to know exactly what everyone else is getting, because I don't want to be taking a big cut if everyone else is not doing the same."

The problem is that if you send the lienholder (e.g doctor's office) a copy of the breakdown sheet, and, the doctor doesn't agree, and, the settlement doesn't go through, the doctor now has in his file a document showing that the other doctors/lienholders are willing to discount 'x' percent. This document is subject to subpoena, and, since the defense lawyer has a a release authorization from your client, privilege will not protect it from production. This document can then end up as a trial exhibit to 'prove' that your doctors are overcharging, etc. So, what to do?

One solution is to go over to the doctor's office in person, show him the breakdown sheet, and tell him you can't leave a copy. Sometimes, this is a no-go, because the doctor thinks you are up to a trick of some kind by not giving him a copy.

In such situations, I have done the following. I will incorporate into the breakdown sheet an introductory paragraph or two loaded up with "poison" that a defense lawyer would not want introduced into trial. e.g. I will add an introductory paragraph such as: "the defendant in this case wants to settle because their present attorney is afraid to go to trial. The defendant is also probably concerned that some sordid issues in his past might come to light if his attorney cannot keep them out of evidence." Of course, this is made up example that is over-the-top, but you get the idea.

BEFORE a settlement is reached, do not, in writing, say something negative about your case or client to the lienholder, in order to convince him about the wisdom of settling his lien now, because that could end up as a trial exhibit. Similarly, if you are speaking to a representative for a big company, be careful about badmouthing your case or client BEFORE settlement has been reached, as this could be written down in a computer log system of some kind, also, potentially discoverable. AFTER a case is settled, it is not risky, in the sense of having it come up as a trial exhibit, to tell a lienholder why you had to settle the case for less than what everyone was expecting, in order to explain the request for a drastic reduction.

CHAPTER SEVENTY-TWO

BUYER'S REMORSE

I have found that in a good many settlements, my clients will seem relatively satisfied at the moment the case is settled (e.g., at a mediation), but then after a couple days, they will call me and say they have thought about it, and are now displeased. Invariably, it will turn out that they have been talking to friends or relatives about the settlement, and the friends or relatives advise them that they made a bad deal, that they should have received more money, etc. Frequently, these 'friends' or relatives were persons anticipating getting some of the money for themselves, either through 'loan' or gift, and they sense that the amount of the settlement will not be sufficient to allow the 'loan' or gift they envisioned getting.

Here are the things that you need to keep in mind when you settle a case utilizing the representation of a reputable, good attorney. The more money you get on the case for the settlement, the more he or she gets for their fee. They are motivated to get as much as they can. Secondly, no two cases are alike, and persons who are not involved in the business, (e.g. friends and relatives who claim to have some knowledge of what 'really goes on') and who do not have a lot of experience representing plaintiffs, are not competent judges of what is and what is not a fair settlement. Third, the things that you read on the internet or hear about on radio shows (particularly right wing radio shows) about "crazy" settlements being given to persons for frivolous injuries, are most of the time "fake news" or highly distorted ('crazy' lawsuit stories are interesting, real lawsuit stories, typically not; and, the large corporate interests who own or support media outlets through advertising have interests that are best served by 'frivolous, crazy' lawsuit stories that might prejudice members of the public who ultimately vote and sit on juries.) Insurance companies are not idiots and they do not hand out big money for nothing, as is sometimes indicated in urban folklore.

My advice after you have settled a case: do not re-think your decision. Turn the page, and move on with your life. Once the settlement is made, you cannot get out of it and change your mind. And, if at all possible, do not share the news of your settlement with friends and relatives who have no absolute 'need to know.' The result of telling people about your settlement is that they will ask you for a "loan," and will resent it if you turn them down. If you do give them a loan, they will rarely pay it back (since they rationalize you already received 'free' money and don't need it nearly as much as they do, after all.)

CHAPTER SEVENTY-THREE

LITIGATION AND TRIAL–
AN OVERVIEW

I suppose every case I have ever litigated has involved client complaints to the effect that "why is it taking so long?" Even when the case goes relatively quickly by the standards of an attorney, to a client it understandably seems like it is taking forever.

Once a lawsuit is filed, there is only so much a lawyer can do to control how fast things go. Even the most aggressive lawyer, pushing things as hard as he possibly can to get the quickest trial date, will not be able to get things done quick enough to satisfy the client. This is because there are court rules that give certain amounts of times for everything to take place, and perhaps more to the point, all our court systems in Las Vegas are busy and the judges can only give so much time for the trial of civil cases. (By law, criminal cases, where persons are in jail awaiting trial, take priority over civil trials.) In some court departments this is more true than in others, but civil jury trials, even

337

the simplest ones, take up a lot of court time, and the court has many other functions to perform other than doing trials (for example, they have to hear civil motions calendars, which take up a lot of time; oftentimes the same court that does civil matters will also be doing criminal matters, so they have to do things such as arraignments, preliminary hearings, sentencings, criminal motion calendar; and there are many types of legal matters other than automobile injury cases that take up the court's time, such as contract disputes, business disputes, real estate disputes, construction defects, medical malpractice, mortgage foreclosure proceedings, etc. In years past our courts of general jurisdiction also had to deal with divorces and child custody problems, but those have now been moved to a separate court system, so the judges who hear personal injury cases do not hear family dispute cases.)

As a general rule of thumb, the bigger the case, the longer it is going to take to go to trial.

There are basically four levels of trials in Clark County for auto personal injury cases: small claims court, justice civil court; the "short trial" program; and regular jury trials.

Small claims court is like "Judge Judy" on TV. The jurisdictional level now for small claims court is $10,000. Up until recently small claims court was only $5,000, and would not award damages other than medical bills and other "special" damages (i.e., things other than pain and suffering, etc.) That limitation has been lifted, so now it is not a bad idea to take the smaller automobile insurance claims to small claims court, as long as the plaintiff is willing to accept $10,000 or less. A small claims court matter can be resolved within two months of the date the complaint is filed.

Justice court civil division can hear civil matters up to $15,000. Previously insurance companies would not request jury trials in justice court, so the cases there went rather quickly. It is now the common practice for an auto insurance carrier to request jury trials in justice court. Generally speaking the justices of peace are not accustomed to conducting jury trials, so having a jury trial in their courtrooms can be rather uncomfortable for all concerned. It is not so much a matter that the judges are any more or less educated or intelligent than the ones in district court, it is simply a matter that their courtrooms, physically, are oftentimes not setup to accommodate jury trials, and the various logistical things involved in getting juries in and out of the courtroom and so forth are not "old hat" for their staffs. Anyway, from start to finish, a jury trial in justice court civil division can take around nine months from time complaint is filed until time trial is accomplished.

In the regular district court system for personal injury cases, i.e., the 8th Judicial District Court of Clark County (what is known as the "court of general jurisdiction" to attorneys), there are two systems for handling auto cases. One system (which I helped to design back in the 90's), is a system which involves court-ordered arbitrations and "one-day jury trials." The case first goes through a nonbinding arbitration process, which usually takes about five months to complete from the time the complaint is filed; and then if either side does not like the arbitrator's award, it goes to a one-day jury trial conducted by a "pro tem" (temporary) judge, and from the time the arbitration is appealed to the time the short trial takes place, this will typically take around four months. So, from start to finish, if you were to file an automobile insurance case with damages of $50,000 or less (the "cap" for the short trial program), it would take about nine months to complete (if not settled in the meantime): five months for the arbitration, and four months for the short trial. These are just basic estimates.

If you go into the "regular jury trial" system for cases worth more than $50,000, from the time you file your complaint to the time you get to a jury trial is typically going to be 18 to 24 months. If you win the case and it is appealed, the time of the appeal will be another two or three years (although with the establishment of the 'new' intermediate court of appeals, that is handling appeals of civil matters involving less than $250,000, the time for appeals is coming down quite a bit for the 'smaller' cases, , and may be down to 12 to 18 months in the near future, or, so I am told by those who know such things.)

Of course, at any time during the complaint to trial process a case could be settled, and usually is.

Sometimes cases in "regular court" can take even longer than the estimated 18 to 24 months, primarily if a particular judge has a particularly busy trial calendar and just cannot handle enough cases.

Our office likes to avoid continuances of cases, but it is common place for the insurance lawyers to ask for continuances. Especially when the stock market is going up, the insurance companies like to hold onto their money as long as they can (so they can invest the "float,") so in times such as this at the time of my writing this book (2018) where the stock market is in a "bull " phase, you can expect insurance lawyers to ask for continuances quite often at the behest of the insurance companies.

CHAPTER SEVENTY-FOUR

THE COMPLAINT

The litigation starts off with the "complaint." The complaint sets forth the most basic allegations of the injured party (plaintiff) case.

When I first became a lawyer, almost 40 years ago, Nevada was just in the process of transferring its civil procedure system over to a virtual copy of the system from the then "new" federal rules of civil procedure. This system involves what is called "notice pleading," which means that the complaints, in Nevada at least, are only supposed to be bare bones allegations of what is the nature of the dispute and the damages. The current Nevada Rules of Civil Procedure, or NRCP, are copied almost ver batim from the Federal Rules of Civil Procedure. For this reason, legal opinions interpreting the FRCP oft times have application to the NRCP, although, particularly with regard to expert witness disclosures, and the Rule 16.1, the two systems have many differences. (To a somewhat lesser degree, the FRE, or Federal Rules of Evidence, were copied by the Nevada lawmakers in our state evidentiary code.) The practitioner who buys or subscribes to the better treatises on the FRE and FRCP, such as Wright and Miller, will oft times find them quite helpful in doing research on the parallel Nevada rules.

(As a side note: there are couple volumes out, from the well know publishers, i.e. West's and Lexis, that purport to be treatises by Nevada attorneys on the NRCP and the Nevada Evidence Code. I have found these books to be of limited value, and, of limited weight in persuading judges. These books were written, in my opinion, by corporate attorney types, and their slant is to favor interpretation of the rules that would, by and large, favor insurance companies. The better known authors of the federal rule treatises are law school professors, and they are more learned, thinking, and less biased, about their interpretations by and large.)

Many attorneys still use complaint forms that trace back to the 1930's, using flowery, 19th century type legal language and stating far more than needs to be said under "notice pleading." I suppose this is to impress clients who might ask for a copy of the lawsuit, as it looks more like a "scary" legal document than a proper notice jurisdiction complaint.

Some states, like California, still follow old rules of pleading which require complaints to have various technical "magic words," but Nevada is like this, except in very rare exceptional cases (which, other than potential fraud claims, or equitable remedies, do not pertain to the vast majority of auto accident complaints.)

Most motor vehicle lawsuits involve a claim of negligence, which basically means "not being careful," and "negligence per se," which means violating a traffic law, such as speeding or running a red light.

In Nevada, one can only ask for general damages, or special damages for that matter, "in excess of $15,000." (It used to be $10,000, but that rule was changed last year.) You cannot, in state court, ask for "a million dollars" or similar in the complaint itself.

The history of this requirement is interesting. Back in the late 70's, we had a very famous local resident: Howard Hughes. It was not uncommon for publicity seekers to make up lawsuits against Howard Hughes and file them in court, asking for "one billion dollars," or some other ridiculous amount, just to grab a headline in the National Enquirer. Howard Hughes had great influence in those days and so arranged for a law to be passed that required all lawsuits filed in Nevada to merely say "in excess of $10,000." This prevented people from making up huge numbers in their lawsuits just to get publicity.

A few states, quite sensibly, allow the plaintiff to name the at fault party's insurance company as the defendant, rather than the other driver, who is not, in reality, the entity truly being sued. These states are called "direct action" states. Unfortunately, Nevada is not yet a 'direct action' state, so the plaintiff must name the other driver as the defendant in the lawsuit, even though, in reality, it is the other driver's insurance company that will pay the damages.

I think it is wise for the practitioner to keep a few things in mind when drafting a complaint.

Although rarely done, an insurance company can enter your complaint into evidence in a trial, and can have it read to the jury. If your complaint has language that would be embarrassing if read aloud, as is the case with many "old form complaints" employing archaic language (e.g. "to wit, the plaintiff did experience great and excruciating pain and anguish of both mind and body"), it could come back to bite you.

The more that you specifically allege about the facts, the more you give the other side to shoot down and ridicule, and leave yourself all the less room to allege other facts when discovery takes place. There is, of course, a balance between specificity and vagueness to be struck, but the complaints I see from other law firms tend to err too much on the side of specificity, reciting facts as though it was a demand letter of some kind. If you will look at the "recommended version" of an auto negligence complaint, which is in the NRCP, you will see that the rule's authors intended for complaints to be very brief and conclusory.

I commonly see other law firms include claims for 'negligent entrustment' against the registered owner of an automobile (assuming that person is different from the driver), when there is no reason to have that claim added, and, no reason to suspect it to be true. This just creates added baggage to the lawsuit, for no good reason.

CHAPTER SEVENTY-FIVE

SERVICE OF THE COMPLAINT

After the lawsuit is filed with the court, then it must be served on the defendant within 120 days. (If it cannot be served within that time frame, then the attorney must petition the court for an extension of time. The various judges, in my experience, automatically grant the first such petition, so long as it is filed *before* the deadline runs. If you file after the deadline runs, most will still grant it, provide it is within a few days or so; but, why take such a chance?)

There is a fictional legal doctrine to the effect that anyone who drives on the roads in Nevada thereby consents to personal jurisdiction in Nevada for any accidents caused here. So, even if the other driver lives out of state, if they caused the accident here, you can sue them here (and serve them in the other state.)

The first effort in any MVA is to try to serve the defendant driver in person. This means you give the complaint and summons to a process server, and the process server tries to serve the other driver. This is just like you see on television, where the process server hands the other person the papers. Unlike subpoenas, which must be served on the actual person, a lawsuit can be served not only on the person, himself or herself, but, can be left at that person's residence household with a person of suitable age and discretion (as long as the person being served actually lives there currently.)

If the process server cannot serve the person after a couple or so attempts (typically because the defendant has moved and no one knows to where, or, more commonly, no one is willing to say where the other person moved, and there is no public record of same– this happens a lot in LV, particularly with persons at the lower end of the economic spectrum) then, the process server does an "affidavit of due diligence." This document, along with the complaint and summons, is forwarded to the DMV, to begin a process known as "service through DMV." The process is laid out in NRS 14.070. There are several more steps, and I won't bother describing them here; if you are interested, just look up the statute. This process is available for unlocatable defendants (even ones from out of state), so long as there is a police report available. The man 'trap' for the unwary practitioner is that the 120 day 'clock' runs on service through DMV, the same as for personal service; so, you need to start trying to serve people early on, as it is going to take you two or three months' time to get all the steps done under service through DMV.

If your process server can not personally serve the defendant, and, if your case does not fit into the situations covered by NRS 14.070 (service through DMV), then you have to 'serve through publication.' (These are those funny notices you see printed in the newspaper classified section sometimes. With actual newspapers going out of business right and left, this process will have to be changed in the coming decades. But for now, we still pretend that everyone reads an actual paper print newspaper.) This process also takes about 90 days to complete, so again, you need to get started early to comply with the 120 day time deadline.

On many cases, when you file the suit, the adjuster will say "don't serve the complaint yet. Give me some time to get some more medical records, and then we will be able to negotiate further." The danger in agreeing to this is that, if the defendant is not easily located and served, you can 'blow' the 120 time limit for completing service through publication or through DMV. You might think: well, if that happens, surely the adjuster will tell defense counsel not to file a motion to dismiss for violating the 120 day rule. Think again. I actually had this happen to me one time, and of course the adjuster and the insurance lawyer apologized for filing the motion, saying that the decision to do so "wasn't up to me. I'm just following orders." Yeah, right.

What if the adjuster says "I need more time to get the prior medical records. Then we can negotiate. I will put in writing that we won't file the motion to dismiss if we go beyond 120 days."

Again, I do not recommend you agree to this. There are other court rule deadlines that can be exceeded if you don't, for example, hold the 16.1 conference within a certain amount of time starting from when the complaint was *filed* (not served).

The better practice is to never hold off on serving a lawsuit to give an adjuster more time to do this or that. Go ahead and serve it. Tell the adjuster that you can give his lawyer an extra month to file an answer so that he can do whatever (giving the defendant an extra 30 days to answer a lawsuit is rarely going to cause any deadlines to be exceeded), if you so choose; but do not put off serving the lawsuit. Too often, a service of process that you thought would be a piece of cake turns out to be a snarly mess, and you don't want to run short of that 120 day rule.

Also, if you need to file for an enlargement of time (extension) to serve, try to get in before the last minute. There are some judges who will deny the petition not only if you file after the deadline, but will deny it if you file, e.g., the day of, or the day before, the deadline, even the delay makes no real difference to the actual parties involved. (Not sure why some are like this, I am guessing that LV is not the only city where such judges exist.)

CHAPTER SEVENTY-SIX

16.1 CONFERENCE

After the defendant in the case is served, (we are required to name the at fault driver, even though the actual defendant is the insurance company), we have what is called a "early case conference," aka "ECC," or "16.1" conference. (The "16.1" refers to the number of the rule requiring this conference.)

Currently in Nevada (I am writing this 2018), a 16.1 conference is technically required for all District Court cases, including for cases going into the arbitration/short trial program. Prior to the (baffling) decision of our Nevada Supreme Court in *Moon v. McDonald, Carano* et al., it was assumed that we did not need to comply with the 16.1 meeting and exchange on arbitration cases (cases with value under $50,000). The Moon decision says that we do have to comply with 16.1 deadlines even on arbitration system cases. Currently, Las Vegas lawyers have come up with a 'work around solution,' where it common practice to stipulate that *Moon* does not apply to this case, and that we will do the case under the "old" rules. The ADR commissioner and the Discovery Commissioner's office, two quasi-judges who are involved with this aspect of the case, approve this 'work around.' Occasionally, I will run across a new associate at an insurance defense firm who has the attitude, "whatever the plaintiff's lawyer asks for, say no, and then start billing to fight him." These types will sometimes refuse to sign the *Moon* work around stipulation. My tactic in dealing with them is to send them a letter stating that this is simply not the way things are done, and they should ask their supervising attorney about it; but, if I do not hear anything soon, I will go ahead and schedule the 16.1 meeting and submit the 16.1 report to the court. When and if we actually go through this stupidity, and the report is submitted the discovery commissioner, the next thing I see scheduled is a hearing by the discovery commissioner to basically ask: what the heck is going on here and who is responsible? At such hearings, the "hardball associate" is routinely given a tongue lashing by the judge for the "fight everything no matter what" attitude.

At the 16.1 meeting the attorneys exchange what evidence they have, and try to agree on a plan for how the discovery (described below) is to take place, deadline date-wise. A report is then prepared and submitted to the court, typically by my office, and the court then uses the report to set deadline dates.

These reports are basically just to give 'headlines' about the case to the court, so that dates can be set. Insurance lawyers, in particular the young 'rookie' sorts that are routinely assigned to cover this stage of the proceedings, oft times want to do extensive re-edits of the reports, as though some particular importance hinges on the wording. (I suppose, they can do no harm by these efforts, and can bill for their time, so this annoyance is commonplace.) Usually, I will put up with a little bit of this "rookie lawyer" time wasting, but if it is too extensive, or goes on for more than a week, I will just submit my own version of the report, and tell them to submit their own version. Typically, the discovery commissioner will reprimand the "rookie lawyer" for making a game out of the 16.1. report in such situations, since the hold-ups and requested edits are usually of the ridiculous variety.

Typically, at the 16.1 conference the insurance company lawyer will present little if anything new, instead, giving the plaintiff's attorney back a copy of the documents he already sent to the insurance company.

There have been a number of confusing court decisions from our Nevada Supreme Court in the last three or so years about what exact language is needed to be put into the 16.1 report form with regard to naming expert witnesses. There are two categories: retained experts and non-retained experts. The "non-retained experts" basically means the treating physicians.

How much needs to be said in the report, and who is a "retained expert" and "non-retained expert" is a matter of great confusion among attorneys right now. There are a couple law firms in town who seem to specialize in filing motions to dismiss based on hyper technical analysis of the language of the 16.1 report. Fortunately, most judges have now become weary and/or tired of these motions and no longer give them much attention.

There is a committee in the state bar that is rewriting the Nevada rules of civil procedure, in particular the 16.1 rules. The committee members with whom I have spoken to said they are well aware of the confusion in this area and are going to rewrite the rules so that they are clear and no longer traps for lawyers who are unfamiliar with the most recent nuances under our (now) confusing supreme court opinions on 16.1 report requirements.

After the initial 16.1 report is given, plaintiff's attorneys are required to give "updated" 16.1 "supplements" when they receive in a new piece of potential evidence, most typically new doctor's records and bills. I have a very excellent staff of legal assistants who perform this job for me, which is tedious, exacting, and time-consuming. If a plaintiff's firm does not supplement its 16.1 reports in an orderly manner, it can lead to admissibility challenges later on.

CHAPTER SEVENTY-SEVEN

WRITTEN DISCOVERY

There are basically two types of "discovery," which is the process by which each side is allowed to find out the facts and expert opinions that the other side intends to introduce as evidence. The original intent of discovery, under the federal rule system that was adopted back in the 70's, was that both sides would know all the important things thing there were to know about the other side's case, and therefore, this would encourage settlements to occur, and shorten the length of trials.

As lawyers oftentimes do, various strategies were invented to impede the other side from finding out much under the new rules , through the use of objections, obfuscation, and misleading answers to questions, etc. This "cat and mouse" game persists to this days, despite the best efforts of judges to derail it.

There are generally two types of written discovery: interrogatories (fancy word meaning "questions");

and request for production of documents, and its "cousin," subpoena duces tecum.

Interrogatory questions ask the other side to give information in written form in response to various questions. Insurance defense lawyers have become so adept at avoiding answering any meaningful question that interrogatories have largely become useless. The answers I get to my interrogatories are, generally speaking, gobbly gook lawyer-ese with little meaningful information. We send them out anyway, not so much to gather information, so much as to make sure that the other side cannot "ambush" us later on with a written document or fact that is not otherwise included with their 16.1 materials.

Requests for production of documents oftentimes are as useless as interrogatories in today's world. The insurance defense lawyers hire armies of young law school graduates to do little more than to think of lengthy non-answers to everything. It is like asking a politician to give you a straight answer. It almost never happens. Again, the RPDs are mostly useful just to make sure that no new documents pop up at time of trial. Sometimes, you get lucky and something new and useful comes in through an RPD, but this is the exception more than the rule.

The subpoena duces tecum is more useful than request for production of documents. This is because subpoena duces tecum are for documents to *non*-parties (i.e. not the person or entity you are suing.) You can send them to, say, the police department to get copies of accident reports; to get copies of contracts and communications sent by the defendant to others; reports with state agencies concerning your accident; DMV records and reports; etc. They are mostly used by my office to obtain *certified* copies of medical records and bills.

There can be procedural problems in getting subpoena duces tecum served, effectively, on out of state entities. My clients oftentimes think I can subpoena virtually anything in the world and "why didn't you subpoena this or that" as though I were a television detective issuing orders to subpoena "all the cell phone tower records for that night." Clients who watch television shows think that I can subpoena DNA samples and surveillance video from "every camera on the block" etc. Even police departments, in real life, do not get DNA and surveillance videos from every person near the scene of an accident. Although very useful, there are limits to documents I can subpoena.

360

There is another form of written discovery called "requests for admission." As envisioned by the persons who wrote the rules of civil procedure, theoretically, these could have been very useful in scraping away the underbrush of every litigation, i.e. things that really shouldn't be disputed, like the authenticity of documents that are obviously authentic. Again, answering these requests has been turned over to 'rookie lawyers' at defense firms by and large, and they pride themselves on not admitting even the most obvious facts, and writing half page legal briefs on why my request is not legally valid. So, they have become essentially useless tools. Yes, I know: at virtually every seminar on discovery I go to, someone will say that these are a "very underutilized tool" and suggest that we could use them for all sorts of things. News flash: in the real world, the insurance lawyers deny every request, and they have armies of rookie lawyers that they pay $35 an hour (and bill at $150 an hour) to make mountains out of molehills if you contest the denial, and in the end, it's just not worth it. It is just much easier and cost effective to take depositions and to get the admissions– at least, the ones that matter most– at the deposition.

CHAPTER SEVENTY-EIGHT

DEPOSITIONS

The deposition is where most of the "real action" in discovery takes place. A discovery deposition is where you can have someone come to your office or to the court reporter's office, and they have to answer questions under oath as you ask them. Because a lawyer does not get to "scrub" every answer, you can actually get some real answers from people.

Oftentimes, insurance lawyers use depositions just to "hassle" people instead of to get information. I say this because I have sat in on so many depositions where my clients are being deposed by insurance attorneys who have computer boilerplate printouts of all sorts of arcane questions, that have nothing to do with the case, and they force my clients to sit there answering truly stupid questions. Fortunately, there are time limits on how long the lawyer can depose any one person, but it can be extremely annoying.

There are some lawyers who will try to personally embarrass the person they are deposing, but new technology is putting an end to that sort of chicanery. Our local discovery commissioner has recently recommended that people install video cameras during depositions not for purposes of taking a video of the deponent (which is possible, although not always justified, cost-wise), mainly for the purpose of videotaping, and thus, dissuading, aggressive or abusive attorneys from over-the-line tactics. A videotape device as simple as a smartphone can be put on the table during the deposition, and you can tell the abusive lawyer that I am going to show this tape to the discovery commissioner if you don't cut it out. This innovation in technology, i.e., the cheap and universal availability of videotaping devices, will, in my opinion, work wonders in curbing abusive tactics used by some attorneys during depositions.

The main purpose of a deposition by a plaintiff's attorney is not finding out the facts of the other side's case (which should have been produced during 16.1 proceedings), but basically to lock in the other side's story (so they don't come up with something different at trial), and to establish, as firmly as you can, the main points you want to make about your own case. Most attorneys do not understand this, and use depositions under the idea that if they drone on long enough, a "smoking gun" or needle in the haystack will be produced. This is a fantasy that inexperienced attorneys have that rarely takes place in real life.

There are whole treatises and weeklong workshop seminars devoted to taking depositions, so, I am not going to cover much in this book, other than to scratch the surface of what I think matters most.

Before you take a deposition, you should write down on a single page the main points that you need to lock in. These are things that you already know, but, you need them in a deposition so that they can used in trial (e.g. in opening statements), or, that you want locked in so that the defendant doesn't change stories later on.

Then, you should write down on a separate piece of paper the "rules of the road" you want to establish with this defendant. Read my above chapter on this subject if you don't know what "rules of the road" means.

Third, you sketch out on a separate piece of paper the things that you just want to ask about to find out what happened, what they know, etc.

So, for the depo you basically have three sheets of paper with some headline type things written on them. Then you take the depo. You check off the 'headlines' when covered. You make sure they are checked off before you end the depo.

You need to listen to what the witness is saying during the depo. You need to be flexible and to ask questions that are prompted by what the witness says. If you are locked into some kind of typed up checklist, you will miss this opportunity. Granted, a typed checklist, taken from a "depo checklist" book (there are many such checklist books available), is far better than going in and just shooting from the hip without preparation (at least, for the younger practitioner it would be); but, I think a checklist of the sort I suggested above is optimal for young and old practitioners alike.

If a witness is evading answering a simple question, you should just ask the question over a couple times, making it as simple as possible each time. The witness who continues to evade will say, at some point, "I've answered your question three times now. This is harassment!" My technique, at this point, is something I have done hundreds of times over the years, and in one form or the other, it always works, even though the defense lawyer will rail against me "making speeches" etc. This is what I do. I will say to the witness something along the following lines. "Look, I have asked you the same simple question three times now. You know, and I know you know, that you don't want answer the question straight out because you think a straight out answer will hurt you some way. I get that. That's understandable. But, at a certain point, we've got to end this game. So, I'm going to ask it one more time. You can answer straight out, and then we can leave this behind, or you can just say, hey, I'm not going to answer that question, and we can move on, and I can take it up with the judge later on. Either way, we deal with the problem for right now. So, what's your answer?" After the defense lawyer finishes his "that's a speech, now let me make a speech..." routine, the witness, usually, not always, just answers the question. If the witness does not, it makes a heck of a record for the discovery commissioner.

Some attorneys use depositions as a way to trick unwary, uneducated, English as second language, or naive witnesses into admitting things by virtue of word games that are being played. Actually, if a lawyer is kind of evil to begin with, this is not all that hard to do, and the insurance lawyers who do this sort of thing all the time think they have a special skill that few possess. I would like to burst their balloon: this is amateur hour stuff, and anyone could do it if they wanted to do it.

As a client whose deposition is being taken, you may encounter lawyers of the sort described above, who try to twist your words or take advantage of any lack of communication skills you might have. For this reason, it is important to have a lawyer with you who will protect you against such abuses. The lawyer has some power to make objections to prevent such chicanery, but this power is somewhat limited. Often, his best tool is to ask you questions at the end of the deposition something along these lines: "Mr. Client, you remember before when Mr. Insurance Lawyer asked you like four times how fast you were going, and you said that you weren't looking at your speedometer and couldn't say for sure, and then he asked you like a fifth time, and said that you admitted you didn't care if you were driving way too fast, and you agreed? Now, I thought that was kind of a trick by him (defense lawyer now makes loud angry objection for show). I want to get this all straight. One, you weren't looking at your speedometer, right? (Client says yes.) Two, you couldn't tell exactly how fast you were going, but you have a pretty good general idea, right? (Client agrees.) Three, you were not going any faster than the flow of traffic and everyone else? (Client agrees). Four, you weren't driving at an unsafe speed. (Client agrees.) So, five, when he said you admitted that you didn't care about whether you were driving too fast, you thought he meant that he was asking again about the speedometer, right? (Client agrees). That was kind of a dirty trick by the insurance lawyer, wouldn't you agree? (Client agrees.)"

Of course, the insurance lawyer will be barking and objecting during this whole exchange, but who cares? You now have created a record on the depo that you can read at trial if the defense lawyer tries to use the trick question at trial.

You might say: I'm not allowed to ask leading questions of my own witness at a deposition, am I? It's cross exam, and in many cases, leading questions are allowed on cross. But, more to the point, the other lawyer can "object to form of the question," but, you can still ask the question, subject to the objection. I think this technique is far more useful than having the client make "corrections to his deposition transcript" later on. Granted, this sort of technique fees into the "plaintiff lawyer is controlling the narrative" defense that every trial contains in some fashion, but, I would rather have this criticism to deal with than a misleading, could-get-the-case dismissed trick question to an ill-educated or ESL type deponent allowed to stand on the transcript, untouched.

CHAPTER SEVENTY-NINE

ARBITRATION

Once discovery is completed, then usually the case is settled. If the case is big enough, the case is usually settled by means of a mediation with a professional mediator. (See above discussion regarding mediations.)

But if the case can't be settled, then it goes to an adversarial proceeding.

Automobile cases with a value of less than $50,000 will go to an arbitration first before regular trial. An "arbitration," in this sense, means a somewhat informal (as compared to a court trial) proceeding in which there is a type of judge, called "arbitrator," who reads the evidence from the documents, and then has a hearing where both the parties can tell their stories, and the attorneys for both sides can make their arguments, and the arbitrator then decides who is at fault, and how much money should be paid. The arbitration decision is non-binding, and either side can ask for a jury trial; but the jury will be informed of the arbitrator's decision.

The arbitration hearings typically take place in the conference room of the attorney who has been appointed arbitrator. In an automobile accident case, the hearings will typically last from 40 minutes in length up to 2 hours. (I have occasionally been involved in hearings that take over 2 hours in time, but this is rare.) The testimony that my client has to give will typically last less than 30 minutes in length. I will generally have my client just describe, in narrative fashion, how the accident happened; how she was hurt; where and why she went to the doctors; and how she feels now. (The arbitrator already has read the police report and the doctor's records, so much of this is superfluous.) The insurance lawyer will have picked out various sections of my client's deposition and medical records that the insurance lawyer thinks cast doubt on the plaintiff's story, and then read these sections to my client and make it into a question like, "do you remember saying that to the doctor" or whatever. These are usually somewhat misleading quotes that the arbitrator, who is usually experienced in car accident cases, will not be impressed by (although, a jury might be fooled by them.) Then, the defendant will testify, usually giving some coached speech to the effect,

"I didn't hit her that hard. I mean, there at the scene she was practically running, nothing wrong with her." Again, the experienced arbitrator knows this is coached, and pays little mind to it (although, again, a jury doesn't know this is the same coached speech they all give.)

Although it may seem as though, from my viewpoint, insurance companies appeal more than half of these decisions, the reality, as I understand it from discussions with the Alternative Dispute Resolution department of our court system, is that something like 70 percent of the cases that go through the arbitration proceedings are concluded after the arbitration, either by the sides accepting the arbitration award, or by the sides settling the case after the arbitration.

The reality is that the arbitration system would be a lot better if the more experienced, "name brand" attorneys volunteered to be arbitrators, as was the case when they system came into being about 25 years ago. But, the pay is so low, and the litigating lawyers now so contentious and rude, that many (including myself) just threw in the towel years ago, and decided to take our names off the list. (In particular, the plaintiffs representing themselves in the lawsuits, "pro per," were the biggest headache. But, in our constitutional democracy, everyone, within broad boundaries, must have access to the court system.)

Truthfully, when people like me complain that the arbitration selection lists are now filled with "people I never heard of" etc; we need to look in the mirror for the root cause.

CHAPTER EIGHTY

SHORT TRIAL

For automobile motor vehicle cases worth under $50,000, if the arbitration award is appealed, or, as it is more formerly known, "de novoed," the next step is the one-day jury trial, otherwise known as a "short trial." This happens at the "real" courthouse with a jury of four members, instead of eight. The trial lasts from 8:30 in the morning to 5:00 p.m. at night, typically. It can be shorter if the sides get done quickly, but usually it takes the full day. Various aspects of a regular trial are truncated. Jurors are selected during a very shortened jury selection process, and witnesses are called. Expert witnesses such as physicians are typically not called because of the expense involved, but insurance companies, with deep pockets, can and do oftentimes bring in their "hired gun" witnesses to testify to the effect that the plaintiff is faking, based on examination of the car damage photos.

The jurors decide the case when three out of four of them can agree on a verdict. The beauty of this system is that it gets things done quickly and with a minimum of wasted time and cost for the parties. The negative is that the jurors oftentimes seem to take the proceedings less seriously than if they were in a "real" trial, and oftentimes will rush their decision on the verdict in order to get back home in time for dinner. It is currently my observation that such attitudes on the part of jurors generally disfavor plaintiffs as opposed to insurance companies, as it is easier to say, "the plaintiff gets zero" as opposed to sifting through all the evidence to decide a real number. But, in an automobile accident case with a value of under $50,000, it is indeed questionable whether it is a good use of limited resources in the courthouse is to have people sit and hear a jury trial for four or five days when the amount involved is relatively small. So, there is a "cost/ benefit" analysis attached to the system.

If the motor vehicle case is worth more than $50,000, then it will go to a regular jury trial in the regular courtrooms, just like the ones you see on TV on shows like "Law & Order." In Nevada, for a civil jury trial there will be eight jurors, and it takes six out of eight to decide the verdict. Typically, there will be one alternate juror sitting with the eight jurors, and it is the job of the alternate to replace a juror who is disqualified or becomes sick.

The voir dire in a "short trial" generally only allows each side about 30 minutes' worth of question. The time is controlled by a clock you might see for appellate arguments, or, more commonly, for official chess matches. A lawyer can ask for more time for voir dire (which I usually do), but the time is deducted from the time for the rest of the trial. The voir time is so truncated that the lawyer barely has time to ask even the most rudimentary questions, so in the end, the jury of four persons that ends up being selected is more akin to just "taking the first four out of the box," as used to be done sometimes in the old day by lawyers wishing to save time. You just don't know, as a lawyer, what, really, you have sitting on that jury. Could be real bad, could be real good; it's a crap shoot.

After the jury is selected, we have opening statements from the lawyers. In a short trial, these generally are less than 30 minutes apiece; I would say 20 minutes is more the norm.

The witnesses typically involve the plaintiff, and the defendant. Testimony from each is typically between 45 minutes and 90 minutes, total. About half of that time is for direct exam, half for cross exam.

376

Sometimes the treating physician is called to testify. Often times this is not done because these guys want at least $2000 to show up, due to the fact that they are losing a day's worth of business for court time. The short trial allows their affidavit to be read into evidence, but this is not as effective as having the live person there. The defense can also call an expert witness, typically a 'bio mechanical expert' or 'professional witness' doctor who will say the plaintiff is faking.

Then, each lawyer can give a closing argument, and the judge reads the jury instructions.
All totaled, this process takes 4 to 8 hours to complete, typically closer to the 8. It is a brutally fast pace for things, and, as an attorney, I am 'wiped out' by the end of it.

The jurors then deliberate and when 3 out of 4 of them agree, they have a verdict. Because the trials are not recorded, either by a stenographer or by video systems, it makes it legally difficult to appeal the decisions, as compared to a 'regular' trial that is recorded/reported.

The judges for short trials are lawyers who are appointed by the court. The list of potential appointees is much shorter and more selective than the arbitrator names list, and is, in general, a pretty good list of 'name brand' attorneys. Frankly, the people on the 'short trial' list are the people who used to be on the "arbitrator list," back when the arbitration system was better.

CHAPTER EIGHTY-ONE

REGULAR CIVIL JURY TRIAL

If you have an auto accident case with a value of over $50,000, and it goes to trial, it will go to the 'regular' civil jury trial procedure in state court, in particular, the 8th Judicial District Court in Las Vegas. (Federal court hears some, but very few, automobile accident cases. In order to have an automobile case in Federal Court, the two parties must be from different states, e.g. one driver is from Nevada and the other is a tourist from California, and, the case must be worth more than $75,000. Typically, plaintiffs disfavor going to federal court for various reasons, and so it is the defendant who chooses to 'remove' appropriate auto cases to federal court.)

(You might be wondering: who decides if the case is worth over $50,000? This is done at the initial stages of the litigation, when the plaintiff files a petition to exempt a case from the arbitration system. The plaintiff will state the essential facts indicating that the case has a reasonably arguable value in excess of $50,000, and the court officer known as the ADR Commissioner, currently Erin Truman, decides whether to grant the petition, or not.)

These jury trials are the real deal, with all the pomp and circumstance you see on TV. Most of my clients are surprised at what a big deal the trial is, with all the various components, such as judge, court clerk, law clerk, videographer/recorder, stenographer (sometimes), marshal (f.k.a. bailiff), multiple lawyers, court watchers, jury pool (usually, at least 50 people initially), video screens, microphones, etc. The trial has to go through numerous formal, and often boring, phases, that take days of time. The trials on TV that take place in seemingly less than a day, which is most person's concept of what a trial looks like, are not reality. The real process involves dozens of people, some paid, many not, a big facility, physically, and lots of time. I would say that most all my clients say, after the first day of trial, "I had no idea it was going to be like this!"

The jury trials first start out with voir dire, which is a process by which the attorneys get to ask all the members of the "venire panel" questions to see if they are good jurors for the case, or not. This process is extremely tedious, as people are asked the same questions over and over, and is very annoying to the people who have to sit through the process for hours and hours. In the typical motor vehicle case, at least in my experience, the voir dire process takes one and a half days of time to complete. Occasionally if the lawyers agree to make it quick, or the judge severely limits things, it take only a half a day, and if the judge has allowed the jurors to fill out written questionnaires ahead of time, so the attorneys don't have to ask a lot of the same questions the process can be shortened up.

In voir dire, most of the questions are asked by the plaintiff's lawyer, simply because he goes first, and, by the time he is done, most of the background questions have been asked. The questions usually involve, mostly, background questions, such as job history of the juror and his close relatives; questions about general attitudes on legal cases, and in particular, automobile accident cases; and juror attitudes about specific issues in the case. There are usually more than a couple eccentric panel members who make outrageous statements of one kind or another that will cause things to be sidetracked; there are usually more than a few people who say things to get off the jury duty, that the judge will question closely, to verify, and in order to make sure that others don't try the same trick; and, the attorneys will usually ask a few questions that are designed to somehow weed out the jurors who secretly hate your side of the case, but who will lie to stay on the jury.

Whole treatises and weeklong seminars are dedicated to how to do juror voir dire effectively. So, I am not going to go through all that in this book. I will say this to the young practitioner. When I tried my first 20 or so trials, I found this to be the hardest part of the case. I stumbled through it in what would be embarrassing fashion, were it not for the fact that the insurance lawyers were just as bad as I was. Then, I started to get the hang of it, and now, it is one of the more enjoyable parts of the case for me. The venire persons typically have a limited set of ways in which they clam up or try to evade answering questions, so once you have worked out a few ways to get around this, you don't have to re-invent the wheel every time. So, if you are new, where can learn how to do it? First, be a court watcher. Find out where some good lawyers are doing a trial, and go watch them. Second, get some trial transcripts of the good lawyers doing voir dire, and study them. Third, get involved with groups that have hands on type training, like Inns of Court, Reptile, and programs offered by AAJ. Last, I would suggest that you hire out some focus groups to sit like real jurors, and you practice on them. You can do it on the cheap by hiring some people through Labor Ready or similar temp agencies (stay away from Craig's List– most of those people don't show up), and spend half a day with this group, half a day with that. At first, it is especially hard to maneuver jurors who you would like to excuse for cause into saying what is needed. Study the techniques used by good lawyers to do this. Lisa Blue's Guide to Jury Selection has some good examples. One thing to keep in mind is that, under the most recent Nevada law on voir dire, there no longer are any 'magic words' that need to be spoken, and, there are no words that, once uttered, make the juror acceptable or unacceptable. In the end, I aim to get the juror to say, "I would have a really hard time being fair," about this or that issue. Once you get that on the record, the judges know it is a very appealable issue if they don't excuse the juror, even if he or she says, "well, I guess if you order me to be fair, I can try my best," or similar. Judges want you to use your pre emptory challenge on a juror, instead of the challenge for cause being granted, so it always a bit of game of chicken as to how far they will push that concern in your case. Without being rude, you need to be somewhat firm about your concerns with jurors who say "they would have trouble being fair." When someone admits that, really, they should be gone, in my opinion.

After the jurors are selected, then the lawyers give their opening statements. It is the conventional wisdom today that after voir dire and opening statements, most of the jurors have already made up their minds about who wins and who loses. Social scientists have studied this for many years and this trope seems to be valid, but, it is no longer the certainty that it is was once thought to be 30 years ago. Jurors will change their mind if the one of the parties, in particular, is particularly bad or good on the stand. Other things during the trial do not matter nearly as much. Rarely do expert witnesses or, closing arguments, act as deverbative factors in the final verdict.

After opening statements, witnesses are called. The plaintiff goes first and calls his witnesses, which usually includes at least one doctor, and the person who was hurt in the accident. Other witnesses can include other treating physicians or expert witnesses, accident reconstructionist, investigating police officers, at the scene witnesses, coworkers who observed injuries on behalf of the plaintiff, economic experts who can testify as to lost future income, etc.

The defense then calls witnesses for its case, which usually consists of the defendant himself, "hired gun" doctors that they have employed, as well as so-called "biomechanical engineers" all of whom basically say the same thing in every trial at which they appear. (I can almost tell you verbatim what most of them are going to say before they testify, since they tend to follow almost a script.) Typically, what they say is that in this particular case it is highly unlikely that the plaintiff was actually injured, and that the plaintiff is faking or exaggerating things.

If the other driver is called to the stand, if the case is one where the fault is glaring and obvious (i.e., drunk driver) the defendant will say they are very sorry for what happened and wish they could wind back the clock, etc. (Usually these people were total jerks at the scene of the accident, but at trial they will be contrite.) If there is any doubt about who is at fault, the defendant will give scripted sorts of answers as to what happened (again, I can almost tell you verbatim what they are going to say before they testify in a given sort of liability situation.)

It is the conventional wisdom of that the most important witness in the case is the plaintiff (the injured person) himself or herself. If the juror "likes" the plaintiff, then the plaintiff tends to win. If the jury doesn't like the plaintiff, then they tend not to win.

Jurors do not like plaintiffs who are caught in lies. This is why I and every other competent plaintiff's lawyers tells our clients over and over not to try to fudge any details, and to be extremely candid about any facts they perceive as negative. Jurors also do not like plaintiffs who are whiny or full of self-pity. If I have a client who starts crying on the stand saying that their life is ruined by the car accident, this is usually a bad sign. If they lost their leg or something really, really horrible happened, then crying on the witness stand or saying their life is ruined is okay. But in the 99 percent of the cases that do not involve amputations or death of loved one, wallowing in self-pity on the witness stand does not elicit sympathy from the jurors, it elicits anger. For better or worse, we now live in a world where sympathy is in short supply. Everyone who sits in the jury box these days is very cynical, and "turned off" by people trying to act out the part of "victim." It is generally better for someone on the witness stand in an injury case to be stoic and underplay the extent of their injuries in their own testimony as opposed to "laying it on thick." This seems to be a hard concept for many to grasp, as it is counterintuitive (as children, we learn that mommy pays more attention to us when we cry and act wounded), but when it comes to adults judging other adults, crying has almost the opposite effect that it has on the mother of a small child.

A young attorney needs to brush up on trial evidence law. The class in "evidence" they teach in law school is mostly about arcane subjects that rarely come up in the courtroom. I very strongly recommend that a young lawyer purchase the set of tapes made by Irving Younger, a now deceased trial lawyer, judge and law professor, who did a series of seminars for trial lawyers on trial evidence. He is brilliant, entertaining, and most importantly, dead on in his teaching. He really gives you the important stuff. The entire tape series is probably less than 15 hours. I frequently go through for review purposes, and I have listened to it at least 12 times in my professional life. The disks might cost a few hundred bucks, but it is the best money you will ever spend.

Young lawyers typically have trouble with two issues regarding witness testimony. One is not asking leading questions on direct exam; and the other is laying foundation. Only experience will fully teach you how to comfortably deal with each, unfortunately. Witnesses are just too darn unpredictable to sum up a 'fail safe' technique to be put into a book. But, a couple helpful hints are in order.

When asking questions of witness on direct, judges are attuned to thinking that any question that can be answered "yes" or "no" is leading. This is not, technically, correct, but it's the way it is in real life. If you simply rephrase a 'yes' or 'no' question as a "tell me whether" question, you can get around the objection. For example, if a you ask a witness, "and the light was red?" and he says "yes," you will draw a leading question objection. But, if you say, "tell me whether the light was read or was it green?" and he says, "it was red," then it's not leading. Just start out your question with the phrase "tell me whether," and usually you will be OK.

As far as foundation is concerned, you have to train yourself that, in the court room, you cannot just go directly to asking someone the final conclusory question. You have to show how they have this or that piece of knowledge. In real life, we skip past this, and, in my observation, newish lawyers skip past it too. They don't even seem to appreciate how it is important (when you practice law long enough, you will understand that people all the time say things that they think are true, but which, they have no way of knowing.) They think that when an objection is made about 'foundation' it is a trick, like a hearsay objection. Judges are much more concerned about lack of foundation, as, say, hearsay or leading question objections. You need to practice, with lay witnesses, asking them, "were you there? Did you see x or y? Did you hear x or y? Do you know this person? Etc." Then, you ask: what did you see? What did you hear? What did you think was going on? Etc.

With expert witnesses, it is more difficult, typically, as the foundation arguments can get hairy in the courtroom. But, basically, I have found that if you can lay on enough foundational sounding things with an expert, the judge will let it in. What are "foundational sounding things?" Things like: you examined this or that document. You read this or that depo. You talked to this or that person. You researched this or that. You have special training or board certification in this or that. You have done over x number of cases concerning this or that. You have been qualified by x number of courts before, in this very area. Generally speaking, if the expert sticks to answering such questions, you'll get whatever into evidence. The thing that goes wrong is when the expert starts to play lawyer and then starts spouting what he thinks is important; this is often times seen by the judge as a "challenge" and then the judge starts cross examining the expert. This can be disastrous if the judge is pre- disposed against your case.

Foundation issues always come up at trial. Do some thinking beforehand as to what you will list out and bring out with questions if foundation is questioned. Normally, defense lawyers will save foundational objections for the really big pieces of evidence that you must get in to survive a motion to dismiss, so if you want to know where to expect a foundation objection, it will be on the big key items that you cannot live without.

After the witnesses have testified, then comes closing argument. This is where the lawyers can really start to act like the lawyers you see on TV, saying clever, sarcastic things and being "dramatic" if they choose to be so. Modern research shows that jurors are rarely influenced by closing arguments as, by that time, they've already made up their minds about most things, but the attorneys can use closing arguments as a vehicle to educate the jury on the finer points of the jury instructions (laws that are read to the jury by the judge), and how to apply them to the facts. The lawyers in closing arguments will typically lay out the facts that favor their side, ridicule the other sides case, and then ask the jury to return a verdict in their favor.

I repeat the wisdom of many other trial lawyers who came before me when I say that the primary goal of closing argument is to arm the jurors who already favor my client with the facts and arguments they will need to stand up in the jury room against those jurors who are favoring the other side. "My" jurors are the ones who will truly 'win' the case for me in the jury room; not me, not my experts, or all my fancy charts. I need to make sure they are equipped to deal with dissenting viewpoints.

The jury then returns to the jury deliberation room, which is a room behind the courtroom, next to where the judge's offices are, where they have a table with many chairs. The rooms are sparsely furnished and any food and snacks available are from vending machines generally.

The jurors in a typical automobile accident case will take anywhere from one hour to six hours to reach their decision. It can be less or more, but I would say that one to six-hour range is typical.

If the trial ends at certain points in the day, the jury is likely to hurry up their verdict to get home before dinner, or, lengthen the decision out in order to get the "free lunch" that is offered. How long a jury takes to deliberate cannot be used as a measure of whether it favors the plaintiff or defendant. I have won cases where juries came back in 20 minutes, I have lost cases where a jury came back in 20 minutes. It is oftentimes a "tealeaf" that the lawyers like to think favors or disfavors them, but really it doesn't matter much.

The jurors will discuss the case among themselves just as you might imagine. There will usually be one or two people who are somewhat controlling, one or two people who are very quiet, and then the other four who are in-between. It takes 6 out of 8 votes to have a verdict in a civil case. There have been numerous experiments and so forth where cameras were allowed into the jury voir dire room, and it is always shocking to the attorneys who watch these tapes. It is common to see jurors discuss the case wherein they focus on facts that, to the lawyers at least, seemed irrelevant. The jurors seem to focus quite a bit on personal observations of the plaintiff, focusing on things such as facial gestures, hand movements, voice inflection, etc.

When the verdict is reached the attorneys are called on their cell phones and they return to the courtroom with their clients. The clients do not necessarily have to appear for the reading of the verdict, but it is typical that they do. The verdict is read just as you see on television. The judge looks at the piece of paper and then the foreman reads it out, or the clerk or the judge reads it out loud. The jurors are then polled as to whether or not they voted in favor of the verdict or not.

After this process it is typical for the winning side to file a motion for attorney's fees and costs to be awarded. It is not uncommon for the losing side to file an appeal of the verdict asking the appeal court to grant them a new trial based on some mistake made by the judge at the time of trial. If the case is appealed, it may go either to the Nevada Court of Appeals, or the Nevada Supreme Court. We have only had an intermediate court of appeals for a couple years now. What I have heard is that the general rule of thumb is that if it is perceived that the case has a value of $250,000 or less, the court of appeals will decide the appeal; if it is perceived that the case is worth more than $250,000, then the Nevada Supreme Court will get it.

It is mandatory for appeals of automobile accident cases to have a settlement conference during the appeal. There are a number of attorneys who are selected to be professional mediators for these appeals. The basic thrust of these meetings is that "you never know if you're going to win or lose this appeal, so it's better to maybe take less than you think you deserve, or to pay more than you think you should, to settle it for sure now instead of waiting and taking a chance later."

Most of my clients think that when they win their case in trial that the insurance company will be around to cut them a check the next week. This is not reality. My experience is that insurance companies almost always appeal verdicts that go against them, in order to have leverage to get the plaintiff to take less rather than wait for his or her money. There is interest running on the money awarded at time of trial, so the insurance company theoretically has a disincentive to prolong appeal, since interest runs on the amount. However, the interest that runs on the amount is a floating rate that is tied to the "prime interest rate." Recently the prime interest rates have been very low, so insurance companies are not all that motivated to settle cases on appeal to avoid interest. However, the day will come when interest rates go up again, and the disincentive will be real. But as long as the insurance companies can safely make more in the stock market than what the interest rate they have to pay is on appeal, they will delay payment.

CHAPTER EIGHTY-TWO

TEN DEADLY MISTAKES TO AVOID ON AN AUTO INSURANCE CASE

1.   Giving recorded statements to adverse party's insurance adjuster.

If you are not represented by an attorney, the first thing the adverse insurance adjuster will try to do is to get a recorded statement from you. Typically, they will act nonchalant about it, as though it was a matter of course, and they will infer, or say if questioned, "well, if you're really telling the truth why would you be afraid to give us a recorded statement?"

The question that a person should ask themselves is "if the adjuster is really just interested in knowing what happened, then why does he need to record it? He could just as easily write or type what I say."

The adjuster knows that in a recorded statement you will probably say something that can be used against you later on. It's not so much that you would not speak truthfully; it is rather that people, when speaking informally, such as they might do on the phone to an adjuster, will oftentimes use loose phraseology that can be twisted by attorneys later on. The insurance company adjusters have questions to ask you that are scripted by their attorneys, which are intentionally made to sound innocuous enough, but are in reality, tricky in their structure. The question sounds like it is asking one thing, but when you read the transcript it later on, appears to be asking something else entirely.

There is absolutely no upside, and only downside, to giving a recorded statement to the at fault parties insurance adjuster.

2.   Believing an insurance company will give you special credit if you don't have a lawyer.

Insurance companies have convinced the American public that there is something unseemly, almost immoral, about hiring an attorney to do a personal injury claim. There is the folklore/perception, created by insurance companies, that people who don't hire attorneys for accident cases are more credible, and treated more fairly, by insurance adjusters.

Think of it: the purpose of an insurance company is to make money. They are not social or charitable institutions. They don't care about you, nor should they. Their job is to make money for their policyholders and their stockholders.

They may fake like they are friendly toward you when you don't have an attorney, but it is an act. They are thinking to themselves "boy, this person is dumb. Let's take advantage of them as much as we can until they wise up."

3. Signing carte blanche release authorizations for insurance companies.

While it is true that if you file a lawsuit on a case, you're required to sign some forms of *limited* release authorization so that the insurance attorneys can get copies of your medical records from *relevant* doctors, a good attorney will make sure that the release authorizations you sign are limited only to certain records, and does not allow the insurance attorney or insurance company to go beyond what they really have a legal right to see. If you are on your own without an attorney, or if you are represented by a poor attorney, you may sign a *carte blanche* release authorization, which the insurance companies will "go to town" using. If you sign a carte blanche release authorization they will "dig for dirt." They may –legally-- access every insurance database that exists. They may— legally– look for things such as records regarding an old child custody proceeding, your military records, your health insurance records going back to when you were a child, any psychological or marital counseling records you have, traffic ticket citations, credit card records, credit reports, telephone company records, etc.

The law in Nevada (Schlatter case) say that just because you are an innocent victim of someone else's negligence does **not** mean that your life is now an open book for use by someone else to "dig for dirt" to use against you. So, do not sign carte blanche release authorizations even if the insurance adjuster or attorney acts like it's just an "informal matter."

4.   Talking about your case on social media.

People somehow have the impression that social media sites such as Facebook are semi-private in some way. They are not. Even if you have a privacy setting, insurance investigators are able to access your social media sites with very little trouble. If you make "jokes" on social media about your case, or discuss your case with other people, in particular, talking about how much money you expect to get, it will come back to bite you, big-time. If you put things on your social media criticizing your doctors, lawyers, etc., it will come back to bite you. Just assume that anything you post on a computer is not going to be private insofar as an insurance company is concerned. As a matter of fact, insurance companies now make it a priority to investigate the social media accounts of anyone who files a claim against them. They have learned that these are real "gold mines" of embarrassing pieces of information and "jokes" that don't look like jokes when you put them up on a PowerPoint in a courtroom.

5.   Making hateful, profane, or otherwise embarrassing social media posts and diaries.

Insurance companies love to get copies of your diary and social media posts, and dig through them looking for things that they can use to try to humiliate you. Do not give them ammunition in this regard. Think twice about what you write in them. You cannot change what was already done, but you can at least control what is put in them in the future.

6.   Abuse of opiates.

Second only to looking into people's diaries and social media accounts, insurance companies now are obsessive about checking into people's use of opiates. They want to get any and all medical records showing whenever you were prescribed an opiate medication. Even the most innocent use of pain medications, e.g., Hydrocodone after a root canal, can be twisted to look like you are a pain pill addict.   In the current society, there is a real negative value attached to any use of opiates, and if you can be labeled a "abuser" of opiates, the insurance company needs to prove little else. Therefore, if you are injured in a car accident, try your best to not take, or limit severely, your use of opiate medications such as Hydrocodone and OxyContin.   If you do have to take these medications for severe, chronic pain, do not do anything abusive, and if the opportunity presents itself for you to "get off" these medications, such as a professional program, it would look very good to a jury later on that you made the attempt to get off the meds.   Right now as I write this book (in 2018) there is a "witch hunt" mentality about insurance companies attacking persons taking opiate medications.   Probably, five years from now, persons who take legitimately take opiates for lengthy time frames will be thought of more humanely by the public at large, but right now the media narrative is to unfairly demonize them, and insurance company lawyers, and, especially their hired gun medical experts, are quick to take advantage of this.

7.   Incomplete disclosure of prior accident claims

The "holy grail" for insurance adjusters and insurance lawyers is to get you on tape, or in some written form, denying that you ever had a prior accident claim, and then they come up with proof that you did.

Insurance companies have computer systems that are very good at tracking any insurance claims that you have ever made your entire life. If you disclose prior accidents, then your attorney can probably keep most of them out of evidence. Accidents that are more than five years in the past, or that did not involve injuries, are usually excluded by judges. But if you say, "No, I didn't have any accidents other than that one last year," and it turns out you had two accidents in California last year, the judge will let evidence of those prior accidents in, not because they have anything to do with your current condition, but because they are arguably indications that you lie or conveniently forget things, and thus it effects your credibility. Jurors tend to feel that non-disclosure of prior accidents is a cardinal sin, and even when done innocently, the insurance lawyer will attach sinister intent behind it.

Even if you had a prior accident claim, the majority of the time, as long as you disclose it fully, judges and juries are not negatively affected in any way. They just figure: if he got hurt before, that just makes him more vulnerable the second time. But, if you fail to disclose right away, they may attach negative inference to the failure.

8.   Incomplete disclosure of prior related medical conditions, e.g. prior back treatment

Again, if you tell the insurance company or the insurance adjuster, or the doctor who is treating you, that "yeah, I had this problem before years ago" or whatever, it can be explained by the doctor that it has nothing to do with your current condition, or that the prior condition made you more vulnerable to injury. However, if you fail to disclose the prior injury or prior condition, and, as invariably happens, the insurance company finds out through its numerous databases, again the insurance lawyer will attach much sinister intent on your part, saying it was part of a scheme to hide

402

things. On the flip side, as long as you disclose it, you and your attorney can put it into the proper context. A jury will put a lot of importance on the fact that you "failed to disclose" a prior injury or prior medical condition if this happens. So, err on the side of disclosure of prior similar medical conditions.

9.   Hiring a law firm who does not regularly go to trial.

Insurance company computer systems keep track of which law firms go to trial and which ones do not. They give much better settlements to those firms who do go to trial on a regular basis such as my firm, as opposed to the many 'poser' firms who only do the 'short' one-day trials, or, no trials at all. There are many lawyers who will go a year or two between regular jury trials.   This kind of reputation gets around, quick, with the insurance companies.

I have even seen lawyers who never go to trial advertise on television inferring that they are real trial tigers, or similar, since they know the importance of this, and they choose their words carefully so they are not outright lying.   I confronted one such fellow who said he had done 'over a hundred trials' on TV when, to my knowledge, he had not done even one. He said, "when I was in the city attorney's office as a deputy, I did well over a hundred traffic ticket trials," and then laughed, like this was a clever deception on his part that I should admire. (Traffic ticket trials are not even close to a jury trial; they usually last about 15 minutes, and the driver is typically not represented.) This to me was truly disgusting.

Unfortunately, there is not a good way for a layperson to find out which law firms actually go to trial and which ones do not, since this information is not kept on easily available public databases. (There are publications that for a price give this information to attorneys who subscribe to them, but the general public does not have access to these publications.) I suppose the best thing to do is this. If you are in the office of an attorney that you are thinking of hiring to do your case, ask him straight out, "How many times have *you* been to *jury* trial where you were the first chair attorney in the last five years?" If his answer is less than 8, you might need to find a different law firm.

If you are lucky enough to know someone who works down at the courthouse, you can ask: who is trying pi cases around here? They know. The people who work for the judges who try civil jury trials, in particular, would be good sources.

10.   Not listening to the advice of a competent lawyer.

If you have hired a good lawyer on your case, then you need to listen to him or her when they tell you that this or that course of action is the best. These attorneys have an interest in getting as much money as possible. They are on your side. They know the system better than you do. Asking well-meaning friends and relatives, or, worse, going on the internet for advice, is not going to get you the best advice. You may get people to tell you what you want to hear, but what good is that if it is not the truth?

ABOUT THE AUTHOR

Steven M. Burris has been an attorney in Las Vegas since 1978. He received his undergraduate degree, A.B. with distinction, from Stanford University; and his law degree, J.D. with honors, from University of Southern California School of Law. He is licensed in both California and Nevada. He was the president of the Nevada Trial Lawyers Association in 1997-98. He is AV rated by Martindale Hubbell, the highest rating by peers available; and is an elected member of American Board of Trial Advocates, which is limited to only the top 25 or so civil jury trial attorneys in Southern Nevada. He was chosen to be a "Super Lawyer," and has been voted as a top trial attorney in Las Vegas Life magazine as well as Desert Companion magazine. His law firm, Law Office of Steven M. Burris & Associates, is comprised currently of four attorneys and it limits its practice exclusively to personal injury cases. Mr. Burris has practiced exclusively as a plaintiff's personal injury attorney since 1983. He has achieved the designation as "Stalwart" in the American Association of Justice;

and is an appointed Judge Pro Temp in the 8th Judicial District Court of Clark County, Nevada. He has published over 25 articles in legal journals, and has been a featured speaker at numerous continuing legal education seminars. Mr. Burris has been married to Melanie for over 35 years, has two sons, and is a proud alumnus of the Boulder City Eagles. He practices law in Las Vegas at the Law Offices of Steven M. Burris & Associates.

9 780692 181362